The Management of a Student Research Project

Third Edition

John A Sharp, John Peters and Keith Howard

Gower

First Edition first published in 1983 and reprinted 1985, 1986, 1987, 1989 (twice), 1991
Second edition published in 1996 and reprinted 1996

Published by
Gower Publishing Limited
Gower House
Croft Road
Aldershot
Hants GU11 3HR
England

Gower Publishing Company
131 Main Street
Burlington VT 05401-5600 USA

John A. Sharp, John Peters and Keith Howard have asserted their right under the Copyright, Designs and Patents Act 1998 to be identified as the authors of this work.

British Library Cataloguing in Publication Data

Sharp, John A.
  The management of a student research project. – 3rd ed.
  1. Research – Management 2. Universities and colleges –
  Graduate work
  I. Title II. Peters, John III. Howard, Keith
  001.4′2

Library of Congress Control Number: 2002100274

ISBN 0 566 08490 2

Third Edition typeset by IML Typographers, Birkenhead, Merseyside and printed in Great Britain by MPG Books, Bodmin

Contents

List of Figures and Tables

FIGURES

TABLES

Preface to the First Edition

The expansion of tertiary education during the last twenty years has seen a significant growth in the number of courses during which the student is expected to undertake project work of one form or another. Although not always designated as 'research' a large proportion, if indeed not the majority; of projects require independent enquiry on the part of the student which would qualify for that description. It is hoped that this book will have something for all students whose aim is to write up and present for examination the results of projects which may last from a month or two to several years.

The aim of the book is to assist such students to manage their projects both more efficiently and more effectively. The motivation to write the book came over three years spent by the authors as Chairman and Vice-Chairman of the large doctoral programme at the University of Bradford Management Centre and their experiences as supervisors and examiners of full- and part-time students working on doctoral and master's theses, master's dissertations, and undergraduate projects.

Responsibility for the co-ordination of the activities of well over 100 research degree students during these three years made it clear that although the students may be working on widely differing topics they shared many problems in common. By reflecting on the experiences of students in various fields and at various levels the authors concluded that a book which was concerned with the management of a student research project rather than with the problems arising from a particular field of research itself should have general relevance. Although the discussion must cater for the highest (that is doctoral) level it was felt that much guidance could be obtained by selective reading of the book by the student working at first degree level.

For projects which are given a mark or must be completed if a qualification is to be awarded the objective of the student is quite clear. At research degree level, however, the situation, until quite recently, has been very different, with the so-called 'apprentice model' influencing attitudes. At its best the apprentice model involves a student working under the direction of a single academic who in addition to being an expert in the area of the study is skilled in research methodology and is able to motivate students to complete their thesis within a prescribed time. At its worst it implies incompetent and inadequate supervision with both student and supervisor being responsible to no-one in particular and resulting in yet another 'failure to complete'.

Although there is a slow trend to central direction or co-ordination of student research it remains the case that the vast majority of students will depend largely for success on their own resources and, as stated, it is the aim of the authors to improve both the standard of the research and the probability of timely completion of the written report by promoting self-management. Our current working environment means that we draw heavily on the social sciences for examples but hope that our earlier backgrounds in engineering and mathematics (together with not a few years in industry) will enable us to establish credibility to student researchers in a much wider field.

We have tried out our ideas on a number of colleagues and would like to express our sincere thanks to Dr Stephen Sobol and Virginia Hayden in particular who caused us to do quite a bit of rethinking. Our gratitude is extended also to Pat Corby and Nigel Howard who were kind enough to criticise certain passages, and to Anne Bennett who offered us some advice on reproduction. Additionally we recognise the valuable assistance received from the Management Centre librarian, Neil Hunter.

A quite separate and distinct expression of thanks should be made to Marjorie Richards who compiled the first draft of the manuscript for us. Coping with contributions from two authors is by no means easy, and quite apart from typing the text she did on occasions undertake duties of a subeditorial nature.

Our thanks are similarly extended to Majorie Kay for undertaking the heavy work involved in incorporating the final amendments into the text.
As a final point we hope that our female readers will not be offended by our use of the masculine form.

K. Howard

J. A. Sharp

1983

Preface to the Second Edition

Somewhat more than a decade after the publication of the first edition the authors are in a position to reflect on changes of significance which have occurred during the period.

In the first instance both of the authors have moved to other institutions and have been exposed to a range of additional approaches to project work.

The greatest impact on the execution of research has, however, been through developments in information technology which have enabled the process of research to be facilitated and enhanced by access to personal computers and information networks.

A further change of significance has been the growth of part-time study, of distance learning through correspondence, and distance teaching where faculty from one institution in one country spend short periods overseas in direct contact with students following their institution's programmes. All of this has led to a considerable increase in students being required to draw upon their own resources to complete their projects. Although nothing can equate with an effective supervisor, immediately accessible, we hope that the written guidance that we offer will help to compensate for any difficulties such students encounter in project work.

A notable intellectual change in the 1980s, as far as this book is concerned, has been the rise of postmodernism with its denial of the existence of a single, human-value free, 'objective' form of knowledge. From its initial beginnings in the humanities and in critical social science its ideas have found increasing support even in the philosophy of natural sciences. From the point of view of research, especially outside the hard sciences (the latter accounting for a diminishing proportion of student researchers) this has led to a discernible tendency towards 'anti-positivist' attitudes to research which emphasise the subjective nature of the interpretation of the individual researcher's research findings. Although the intellectual arguments for this position are of considerable interest at the higher levels of research, at least, they are, in our view, of limited use to the student researcher because they presuppose a familiarity with positivist approaches to science. Indeed, one of the major reasons for requiring students to undertake a research project is to provide familiarity with this approach. This book undoubtedly has a positivist orientation which is intended to support such training. We accept that student researchers may eventually go beyond positivist views but remain convinced that they do need first to familiarise themselves with what traditionally constitutes good research practice.

The continued success of the first edition and the comments of many of our colleagues who have used it encourages us in the belief that this view remains widely shared and that there is a very real need for a second edition. More even than the first it has benefited from the comments of our students, our immediate colleagues, and colleagues in other institutions both within and outside the UK. to single out particular individuals would be invidious but we would like to dedicate this second edition to all of them.

J. A. Sharp

K. Howard

1996

Preface to the Third Edition

There have been many changes since the second edition of this book was published, changes which have called for a revision of several important sections as well as a the update and freshening-up which any publication of this kind requires from time to time.

The second edition of *The Management of a Student Research Project* brought on stage information technology and the use of the personal computer, and touched on the emergent use of the Internet by student researchers. Today, use of electronic media has clearly moved towards centre stage for researchers. But in addition to the huge opportunities afforded it has brought with it a whole range of problems, issues and protocols. How exactly should websites be cited in a reference list? What does 'published' mean? Are the problems of insufficient information of a similar or different nature to those of too much information? How can a search engine be best used for research? The fact that definitive answers do not, in many cases, yet exist has not prevented us from addressing these issues.

'Quality assurance' has become part of life around universities and colleges. How supervision, research and formal assessment of such research is undertaken by funding bodies within QA frameworks is also addressed in the latest edition.

We have taken account of the many helpful comments and thoughts of readers in framing the new edition. We have, inevitably, updated language and terminology while seeking to retain the overall tone and approach of the book. We acknowledge the useful suggestions made by anonymous reviewers from the Open University, and we would be remiss to not mention the contribution from those at Gower; especially Ellen Keeling, Helen Hodge and our publisher Jo Burges.

A third author, John Peters, has joined the two original authors. John's background includes university teaching, research and supervision, business consultancy and management.

Yet amongst these changes much remains the same. The skills and techniques of planning and management remain as the cornerstone of the book. While the second edition made a proper reference to the increasing importance of newer and non-traditional interpretations of research – which continues in the Third Edition – such an approach strengthens, not lessens, the need for clarity, transparency and discipline. We believe that the value of systematic research – *'seeking through methodical processes to add to one's own body of knowledge and, hopefully, to that of others, by the discovery of nontrivial facts and insights'* – sustains.

The aims of this book remain – to provide a clear, comprehensive and useful guide to students undertaking research projects to improve the chances of a successful outcome.

J. A. Sharp

V. J. Peters

K. Howard

2001

Part A

Preparation

1

Research and the Research Student

THE AIM OF THIS BOOK

Students in higher or further education, whether full- or part-time, may be required to complete projects of one kind or another. In some instances the project forms a relatively minor part of a course; in others, the project is virtually the whole basis on which an award is made. At either extreme, the primary purpose in making a research project part of a qualification is to foster the personal development of the student. With a research project, at whatever level, the agenda is set by the student to a greater extent than is possible in the ordinary taught course. Similarly, the student bears responsibility for the quality of learning that takes place in the project and for the eventual written outcome.

Whether the student is seeking to write a report at undergraduate level, a dissertation as part of a taught master's course, or a thesis at master's by research or doctoral level, two key factors which must be borne in mind are timing and quality. In some instances the time constraint is inflexible. If the report is not presented by a particular date the qualification sought is not obtained. When deadlines of this nature apply, compliance with them can lead to content which is sub-standard if an ineffective approach is adopted.

THE TWO KEY FACTORS IN SUCCESSFUL STUDENT RESEARCH ARE TIMING AND QUALITY

Recognition that PhD and masters' theses must be of high quality sometimes results in inordinate lengths of time being taken for completion. Indeed, the task of finishing theses proves to be too much for many students and has been the subject of some discussion in the UK for many years. An unpublished survey carried out several years ago by two of the authors of this book found that only about 30 per cent of students who had been researching full-time in the social sciences were awarded higher degrees (in some cases up to a decade after commencing their studies).

Unsurprisingly, the problem is international in nature. In the US the National Research Council saw fit, in 1991, to establish the Ad Hoc Panel on Graduate Attrition Advisory Committee. Its findings were reported in 1996 by the National Academy Press, from which the following is taken:

> There is growing concern among educators and policy makers over recent levels of attrition from PhD programs as reported by some US universities. Of the studies currently available, some institutions place graduate attrition at 50 percent for selected fields in the sciences and humanities; others have documented attrition at levels well over 65 percent for some programs ... the rates reported by these institutions are considered 'high' compared to estimates provided by faculty and deans in 1960 when they placed attrition at 20 to 40 percent.

Identical views were expressed at a forum held in Perth, Australia in 2000, the opening sentence of one presentation being:

> A major concern of university administration in regard to postgraduate research is the completion rates of doctoral students.
>
> (Styles and Radloff, 2000)

As pressures for quality audit in higher education grow, similar problems of unwarranted delays in the completion of research projects are also occurring in many coursework-based degree and diploma programmes. This problem of delay in completion is, then, a general one, and is one of the major issues with which we are concerned. It is assumed that admission procedures imply that student entrants have the potential to complete their studies satisfactorily. What, therefore, are the reasons why sub-standard work is submitted or students fail to complete? Much of the explanation must lie in the inability of students to plan and control – that is, to manage – their work. By 'manage' we mean the manipulation of all resources available to students, both material and human. The most

4

important of the human resources are the students themselves and the person who, in many instances, is designated to supervise their work.

Our aim is to provide degree and diploma students (and their supervisors) with guidance in the identification of feasible research projects and on how to complete them.

> THE DEMANDS MADE OF STUDENTS IN TERMS OF TIMING AND QUALITY WILL VARY ENORMOUSLY ACCORDING TO THE LEVEL AT WHICH THE RESEARCH IS UNDERTAKEN

The demands made of students in terms of timing and quality will vary enormously according to the level at which the research is undertaken, but all research projects have certain features in common. Where possible, the book is addressed to all types of student researcher and will often refer to the 'research report' rather than to a 'thesis, dissertation, or report'. If the remarks are directed specifically to the research degree student 'thesis' will be employed, while 'dissertation' will be used to refer to the type of research report produced in connection with postgraduate taught courses.

Though part-time study for masters' and doctoral degrees has been possible for many years, we could not have envisaged when writing the earlier editions of this book how part-time study would grow during the ensuing two decades. Increasing acceptance of the ability of students to combine other work with that leading to a qualification has had a profound effect on teachers and learners alike. But that is not the whole of the matter. Off-campus work has changed quite dramatically as a result of the advent of the Internet, which has influenced both the approach to learning and the location in which it may be undertaken. The implications which these changes have for the successful completion of projects will be considered throughout the book.

THE STRUCTURE OF THE BOOK

Research is not a straightforward process made up of a series of distinct steps, each of which is part of a clearly defined sequence. Quite apart from opportunities to undertake several activities at the same time, blind alleys will from time to time necessitate a return to an earlier stage.

This does not mean, however, that students should use the inevitability of uncertainty as an excuse for not adopting a systematic and logical approach to their work. The latter is the essence of planning, a process demanded by all project work.

This book has been divided into three parts, each of which is concerned with a broad aspect of student research. It can be argued that certain activities are more or less common to research regardless of the field in which it is pursued. Thus, all students have to select (or at the very least understand the implications of) a topic. They will then need to use the particular skills and techniques which the specific nature of their research demands. Finally, they will have to undertake their work within a certain environment before reporting upon the outcome of their studies. Figure 1.1 shows the extent to which it is realistic to cover, in a book aimed at student researchers in general, the range of problems encountered by the student at each of these stages of their research.

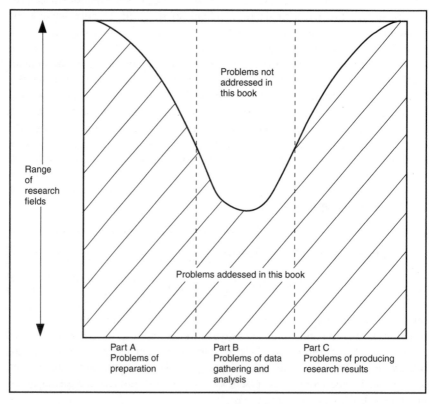

Figure 1.1 The extent to which problems common to a range of student research are addressed in this book

The inference to be drawn from Figure 1.1 is that the preparation, production and publication phases of student research have (for a given level) much that is common across all research fields. That which primarily distinguishes one type of research from another is the activities needed to track down, collect, and analyse data. These activities, as depicted in Figure 1.1, are the subject of Part B which comprises the chapters on analysing and gathering the data. In addition to the present chapter the other chapters to be found in Part A are selecting and justifying a research topic, planning the research project and literature searching. Part C, which is concerned with research output, covers executing the research, common problems encountered in research, specific issues of dealing with supervisors and presenting the results of the research.

Part B presented the greatest difficulty in our attempt to be relevant to the broad field of student research. We have, however, concentrated on the management of data gathering and analysis. In our coverage of analytical methods we recognise our bias towards the social sciences but would claim that many of the techniques referred to have a broader application, not least because of the growing importance of subjects such as management in fields of study like engineering or environmental studies.

We do not propose that this book should be read from cover to cover at one go. Much will depend on the experience which has been accumulated by the student. Sections of the book have been designed to impart skills (such as those needed in literature searching and formal planning), others to add to the student's knowledge (for example, the chapter on analytical techniques), and still others to describe the environment in which the research will be conducted (for example, the problems encountered in executing research). Thus, the book may be seen as a reference work, to be picked up at intervals during the course of the study.

WHAT IS RESEARCH?

> RESEARCH IS SEEKING THROUGH METHODICAL PROCESSES TO ADD TO ONE'S OWN BODY OF KNOWLEDGE AND TO THAT OF OTHERS, BY THE DISCOVERY OF NONTRIVIAL FACTS AND INSIGHTS

Most people associate the word 'research' with activities substantially removed from day-to-day life and which are pursued by outstandingly gifted persons with an unusual level of commitment. There is, of course, some truth in this viewpoint, but we would argue that the pursuit of research is not restricted to this type of person and indeed can prove to be a stimulating and satisfying experience for many people with an enquiring mind.

While it is the case that the major contributions to knowledge do tend to come from highly intelligent and committed investigators, significant advances are the 'tip of the iceberg' insofar as the total volume of effort is concerned. Indeed, top-class investigators often fail to achieve firm conclusions, while by far the greatest amount of activity is much less ambitious in nature. Fundamental additions to knowledge frequently draw upon prior studies of restricted scope carried out perhaps by workers of limited research experience.

We define research as

> seeking through methodical processes to add to one's own body of knowledge and, hopefully, to that of others, by the discovery of non-trivial facts and insights.

At the higher levels of student research a necessary condition of success is that the research actually adds to existing knowledge rather than simply reporting conclusions which have been reached in a particular context and whose general relevance has not been addressed. This requirement will be considered at some length in Chapter 2.

The Higher Education Funding Council for England (HEFCE) considers, every four to five years, how research funds should be distributed among universities and colleges. The distribution is based upon the Research Assessment Exercise (RAE), which allocates funds on the basis of perceived quality of research output within institutions.

The RAE definition of research adopted for 2001 is much longer than the one proposed above and is concerned with research at higher levels. It is cited here in view of the extent to which it gives substance to what may be taken to be 'non-trivial facts and insights'.

> Research for the purpose of the RAE is to be understood as original investigation undertaken in order to gain knowledge and understanding. It includes work of direct relevance to the needs of commerce and industry, as well as to the public and voluntary sectors; scholarship*; the invention and generation of ideas, images, performances and artefacts including design, where these lead to new or substantially improved insights; and the use of existing knowledge in experimental development to produce new or substantially improved materials, devices, products and processes, including design and construction. It excludes routine testing and analysis of materials, components and processes, e.g. for the maintenance of national standards, as distinct from the development of new analytical techniques. It also excludes the development of teaching materials that do not embody original research.
>
> *Scholarship for the RAE is defined as the creation, development and maintenance of the intellectual infrastructure of subjects and disciplines, in forms such as dictionaries, scholarly editions and contributions to major research data bases.
>
> (RAE Circular 5/99, Assessment Panels' Criteria and Working Methods, Section I, HEFCE, 1999)

Addressing the nature of research (as discussed later in this chapter), a further extract from the RAE website (h-w.rae.ac.uk/pubs/briefing/note14.htm) is: '... all research, whether applied or basic/strategic, should be given equal weight' (*RAE Circular 5/99*, Assessment Criteria and Working Methods, Section II, HEFCE, 1999).

Following the RAE conducted in 1996 the HEFCE consulted with higher education institutions and received nearly 100 responses. On the theme of relevance it found that:

> A large majority agreed with the assertion that there should be no *additional* [their italics] credit given in the RAE to the utility of research. However, many pointed out that in some subjects ... the question of relevance or utility is integral to any understanding of research quality. Therefore, ... criteria should articulate what recognition will be given to usability or application as an indicator of research quality.
>
> (*Research Assessment Exercise in 2001: key decisions and issues for further consultation*, HEFCE, 1998)

Though there is widespread support for research having relevance, the traditional view within academe – that it is for others to find practical applications for research outcomes – remains strong.

Another area within the RAE where some confusion exists is that of interdisciplinary research. Sixty-nine distinct subjects or disciplines are recognised by the HEFCE, each being the responsibility of a 'panel'. Concern has been expressed that the difficulty of evaluating quality over one or more subject boundaries (the consequence of interdisciplinary research) led to the commissioning of a survey following the 1996 RAE. Findings (HEFCE, 2001, *Briefing Note 14*) include:

1. Interdisciplinary research is pervasive throughout higher education. Around four-fifths of researchers report that they are engaged in at least some interdisciplinary work.
2. Departments and researchers widely believe the RAE inhibits interdisciplinary research.
3. Despite these beliefs, there is no evidence that the RAE systematically discriminated against interdisciplinary research in 1996....

We make these points in order to stress that student researchers at higher levels should ensure that if they are to pursue research of an applied and/or interdisciplinary nature it is vital to ensure that supervisors and, as far as can be predicted, internal and external examiners are sympathetic to the course of study to be followed.

SOME FEATURES OF STUDENT RESEARCH

The concern of this book is with student research projects and, although a commonness of process is evident, account must be taken of constraints which are imposed by the particular environment in which the student will be working. For example, all or some of the following factors may be relevant.

1. The research topic may be imposed on the student.
2. The research (if it is to be rated a success) must be completed within a given time period: for example, four weeks, six months, three years.
3. Funds for experiments, travel, postage and so on may be limited or even non-existent.
4. The results of the research must be presented in a specified manner.
5. The student may possibly have to relate to an academic supervisor who may lack competence within the field of study chosen or with the process of research itself.

Problems such as these will be addressed throughout the book, particularly in Chapter 7, much of which will be devoted to student-centred issues.

Research work outside the educational system is primarily concerned with adding to knowledge. Within the educational system, however, an additional factor is present, namely the need to demonstrate research competence. Indeed, at all levels except higher degrees by research, the need to demonstrate research competence outweighs that of adding to knowledge. Short comments on the various levels of study are apposite at this stage. A closer look at the criteria to be satisfied at each level will be taken in Chapter 8.

First Degree and Diploma Projects

This category includes studies which form part of courses at the first level of higher education, many of which are referred to as 'degree equivalent'. Although analytical rigour is not usually demanded, independent enquiry and exercise of judgement is expected as, too, is a reasonable standard of presentation of the results. In some cases, students will be expected to display competence in specific areas – for example, the ability to collect data. It is customary for the projects to comprise part of the student's assessment. Rarely will projects represent less than 10 per cent of a particular year's assessment. In some instances (for example, the sandwich course with a whole year in industry) the project may be the only academic assessment made during a part of the course.

> IT IS IMPORTANT TO DEVOTE TIME TO STUDYING THE RESEARCH PROCESS ITSELF

With the requirement for independent enquiry comes the need for planning how the enquiry should be pursued. There is some force to this argument but what is often not appreciated by tutor or student is that there is much more to research methodology than may initially be supposed. Time devoted to studying the research process is therefore a worthwhile investment.

Although research is a vital element of further education it should not be assumed that all tutors have had significant research experience. Academic staff may have been overseeing first degree or diploma projects for many years but this does not guarantee competence in research methods.

Taught Masters' Degree Dissertations

A feature of recent decades has been the growth in masters' degrees obtained by 'study and dissertation', such as the Master of Business Administration (MBA). Thus, typically, a one-year full-time course may comprise nine months of taught courses, with three months being available for a project to be written up as a dissertation. A period of the order of three months is insufficient to enable tasks to be undertaken which will form a sufficient basis for the 'thesis' required for the master's or doctoral research degrees. Little more than a descriptive account can be given of some line of enquiry and the absence of validation and generalisation distinguishes dissertations of this type from the thesis of the pure research degrees.

Where the elapsed time made available for a postgraduate dissertation is rigidly controlled, students need to plan their project very carefully and in particular should avoid being over-ambitious. There are, however, some courses which permit a student to take much longer over their dissertation (possibly to include an additional two or more years of part-time study). Although the dissertation may then be more substantial due to a greater opportunity to collect data, the probability of completion can be reduced by the competing demands of employment and remoteness from an academic environment.

Masters' Degrees by Research Theses

The requirements for the successful completion of projects in a master's degree by research are in some respects difficult to establish. In particular, the amount of originality needed and the extent to which generalisation of the results is possible may be unclear. At the very least any conclusions which are reached must be capable of validation. Certainly, the contribution to knowledge of a master's thesis should be of some significance, particularly in view of the fact that it is likely to serve as a reference work.

11

Externally, assessors will give attention to the thoroughness of the research as indicated by the list of references, in addition to the analysis, conclusions and the standard of presentation.

Doctoral Degree Theses

This is the highest level of student research activity and, although students may proceed to careers in research itself, the doctoral project will probably be the last occasion when they are formally assessed on the grounds of both research competence and originality. The major aim is to present a thesis for external assessment which will prove to be satisfactory in both respects. A subsequent aim may be, through publication, to become recognised as an expert in the field of study chosen. The requirements are, inevitably, more demanding than those of the master's degree by research: for example, the University of Manchester's Ordinances (2000) page states that:

> the degree of Doctor of Philosophy (PhD) is awarded by the University in recognition of the successful completion of a course of supervised research, the results of which show evidence of originality and independent critical judgement and constitute an addition to knowledge.

The achievement of a doctorate in any subject will represent a major investment in terms of time and effort. Usually, the process requires at least three years and there is no guarantee of a successful outcome. Failure to complete is a disturbing feature of doctoral study; a major aim of this book, as stated earlier, is to reduce the chances of this occurring.

Projects and the Part-time Student

During the 1980s, the number of part-time programmes in higher education, particularly at master's level, increased dramatically in the UK. By implication, students in this category devote part of their time to academic study and the remainder usually to employment. Predominantly, they are managers or professionals who wish to add to their career potential by supplementing a qualification at degree or equivalent level with a higher degree.

Although there is a significant trend towards the inclusion of formally assessed projects within first degree programmes, which has exposed students to aspects of the research process, an equally important trend has been the growth of masters' projects undertaken by part-time students in employment. The dual status of student and employee provides opportunities not hitherto available, as the researcher might well be in a position to move beyond recommendations to assuming responsibility for change within the organisation. If this is the case, action research, rather than applied research is in prospect. In the following section, 'Classifying Research', comment will be made on this approach.

> MOTIVATION TO COMPLETE LONG-TERM PART-TIME STUDY NEEDS
> TO BE VERY HIGH

Whilst positive advantages can be created by part-time study, difficulties can arise, often created by the absence of a high measure of contact with faculty and fellow students. The motivation needed to sustain research effort over, possibly, a five-year period, has to be of a high order. Access to facilities and supervisors is much more restricted than is the case with full-time students and the value of self-management of the research project is therefore greater. Further comments are made on this aspect in Chapter 7.

CLASSIFYING RESEARCH

The majority of student research projects are completed without much thought being given to the type of study which has been followed. In this section we examine research from four points of view:

1. The field of research.
2. The purpose of research.
3. The approach to research.
4. The nature of research.

Each of the four will have a different bearing on the successful management and completion of a study.

The Field of Research

Research is most frequently classified by field but this is little more than a labelling device which enables groups of researchers with similar interests to be identified.

Fields are often grouped for administrative purposes into categories such as the social sciences, life sciences, physical sciences, engineering and the humanities. It was suggested earlier that a significant proportion of research may fall into more than one of these categories (interdisciplinary research). This is particularly so at the higher levels of study where the project may often involve the translation of ideas from one field to another.

As far as this book is concerned, classification by field is of the least relevance. This does not mean that researchers do not need a comprehensive knowledge of their own subject. Rather, it reflects our intention to concentrate on those aspects of research that are common to most fields and the majority of research projects.

The Purpose of Research

A research project has many different purposes. Four common ones are:

a)   to review existing knowledge;
b)   to describe some situation or problem;
c)   the construction of something useful;
d)   explanation.

The review of existing research findings is a very common type of student research project, particularly in diploma, undergraduate and taught masters' courses. It can provide excellent research training with the added advantage that it requires little by way of resources save access to the relevant literature.

Although *descriptive research* may appear to be less demanding than other types this is often far from the case. However, due to the lack of knowledge of a subject or research methods, or both, it is quite possible that the purpose of a student's first study will be to describe something, particularly if there has been little previous research in the field.

The construction of *something which is useful* is an outcome of research which increasingly is being favoured by sponsors. In the physical sciences and engineering, students may be recruited to pursue a particular line of research such as the construction of a new type of optical system.

Explanation is the ideal of all professional research workers. It is only when causal rather than statistical relationships are identified that generalisations may be made or laws formulated.

The Approach to Research

Another way of classifying research is by the major research approach used. Approaches encountered in student research are:

a)   the laboratory experiment;
b)   the field experiment;
c)   the case study;
d)   the survey.

The *laboratory experiment* is relevant to all the major research subject groupings (with the possible exception of the humanities) but is primarily used in physical science, life science and engineering research.

In the context of research methods a *field experiment* suggests that an investigation subjected to certain controls is conducted in non-laboratory conditions. For example, a new detergent may have been developed as a result of laboratory research and a field experiment may be set up to see how well it works in actual use.

The *case study* is often the basis for student projects, particularly in the social sciences. In this type of research students may spend a period in an organisation and the comments and conclusions which emerge will be based solely on their experiences in that setting.

There is some connection between the *survey* and the field experiment in that techniques relevant to the latter may be used in the former. However, whereas the field experiment implies controls and need not necessarily involve people the survey is viewed separately here as a method of extracting attitudes and opinions from a sizeable sample of respondents.

The Nature of Research

Our fourth view of research is by nature and type of contribution to knowledge. A further label is the category in which the research falls. Figure 1.2 includes classifications proposed during the final decades of the twentieth century. We have made an attempt to categorise according to Clark (1972), elaborated by Grinyer (1981), and the UK Universities Funding Council (1992) and restated in the RAE 2001 exercise undertaken by the HEFCE (2001), but we make no claim for exact comparability.

Grinyer suggests that the opportunity of a truly original contribution to knowledge (which is related to our concept of value to be presented in Chapter 2) decreases as we go down the list, whereas the prospect of successful completion increases. Both Clark and Grinyer were mainly concerned with research in the social sciences, whereas the definition proposed by the HEFCE is intended to cover all fields of research.

Our three categories of research as indicated in Figure 1.2 are, then, defined as follows.

Category 1 is concerned with the development of theory, without an attempt being made to link this to practice. The findings are usually reported in learned journals.

Category 2 might take the outputs from Category 1 and seek to draw general conclusions about the prospects for application. Academics will be interested in the findings, but so too will be relevant professionals working in industry, commerce or government who will wish to evaluate the potential for transfer of the findings to their own settings.

15

Category	Clark	Grinyer	UK Universities
1	Pure Basic Research	Pure Theory	Basic Research
2	Basic Objective Research	Testing of Existing Theory	Strategic Research
3	Evaluation Research	Description of the State of the Art	Applied Research
	Applied Research	Specific Problem Solution	
	Action Research		

Figure 1.2 Classification by the nature of research. After: Clark (1972) as elaborated by Grinyer (1981); UK Universities Funding Council (1992).

Category 3 embraces research undertaken with a specific practical objective in mind. For some purposes, as Grinyer suggests, it may realistically be divided into three sub-categories, with the 'Evaluation/Description' sub-category possibly overlapping our Category 2. 'Applied Research', at the middle of Category 3, is an activity in which professional and student researchers might be involved, with the output being recommendations for action by others. The final sub-category, 'Action Research', as its name implies, leads to change, and the researcher is a participant in the change process rather than an observer of it. Clearly, this will demand skill, and experience which many students will not possess.

THE PROCESS OF RESEARCH

Deeper understanding of research will come from consideration of the process by which it is conducted and, of course, from embarking upon an actual study. Despite the wide variety of field, purpose and approach, some common features of the research process can be identified, and if a student departs significantly from a general systematic approach the research will be inefficient and quite possibly ineffectual.

Several conceptual models designed to serve as a basis for a systematic approach to research have been proposed. Rummel and Ballaine (1963), drawing upon suggestions made by J. L. Kelly and J. Dewey, proposed a model with six steps: a felt need; the problem; the hypothesis; collection of data; concluding belief; and, general value of conclusion. This is a robust view which stands the test of time.

The model outlined in Figure 1.3 demonstrates some similarities with Rummel and Ballaine's proposal but contains different emphases. Steps 1 to 4 of the model may be described as the planning phase, with the remaining steps, numbers 5 to 7, as the effectuation phase, that is, the doing. Much work, notably a search of the literature, is involved in the planning phase, and this should be highly relevant to parts of the effectuation phase. Until the end of Step 4 it is often the case that the researcher finds it necessary to return to one of the earlier steps before proceeding further. Reversion from the effectuation to the planning phase may, however, prejudice the prospects of completion given the time constraints within which most students must work.

Each step should be viewed as being less reversible as progress is made from the beginning of the project to the end. A research project, however, always involves novelty – at least for the student – and the researcher will frequently find a need to return to an earlier step because later experience has shown how the project can be more closely defined. It will be appreciated that such a return, though it may expedite future work, does not constitute progress. Too frequent reversion to earlier steps is a sure sign that the initial steps of the planning phase have been inadequately carried out.

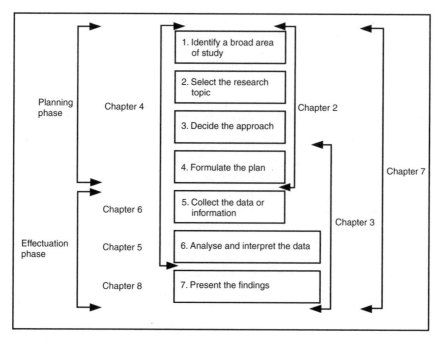

Figure 1.3 A systematic approach to research – a process model (the chapter numbers indicate where each step is discussed in this book)

'Inadequately' is a strong word to employ, and we would point to it having different force at the various levels of research. Although, for example, an undergraduate might not be deemed to have been inadequate in having failed to uncover that a similar study reaching significant conclusions had been completed elsewhere, a doctoral researcher who remained in ignorance of such an achievement could definitely be labelled 'inadequate'. We emphasise this point to stress the commitment which students must give to the planning phase.

The seven steps in Figure 1.3 should be comprehensible to all students though the relative importance of individual stages will differ from one project to another according to the aims and approach, as we shall see later. The figure contains reference to Chapters 2 to 8 indicating where each of the steps will be considered in some depth. Although during a project the research plan will precede data collection and analysis, it is suggested that before formulating the plan, students should first read the chapters which address these topics (5 and 6) so that they will have some understanding of the methodology and tools of research before they decide upon the direction and duration of their study.

Careful compliance with the model should considerably improve the prospects of successfully completing a piece of research. It is difficult to avoid the temptation to skip steps or to proceed having only partially completed stages. Thus, though the research topic may have been only vaguely formulated a student may commence to organise a project in the hope that an appropriate topic will emerge after data have been collected; or a researcher may reach conclusions after collecting only part of the data planned and, as a result, discontinue further collection, only to find that the initial interpretation was incorrect.

THE SUCCESSFUL COMPLETION OF STUDENT RESEARCH

One immediate question is: 'What is success?'

Below master's level, success is measured by formal recognition that examination requirements have been satisfied. At master's and doctoral level, when dissertations and theses are to be displayed in libraries, success often means also that students are satisfied that their own standards have been met.

A further question is: 'What are the factors that affect success as thus defined?'

A useful vehicle for providing an answer is a survey of PhD students in which two of the authors were involved. Stimulated by the widespread concern over completion rates (particularly in the social sciences) the Doctoral Committee at the University of Bradford Management Centre devised a questionnaire and sent it to 45 students whose full-time studies had terminated and to 28 full-time students who were currently doing research. From the former category 19 replies (42 per cent) were received and 18 (64 per cent) from the latter category. The 19 students who had ceased to research full-time included 10 who had transferred to part-time registration in an endeavour to complete their studies.

Students were asked to indicate for 20 factors whether these had affected research progress beneficially, neutrally or adversely. The factors included:

1. The subject chosen.
2. The research design.
3. Quality of supervision.
4. Quantity of supervision.
5. Availability of funds.
6. Teaching.
7. Running tutorials.
8. Writing papers.
9. Attending conferences.
10. Own level of motivation.
11. Own abilities.

The implications of these and other factors will be examined in other parts of this book, particularly in Chapter 7.

In order to effect a measure of interpretation, beneficial responses were scored +1, neutral responses 0, and adverse responses −1. By simple addition a total score was obtained for each factor, and factors were on this basis assigned to the categories of those having an adverse effect on progress and those having a beneficial effect. The results are shown in Figure 1.4 ranked for each category in descending order of importance.

Different perceptions will be noted from the above rankings where, for example, successful students rated four individually centred activities as having been most beneficial to completion.

Of some interest is that only in the case of students who were currently researching full-time was the subject chosen fairly beneficial to progress. Even for those who had successfully completed their studies the factor was located no higher than the mid-point of the rankings and thus does not appear in Figure 1.4. As might be expected the nature of the subject chosen was ranked even lower (twelfth of twenty) following the aggregation of the responses of erstwhile full-time students who had yet to complete their research.

In Chapter 7 obstacles to successful completion ranging from departure from the research plan to supervision issues will be examined.

The study by Styles and Radloff (2000), which focuses on how doctoral students at two Australian universities feel about their theses, is of particular value in its implications for the relationship between supervisors and research students.

Category of respondent		
Students who had completed their doctorates	Ex full-time students who had not yet completed	Current full-time students
Adverse effects		
None	Availability of funds	Teaching/Running tutorials
Beneficial effects		
Own level of motivation	Writing papers	Attending conferences
Own abilities	Own abilities	Own level of motivation
Writing papers	Quality of supervision	Quality of supervision
Attending conferences	Quantity of supervision	Writing papers
Quality of supervision	Own level of motivation	The subject chosen

Figure 1.4 A survey response indicating factors which influence student research progress

TYPES OF RESEARCH AND THIS BOOK

Having examined research from four different viewpoints it will be noted that only in one case was it necessary to refer to the subject of the research. Even when research is classified by field, there are still many acceptable styles of research project.

This book aims to meet the needs that are common to most student researchers. In particular we have drawn heavily on the process model of research (Figure 1.3) in the organisation of the remaining chapters.

This chapter commenced with references to the two key factors of timing and quality. The implications of being unable to satisfy the former are readily apparent – that is, no report, no qualification. We believe that by the adoption of careful management the prospects of earlier and successful completion will be much enhanced.

What is more difficult to grasp is how the quality criterion can be satisfied and, indeed, how it can be measured. For combinations of research approach and purpose that are legitimate in a particular field each combination will carry with it different implications in terms of constraints and opportunities for research with potential quality. Which is selected will depend in part on student preference and attitude towards risk. An important point to stress is that, where research degrees are concerned, the topic should preferably be chosen by the students rather than being foisted upon them, otherwise motivation (which was rated highly in both the surveys referred to above) will be difficult to sustain.

In Chapter 8 we shall be considering the range of requirements which need to be satisfied at the different levels of research. These will provide a fairly specific list of criteria against which a prospective topic can be evaluated. A rather different view of quality will be taken in Chapter 2 when we will suggest that research may be judged in terms of its potential value and the surprise element which will arise from a change in previously held beliefs. Clearly, research which is likely to be rated lowly in terms of both value and surprise will have limited prospects of success at research degree level, even though the methodological quality proves to be high.

An important factor that needs to be taken into account in assessing quality is that value and surprise do not exist in isolation – they are subjective. As suggested earlier, this points to a need for the student to give some thought to the person or the type of person who will assess the research.

The aim should be, therefore, to maximise the probability of timely and successful completion by identifying as soon as possible a research topic with high potential quality. This, taking account of the resources available to the student, should seem, with good management, to be capable of being concluded within the stipulated period. The planning and control of quality is just as important as the planning and control of resources. All of these aspects are examined in the chapters which follow.

THE REQUIREMENTS TO BE SATISFIED

At several points in this chapter we have stressed that forward planning should feature throughout the research. It is, sensible, however, that before embarking upon what we describe in Figure 1.3 as the effectuation phase the student should reflect at some length on the activities to be undertaken and the requirements to be satisfied. As far as is possible a clear and unambiguous vision of what will be needed should be sustained throughout the research.

As the student moves beyond planning there is a prospect that immersion in literature searching, primary data gathering and analysis will cause sight to be lost of the totality of the research. We suggest that writing should commence as soon as is realistically possible but would argue strongly that the student should view the separate chapters as an integral part of a final whole. Far too frequently examiners are presented with reports, dissertations or theses which are disjointed, inconsistent or fall short on logical and coherent argument.

In Chapter 2 a logical structure of a thesis is proposed in which content is considered within six areas. Here, a few words are appropriate on what constitutes a good research report, a standard which the student should seek to attain.

The Aim of the Research

The researcher and, subsequently, the reader should be convinced that the study is well worth undertaking. Throughout the programme the student should never lose sight of the aim; everything that is written should be subordinated to this. The aim should be clearly stated.

Appropriate Use of the Literature

At lower levels of research recognition may be given to an effective review of the literature on its own account, albeit that it must be linked to the study. Research theses demand full integration of existing literature at all stages of the thesis. It is likely that a chapter of a thesis will be devoted to establishing the existing state of knowledge as a datum but references to the works of others should, as appropriate, appear throughout the text.

> A STUDENT SHOULD ACTIVELY SEEK CONFLICTING VIEWS ON A PARTICULAR ISSUE

If full impact is to be achieved the student must actively seek conflicting views on a particular issue. Evaluating and synthesising the views of others when embarking upon an attempt to add to knowledge in a given field calls for considerable critical insight – and in historical studies may, indeed, be the whole basis for satisfying a research objective.

Research Methodology

The researcher has to identify different and potentially applicable designs and then explain the reasons for choosing a particular methodology – which may involve several different approaches. Thus, an in-depth case study may be supplemented by a mailed questionnaire, or a number of interviews may be followed by a series of research workshops. The researcher must address the question: 'What bias might arise from conclusions reached by adopting a certain methodology?', not least because that might well be a matter raised by an examiner.

Presentation of the Research Results

The completion of the data-gathering phase will see the researcher in the possession of a substantial amount of data, intelligence and information. The seeds of the analysis are contained herein and no small measure of skill is needed to order and present the results in a form which is consistent with the thesis or dissertation. Normally primary data whether these be, for example, instrument readings or questionnaire responses, are not included within the report; but it must always be understood that examiners may insist upon, and other researchers might request, access to the data collected. The argument will be sustained if simple data are included in appendices, but it is customary to process and present data in such a way that their interpretation is possible from the text. Graphics, tables and the outcome of mathematical or statistical analysis may be employed to achieve the desired effect.

Analysis of the Results

Although the analysis will have commenced with the initial processing of the primary data the value of the research will be dependent upon the researcher's interpretation, leading to conclusions and recommendations. It will need to be appreciated that only rarely is the researcher confronted with a 'puzzle', for which there is a solution. More often there is a 'problem' in respect of which a number of conclusions might be possible.

In large part the ability of the researcher will determine what conclusions are drawn from the data. It is possible that quite different findings would be reached in certain cases by different researchers. There may, for example, be several plausible causes of most of the major wars throughout history. The quality of a thesis would be undermined if there was evidence that the researcher had adopted a 'blinkered' approach and had failed to review and explore alternative arguments and possibilities.

It is always sensible to comment on the limitations of the analysis. At higher levels this may be due to a rather limited response to a questionnaire; at lower levels it could be that the student felt that the research could be satisfied by employing simple rather than more advanced statistical techniques. The student should, however, never leave the analytical phase without feeling confident that the aim of the research has been satisfied sufficiently for the qualification being pursued.

Conclusions and Recommendations

The thesis or dissertation ends with conclusions reached by the researcher. These should be presented with clarity and emphasis and should be related to the aims as stated at the outset. It is the duty of students working at postgraduate level to identify prospects for further research to provide impetus for those who will tread the same path.

For the categories 'Applied Research' and 'Action Research' listed in Figure 1.2, conclusions should be followed by recommendations for application.

At this stage it is suggested that the student should refer to Figure 8.1 which lists the criteria to be satisfied for successful completion of the different levels of degree.

CHAPTER SUMMARY

RESEARCH IS: a process by which researchers extend their knowledge and possibly that of the whole community. Student research is encountered from first degree or diploma level though to doctoral level. It involves the development of competence in undertaking research and in adding to knowledge. In general the former is more important at lower levels, the latter at higher levels.

RESEARCH CAN BE CLASSIFIED:

by field
by purpose
by approach
by nature

Combinations of these categories create a large number of different types of research project. Not all are feasible given the student's expertise and the resources and time available.

THE IDENTIFICATION OF A GOOD RESEARCH TOPIC: requires that thought be devoted to its quality which will be assessed by taking into account such factors as standards, value and the element of surprise.

A SUCCESSFUL OUTCOME TO THE RESEARCH PROJECT: is more likely if it is conducted as a series of logically ordered steps which in large part are common to all types of student study. A range of factors (many of which are under the personal control of the student) will have a bearing on the outcome.

UNDERSTANDING THE REQUIREMENTS: of theses, etc., is essential to a successful outcome.

2

Selecting and Justifying a Research Project

Because of the very different time-scales of research degree and undergraduate or master's research projects there are significant differences in the way that the choice of research topic is made. Accordingly, we will treat the two types separately. For convenience, undergraduate and master's projects will be referred to in the rest of the chapter as dissertation projects.

PERSONAL VALUE OF THE TOPIC

The educational benefit of conducting a research study has already been noted. However, it is up to the individual student to obtain the maximum self-development from the research project. A key factor in this respect is the choice of research topic. Other things being equal, a project that is closely allied with the student's career aims is better than one that has no obvious relevance. Thus students who intend to pursue careers as, for example, business consultants, are clearly well advised to familiarise themselves with the 'state of the art' in some field which has high relevance to the future rather than studying a topic which has little interest to practitioners.

SELECTING A PROJECT TOPIC

The primary aim of a project is to develop the individual student's ability to conduct independent research. It is not expected that there will be a significant contribution to knowledge; indeed, many good dissertations do no more than review systematically and impose some structure on a field of interest or demonstrate that the student can carry out the processes of research adequately.

OTHER THINGS BEING EQUAL, A PROJECT THAT IS CLOSELY ALLIED WITH A STUDENT'S CAREER AIMS IS BETTER THAN ONE WHICH HAS NO OBVIOUS RELEVANCE

In many cases, the student who is involved in a research project for a taught course will find that a list of topics is made available by academic staff. The student can choose from this list in the light of personal interest, career plans, etc. In such cases, it is safe to assume that the topic is viable provided that the research project is conducted competently.

In other cases, especially where the course is part-time and students are sponsored by their employers, the dissertation is often expected to provide a solution to some problem in their own organisation. In our experience, the selection of a dissertation topic under these circumstances has something in common with the topic selection process for the research student as discussed below. Considerations of novelty are not important because the topic will be specific to the sponsoring organisation. There is, however, a need to ensure that the dissertation topic is consistent with the academic aims and standards of the course.

RESEARCH DEGREE TOPIC SELECTION IN OUTLINE

Until a topic has been selected the research cannot be said to be underway. Despite this obvious comment it is not uncommon to find full-time research students who have yet to make a real start on their study a year after commencement. True, they may have done an enormous amount of reading, thinking or travelling, but in no sense could this be seen as making significant progress, which only really occurs after the research topic has been selected (see Figure 1.3). Research plans may founder because of the unexpected but this possibility should not be confused with an inability to identify an appropriate topic with reasonable speed; yet, in our experience this is one of the most common problems encountered in student research.

The prospects of selecting a suitable topic will be enhanced if a systematic approach is adopted. Figure 2.1 expands upon the first stages in Figure 1.3. In the

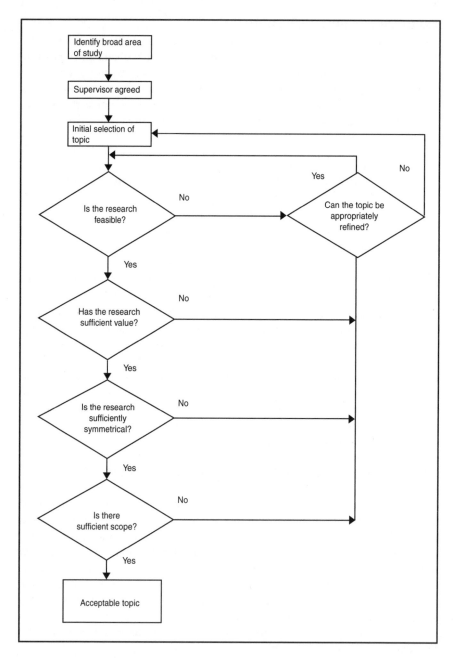

Figure 2.1 The process of topic selection

first place the broad area of study will suggest likely supervisors, who normally will prefer to supervise studies in fields which are related to their main interests. Thus, a lecturer in marketing who has inclinations towards quantitative methods may be prepared to undertake supervision of a student who wishes to develop a mathematical model of advertising effectiveness but may not be prepared to supervise a student who wishes to research into the development of consumerism.

The significance of the various stages included in Figure 2.1 will vary considerably according to the level at which the research is to be undertaken. An undergraduate may be presented with a research topic which would obviate the need for thought to be given to any of the stages. By contrast, each of these stages will feature prominently during the early part of a doctoral study, consuming perhaps 20 per cent of the time ultimately spent on the research.

APPOINTING THE SUPERVISOR

Most books on research methods pay little regard to the role of the supervisor in research studies. In part, this is because such books are addressed to all researchers, many of whom are solely accountable for the work they do. Almost by definition, however, any student within a formalised education system must be complemented by a teacher. In the particular context of student research activity the teacher is usually referred to as the supervisor, although other descriptions such as project director may be encountered. In this book 'supervisor' will be used to imply the individual to whom the student will turn for regular guidance. It is, nevertheless, appreciated that many students will receive a minimum of supervision during their projects and we will seek to provide guidance in these situations.

More is written in Chapter 7 on the relationship between the student and the supervisor. Comments in this chapter will be limited to the supervisor's role up to the point when the topic is finally agreed and the research proposal accepted. The extent of the dialogue between student and supervisor will normally be related to the level at which the research is being undertaken. Thus, academic staff may have a list of topics which are appropriate for students below research degree level, whereas research students are more likely to be expected to have a clearer idea as to what they would like to do. Although topic selection at research degree level may be an arduous process the likelihood is that the precise topic which eventually emerges will in large part have been identified by the student, and as such will provide an opportunity to establish an academic reputation in a specific area.

The 'apprentice model' in which a doctoral student relates directly to one, occasionally two, but rarely more, supervisor(s) throughout the whole of the project (with which the supervisor is concerned from the outset) is traditional in the UK educational system. By contrast, North American doctoral students attend taught courses for the first half or even two-thirds of their period of study before commencing their projects under the direction of a member of staff. This model is increasingly being adopted in the UK with the first year of PhD studies being devoted primarily to taught courses. Indeed, this process has been given some encouragement by the introduction of one-year Master of Research degrees aimed at providing research training as proposed in the 1993 UK White Paper on science policy.

ACADEMIC SUPERVISORS MUST GRADUALLY STAND BACK FROM RESEARCH AS IT PROGRESSES; IT IS NOT THEIR CONTRIBUTION TO KNOWLEDGE THAT WILL BE ASSESSED BUT THAT OF THE STUDENTS

At the outset, however, doctoral research students should recognise that the thesis eventually written should be seen as their work. Whereas craftsmen may work alongside their apprentices throughout the period of their indenture, and may well be associated with the output of their joint endeavours, academic supervisors must gradually stand back from doctoral students' research as it progresses; it is not their contribution to knowledge that will ultimately be assessed but that of the students themselves.

In the case of undergraduate and postgraduate taught course projects, it is normal for the student to have only limited access to a supervisor. A 'budget' of a few hours of a supervisor's time is usually the best that can be expected. The input of a supervisor, at this level, is usually confined to ensuring that the student conducts the research satisfactorily and that the research report is properly structured. It is relatively rare that there is any need for the supervisor to have a deep knowledge of the subject under study. At research degree level, however, both student and supervisor should share common interests. The problem of matching the interests of student and supervisor is a feature of the apprentice model and can result in strong candidates being lost to research or, equally unsatisfactorily, embarking upon a line of research to which they are not fully committed. A clear advantage of models of study which delay the setting up of a formal student/supervisor relationship is the opportunity which arises for 'breaking the ice' before commitment is made.

The opportunity cost of pursuing a research study full-time for from one to three years (that is the 'cost' of not doing what otherwise might have been done) may be very high if a successful outcome is not achieved. In this respect the importance to research students of obtaining an appropriate supervisor cannot be overstated. It would be the first indication of bad management of their research if students were not to obtain answers to the following questions about prospective supervisors:

1. What are their records in terms of student completions?
2. What are their views on the management of student research – and, in particular, the supervisor's role in it?
3. How eminent are they in their specialisms?
4. In addition to being knowledgeable about their subjects, have they high competence in research methodology?
5. How accessible are they likely to be?

FIND OUT A SUPERVISOR'S:

COMPLETION RECORD
VIEWS ON THE SUPERVISOR ROLE
KNOWLEDGE OF SPECIALIST SUBJECTS AND RESEARCH
   METHODOLOGY
ACCESSIBILITY

Since individuals respond in different ways to the uncertainties of research, students will need to base their decision, in part, on the type of relationship to which they respond best. Thus, the highly creative, independent student might put most emphasis on Question 3, whereas a student who responds best to a fair degree of direction will probably place more weight on Questions 2 and 4.

If students are intending to conduct their studies part-time they should recognise that supervisors will often feel less committed. Although, in the UK, the apprentice model will still normally apply, it will need to take account of the greater duration of the research which will render the findings both remote and uncertain. Part-time study can be very demanding but can be much facilitated if students are prepared to sustain a strong initiative in their dealings with their supervisor.

INITIAL SELECTION OF A TOPIC

This section deals with the situation in which students must develop a topic for themselves. The short time-scale of taught masters' programmes mean that such students will be offered a list of topics on which they can draw. Undergraduate students may well be presented with such a list. Often, there will be some possibility of refining or adapting the topic to meet more closely the student's own interests, in which case some aspects of this section may be relevant.

It would be almost tautological to claim that the eventual successful completion of a research study will be seen to have depended on the selection of an appropriate topic. For each student, however, a range of possible topics will exist and some will prove to be more 'appropriate' than others. The possibility that a student who has been accepted by an institution should fail due to an inability to identify a workable topic is wholly inconsistent with the responsibility which the institution has itself in this matter. Nevertheless, the student, particularly at the higher levels, has a significant part to play in topic selection and it is our contention that by adopting a thorough and well-ordered approach the chances of selecting a topic that will enhance completion prospects will be much improved. In what follows we are proposing a mechanism which should greatly assist in the identification of a line of study which will be consistent with the student's interests and abilities.

Figure 2.1 suggests that a logical sequence should be followed before a topic is finally selected. In practice, researchers will probably subject their ideas to the tests indicated without necessarily being aware that they are doing so in a particular order. Nevertheless, before finally selecting a topic it should be rigorously exposed to the tests listed.

The first step is to identify areas which seem to have potential. The supervisor should, of course, be involved at this stage and may in fact have a ready-made topic which appeals to the student. If this is not the case, then students must, particularly at research degree levels, be able to:

1. Identify an apparently novel topic.
2. Convince themselves and others of the novelty of the topic.

In this, requirement 1 implies a degree of creativity, the extent of which will relate to the level at which the research is to be undertaken; and requirement 2 will involve a systematic search of the literature along the lines to be described in Chapter 4. It is customary to consider several topics during the selection process and it is sensible that students should identify as many potentially rewarding lines as they can.

Only at the level of the research degree does it become necessary to add to the body of knowledge to any significant extent. Therefore, at this level, an early step must be to determine what the body of knowledge is. The supervisors have an obvious contribution to make at this stage.

There are numerous sources of ideas for research. It is assumed that the supervisors will discharge their responsibilities appropriately at this stage by being both proactive (putting forward their own suggestions) and reactive (responding to the student's findings).

Suggestions for research topics may arise from the following sources:

1. Theses and dissertations.
2. Articles in academic and professional journals.
3. Conference proceedings (including internet conferences) and reports generally.

4. Books and book reviews.
5. Reviews of the field of study.
6. Communication with experts in the field.
7. Conversations with potential users of the research findings.
8. Discussions with colleagues.
9. The media.

The type of study being followed will affect the extent to which students use the sources listed above. PhD students must expect to cover most if not all of them, as it is vital to establish that their work is original. At other levels convenience and access are likely to dictate the action taken.

Sources 1 to 5 imply access to relevant literature. For most students this will normally be obtained through a high-quality library – the quality being measured in terms of the library's access to literature and the ability of the library staff to advise on use of the library resources, including on-line databases.

All *theses*, many dissertations and other student reports will generally contain suggestions for additional research. *Journal articles* sometimes include recommendations for further work and, as they are reasonably up to date (appearing a year or so after the completion of a study), should be given careful attention by the researcher. Reports, particularly of government-sponsored bodies, although often the outcome of protracted enquiries, are usually published with some speed. Again, these often contain recommendations on which research can be based. *Books* give a detailed account of particular fields and consequently will figure prominently in a researcher's studies; books do, nevertheless, possess the disadvantage that they are not as up to date as the other written sources mentioned, and their contents may have become known to other researchers. It will be noted that the list above includes *book reviews* as well as books. The reviewers of a book are usually able to evaluate the extent of its contribution to knowledge and can provide a useful service for students seeking ideas for topics. Citation indexes (see Chapter 4) provide listings of book reviews and may well be worth consulting for this purpose alone. The essential step of gaining access to relevant published material will be examined in depth in Chapter 4.

Reviews of the field of study provide a very useful guide to the researcher as to what is known in the field and what are still matters of conjecture; and of what has been discovered by previous researchers and where research is needed. There seems to be a definite trend with the proliferation of research subjects for academic journals to publish review articles by leading experts in the field.

Sources 6 to 8 require rather more initiative than does a mere search of the literature. The notion that research can be pursued from behind a desk may appeal to some students (and indeed may be all that is expected for a dissertation) but whatever the field, at research degree level, much advantage may be gained from *discussions with others*. Active researchers are usually sympathetic towards students who are undertaking studies in an area of mutual interest. Ideas for research can sometimes be tested during a brief conversation on the telephone or at conferences and seminars but ideally an appointment should be sought where potential topics can be discussed more fully. These comments apply with particular force to doctoral-level students who are able to identify individuals from other institutions or organisations who are obviously leaders in their field. In these circumstances a journey of some distance may well prove to be a highly useful investment.

ELECTRONIC CONFERENCING CAN HELP IN EXPOSING THOUGHTS ON A POSSIBLE RESEARCH TOPIC TO OTHER RESEARCHERS

The growing practice of electronic conferencing can assist students who wish to expose their thoughts on prospective topics to those researching round the world in specified fields. Increasingly, use is being made of the Internet for this purpose (see Chapter 4). Although there will be some circularity in the sense that the nature of the research will not be defined until the topic has been selected, the field in which the student is working will probably favour certain categories of research which might be linked to potential *users*. Thus, a research student in biochemistry might make contact with the research departments of companies manufacturing pharmaceuticals, or an engineering student could initiate discussions with a company making hydraulic valves.

Much may be gained when a few ideas have been generated by discussing them informally with *colleagues* (students and staff). In this respect the advantage of working within a research group is obvious and the need for greater initiative on the part of the lone research student is highlighted.

The media should not be ignored as a potential source of topics. Researchers are disinclined to publish their findings until they have been sufficiently substantiated but newspapers, popular journals, and radio and television may report on research progress which is felt to be of general interest. Additionally, findings may be reported by the media perhaps twelve months before scholarly accounts appear in learned journals. Students in the social sciences in particular may through awareness of the media be able to identify issues within which research topics might be located (see Chapter 4).

TECHNIQUES FOR GENERATING RESEARCH TOPICS

Experience suggests that methods of evaluating topics, and suggestions as to where to look for them, are often ineffective. Students need specific methods that will guide them in the topic selection process. These methods should be capable of providing useful guidance for two very different types of student: the under-focused, whose ideas of a subject area are not specific enough to form the basis of a viable topic, and the overfocused, who has a single-minded aim of pursuing a particular topic.

Underfocused students need ways of refining rather vague and often somewhat grandiose notions of a research area. The methods that are useful to them are those enabling them to identify a researchable 'niche' which they are capable of exploiting with the time and resources at their disposal.

The overfocused student might seem, by contrast, to have the ideal attitude for successful research. It must be remembered, nevertheless, that research is a specialised business and that it is by no means unknown for research students who have a clear idea of the research they wish to do to find, belatedly, that it has been done already or is not feasible, a fact of which they are unaware simply because of unfamiliarity with the frontiers of the subject. Where a supervisor has indicated an area for study this is less likely to be a problem but the implication of Figure 2.1 is that there are occasions when the best decision a student can make about a possible research topic is to drop it.

For both types of student there is virtue in having methods that are capable of suggesting alternative themes given a starting subject. The techniques that are helpful in topic selection are essentially part of the field of creativity or problem-solving theory. Useful detailed discussions of these fields can be found, for instance, in de Bono (1988), Ackoff (1978), or Van Grundy (1988).

Three approaches of considerable use to the researcher will be discussed here in more depth: the use of analogy, relevance trees and morphological analysis.

The Use of Analogy

Analogy plays an important role in many types of research. It aids the research process in two ways: firstly, it may suggest a fruitful line of enquiry in a particular subject area based on a perceived resemblance to some other area; or, secondly, it may suggest methods of analysis devised for use in one field which may profitably be employed in another. This latter role is exemplified by certain statistical techniques and will be discussed further in Chapter 5.

The use of analogy in topic formation is the principal interest here. An example of this process is the case of the researcher with an interest in small busi-ness innovation who notes that many experts have suggested that the advanced equipment used in the West is inappropriate in developing countries and that the latter need 'intermediate technology' better suited to their less developed tech-nical infrastructure. On reflection, the researcher perceives that the gap between the most advanced small businesses and the least is by no means dissimilar to that between the West and certain of the developing nations. From there it is a short step to speculate about 'intermediate technology' in the small businesses and the forms it might take (for example, in production management methods).

Relevance Trees

Though 'relevance trees' originated in the field of research and development management, their attraction is that they are excellent models of one of the ways people think about problems. Essentially, a relevance tree suggests a way of developing related ideas from a starting concept. To be most effective, the starting concept should be fairly broad. The relevance tree then serves as a device, either for generating alternative topics or for fixing on some 'niche'. The importance of both functions has, of course, already been noted.

Figure 2.2 shows an example of a relevance tree. Starting from the broad area of 'Demand for transport' the researcher first identifies two major factors affecting it, 'Need to Travel' and 'Individuals' ability to afford travel', which in turn can be related to 'Income' and 'Cost of travel'.

The first factor splits again into 'Leisure journeys' (also affected by the ability to afford travel) and 'Work journeys'. Determinants of the latter factor are seen to be 'Location of work' (where it is carried out), 'Location of people' (where they live) and 'Work activities'. This last set of ringed variables might suggest to the researcher a possible topic, namely the extent to which changes in the forms of work activity, for example those brought about by the introduction of intranets and extranets into large organisations, will affect in the longer term where people live and how far and how frequently they travel to work.

Morphological Analysis

Morphological analysis is another technique originally developed for use in industrial research and development. It relies upon a threefold process:

1. Defining the key factors or dimensions of a particular subject.
2. Listing the various attributes of the factor or ways it can occur.
3. Defining all feasible combinations of the attributes.

Figure 2.3 shows an example of morphological analysis for defining valid types of management dissertation. It is supposed, for the purpose of illustration, that the body of knowledge to be used is already known but that it is desired to identify a topic of sufficient potential for a master's degree. The researcher has selected three major factors defining type of management research:

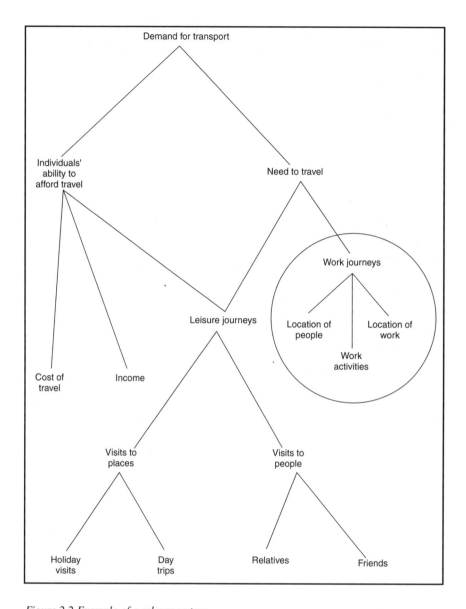

Figure 2.2 Example of a relevance tree

1. Focus: the group or activity which is to be researched.
2. Objectives: what the student intends to do in the dissertation.
3. Design: which methodology is employed.

FOCUS	OBJECTIVES	DESIGN
Issue	Description	Desk research
Management Function	Identify Key Dimensions	Mail Questionnaire
Market	Post Audit, Lessons for Management	Questionnaire Survey
Markets	Identify Barriers/Benefits	Case Study
Organisation	Forecast	Comparative Analysis
Several Organisations	Develop Tool	Modelling
Technology	Technique Development	
Decision	Technique Application	
Project	Develop Business Plan	

Figure 2.3 Example of morphological analysis. Types of management research dissertation

Various possible attributes of each factor are listed and different types of research project can then be generated by taking one attribute from each of the three columns of Figure 2.3. For example:

Several Organisations / Identify Key Dimensions / Comparative Analysis

which, clearly, would involve the researcher in attempting to determine the key dimensions of some phenomenon by comparative analysis of data drawn from several organisations.

In practice, not all combinations are feasible: for example, the limited scope for comparative analysis within one project. However, it will often be found that combinations involving two or more attributes of one or several factors are attractive. For example:

Modelling

Issue / Technique Development /

Case study

is a design frequently encountered in practice because of the opportunity it gives for testing the performance of techniques developed in actual situations.

Morphological analysis is capable of generating a very large number of alternatives. For this reason it is necessary to define only a few key dimensions or factors and to restrict the aspects of each that are considered. This forces the user to structure the problem and is thus particularly useful to the underfocused student who finds it difficult to get to grips with topic selection.

FEASIBILITY OF THE RESEARCH PROPOSED

There is little purpose in attempting a full evaluation of a topic unless the research to which it leads is feasible. The student should therefore consider the following factors.

1. Access to and availability of data and information.
2. Opportunity to pursue a particular research design.
3. Time needed to complete the research.
4. Technical skills needed.
5. Financial support.
6. The risk involved.

The six factors may be relevant to all levels of research and the first two can be insurmountable obstacles.

Access and Availability

The first factor may be exemplified by a student who has selected as a research topic variation in manufacturing costs in different countries within multinational car firms. Some car companies may be prepared to state in which countries costs are particularly high but it is unlikely that sufficient companies, if any, would disclose detailed data. This may be an obvious example but students should satisfy themselves that there is reasonable prospect of access before proceeding further. A more difficult assessment for the student to make at this stage is whether data or information which will be essential to the research actually exist. Planned approaches involving the analysis of secondary data (which are not gathered by the researcher) will be impossible if the data have not been recorded or are unreliable.

Opportunity for Research Design

The student may be inclined towards a topic in which a laboratory features and in many cases such researchers will be able to set up experiments in their own institution's laboratories. If, however, the student intends to conduct a field experiment, some degree of cooperation will normally be needed. For example, pricing policy for books may well be felt to be a suitable topic for research but it would be unlikely that a publisher could be found who would agree to handing over control of pricing to a student. Similar difficulties may be encountered in attempts to arrange a survey. Thus, a researcher may wish to study member/ officer relationships within a particular local authority. Before proceeding further, permission must be sought to approach the subjects of the investigation. To attempt to proceed without approval is likely to lead to complete frustration of the plan.

Time Available

A prime aim of this book is to assist students to complete their research within the time available to them. In some instances, research is designed without proper thought being given to the time needed for its completion.

For example, the development of an anti-corrosive paint could be an appropriate outcome of a research study but the time required to assess the anti-corrosive properties added to the development period may far exceed the time available to a student researcher. Very often the student's department will have recognised the problem and broken down the task into a set of consecutive projects, each of which can be undertaken by a different student. Where this is not the case the student will need to consider whether it is necessary to undertake another project. Another question is whether too much is being attempted within the time available for research. When the topic has been selected, much is to be gained by drawing up a research plan which will indicate whether the deadlines can be met (see Chapter 3).

Technical Skills

It is reasonable to assume that student research at any level is more likely to succeed if the topic chosen will utilise skills and knowledge already possessed. There would, for example, seem to be greater prospects of satisfactory completion if a student with a first degree in physics were to research in this subject rather than in botany. In some instances, however, it is impossible to avoid having to acquire new skills if a topic is to be researched effectively. This is particularly so in the social sciences where skills often require to be developed in statistics, mathematics and computing. Students should, therefore, consider very carefully whether the topic chosen matches the skills they possess or will have time to develop during the course of their study. If doubt exists, the supervisor should be able to give guidance.

Financial Support

> BEFORE A TOPIC IS FINALISED, THE QUESTION OF THE COST OF CONDUCTING THE STUDY MUST BE EXAMINED

Much research has foundered because of a lack of resources. In student research where the prime resource is the individual concerned, it is essential that the financial support needed for the study should have been resolved before work is started. The student's budget will include funds to support normal research expenditure which may involve travelling, purchase of books, cost of transcriptions and so on. Many sponsored students are unclear as to what expenditure will be covered by their sponsor but this is unlikely to cover the purchase of expensive equipment or materials, or unlimited travel and subsistence, and may not even extend to postal questionnaires. Before a topic is finally selected, therefore, the question of cost must be examined. Inability to undertake certain activities due to a shortage of funds may prejudice a potentially successful study if the problem is not anticipated and resolved at the outset.

The Risk Involved

As a final point, the student should consider the risk that for any reason the project will prove impossible to complete. It will be remembered that, in discussing the nature of research in Chapter 1, we made the point that some types of research are perhaps inherently more risky than others; the student should, therefore, at least decide whether the risk of the project proposed is acceptable.

These comments on the six factors have been made particularly with full-time research in mind. They apply with even greater force to part-time researchers with the one exception that in longitudinal studies involving an evaluation of some phenomenon over time the part-timer may have an advantage because of the longer duration of the study. In the UK, for example, most degree-awarding bodies, although preferring a part-time doctorate to be completed within five years, would be tolerant towards a longer period of registration providing evidence of progress could regularly be given and there was no likelihood of the research becoming out of date. Social, economic, or political 'experiments' often need lengthy periods of evaluation, and as such would exceed the two or three years available to full-time research students.

No apology is made if the observations appear to be somewhat negative. By giving systematic consideration to the feasibility of the topic and the risks it entails the student will be forced to think carefully about the purpose of the research and the approach to be adopted. If the topic can satisfy the demands of feasibility, as described, the student will be well equipped to complete the planning phase (see Figure 1.3); if not, the prospect of a future disaster can be avoided by refining the topic or selecting another.

SOCIAL VALUE OF THE RESEARCH

Having satisfied themselves that the topic is feasible, students next need to consider whether it has sufficient social value. In some respects the student is in a privileged position in that the value of research may be judged purely on its contribution to academic knowledge with the question of its wider, social utility being unimportant. At the level of the undergraduate or the postgraduate dissertation, the question of value may be resolved even more easily as the prime aim may be to demonstrate a measure of research competence or problem-solving ability (through, for example, a literature search or a case study).

The right of researchers to select topics which have no apparent value for the community at large is, however, being increasingly questioned. For example, the 1993 UK White Paper on science policy laid upon the UK Research Councils the duty of taking account of the need of publicly funded research to support the wealth creation process.

There is little point in studying apparently irrelevant and trivial topics if alternative topics of 'importance' can be identified. A further advantage of working on a topic of some significance is that the student is much more likely to be motivated, a frame of mind essential for successful completion. In addition, the supervisor (and ultimately any external examiner) is likely to take a greater interest if the research outcome is of undoubted value to the community. The PhD student who elects to pursue a topic that has little obvious social value must expect in today's research climate that this aspect of the research will at examination receive much more attention than hitherto.

It is indicative of a thorough approach to a study if the student is convinced that a topic of social value has been identified. In realising this situation advice will normally have been taken from experts in the area in addition to that offered by the supervisor. The model depicted in Figure 2.1 is, however, an idealised one and it is possible that changes made to the topic for one reason (for example, infeasibility) may fundamentally alter its ability to satisfy other requirements including social value. For example, it may have been agreed initially between a doctoral student and a supervisor that the research would focus on the relationship between local authorities in England and central government. The student, after considering the extent of the fieldwork involved, may have decided to examine the relationship between one local authority only and central government. Although studies in depth have their own attractions and advantages, value would probably be lost because of the restricted scope for generalisation afforded by a single case study. In order to avoid such an eventuality it is evident that second opinions should be sought at each new stage or redirection.

There is, unfortunately, no easy way to measure the social value of research, and indeed its importance in student research is related to the level of the activity, being much more important in the case of doctoral studies. The best advice to students is probably for them to continue to search for an alternative topic if the one under consideration seems to be of doubtful social value.

RESEARCH SYMMETRY

Even though a student may be satisfied that research is both feasible and potentially valuable, Figure 2.1 suggests that there are still two stages of the idealised process to go through before a topic is finally selected. The first of these stages requires that the alternative outcomes of the study should be identified. Although below research degree level there may be only one outcome – for example, the writing up of a literature search or a case study – in more advanced research two or more outcomes may be possible. For instance a hypothesis may be accepted or rejected, or an experiment may provide a definite result or may be inconclusive. Preferably each of the outcomes should represent findings of value in which case the risk involved in the research will be reduced.

THE EXTENT TO WHICH RESEARCH OUTCOMES ARE OF SIMILAR VALUE – SYMMETRY – IS AN IMPORTANT ISSUE

The extent to which the outcomes are of similar value is an indication of the symmetry of the research. The research student should seek to select a topic which promises high symmetry, but the prospects will be affected by the research approach which is adopted. Thus, some research work of an experimental nature undertaken in laboratories by scientists and engineers may be highly asymmetrical and may ultimately fail to achieve a positive result. Alternatively, a student may be unable to validate an econometric model which has been developed, perhaps mainly from theory. In both of these instances this would lead to there being no basis for the award of a research degree.

Symmetry depends in large part on prior beliefs about a topic which are held within a field of study. If, for example, there exists strong support for the view that the eating of sweets damages children's teeth or there is little belief that the phases of the moon affect work output, experiments which confirm strongly held opinion will not be rated highly even though the design and conduct of these experiments cannot be criticised. Obviously, if the research findings were to contradict current belief they would be of potential value. An example of a symmetrical research topic would be one concerned with the effect on career progress of students who attain the degree of Master in Business Administration (MBA). If it were found that the MBA had no effect on career progress this conclusion would be of considerable value as would the contrary finding (although note should be taken of 'Scope for Research' as discussed in the next section).

One possible outcome of research is that the findings are inconclusive. Research students should satisfy themselves that the probability of this type of outcome is sufficiently low. As an example, we can consider a student seeking to establish whether a theory of leadership based on research within a number of companies in the private sector is applicable also to management in the public sector. If a hypothesis to this effect were to be confirmed or rejected either finding could be of considerable value. Although the topic may be symmetrical with regard to conclusive outcomes the research student may feel that there is a distinct possibility of an inconclusive outcome and that this makes the research insufficiently attractive to pursue.

At doctoral level, symmetry is to be preferred if the research lends itself to it, because it reduces the risk of an unsuccessful outcome to the research. In this way research which satisfies all other criteria should lead to a successful outcome. We do not wish, however, to imply that success or failure always involves symmetry. Research which is of an exploratory or descriptive nature will normally have only one outcome which will be assessed at some point on a scale ranging from acceptable to unacceptable.

SCOPE FOR RESEARCH

The final test of a research topic, as is suggested in Figure 2.1, is that of assessing whether sufficient scope exists. In large part, scope will be related to work already completed in related areas. As a result of such work prior beliefs will be held and these will affect the reaction to the research outcome in terms of novelty and surprise. Prior beliefs may range from certainty (for example, that the earth moves round the sun) to complete uncertainty (for example, whether life exists elsewhere in the universe). Scope should be seen as the opportunity to increase confidence in, reduce confidence in, or even confirm current beliefs.

In considering scope, research students should reflect also on the value of their potential topic. If this is high there may be sufficient scope even if prior beliefs are strongly held (for example in the case of the effect of dietary fat on health). It goes without saying that findings which overturn strongly held beliefs on matters of importance will be rated highly but these opportunities will present themselves only rarely to the student researcher. The topics to be avoided are those which are potentially low in both surprise and value (here in the broadest sense). Thus, a researcher might select as a topic the speed of learning of a foreign language by child expatriates. It would come as no surprise, and would be of little apparent value, to find that English-speaking children in families living in France or Germany gain a more rapid command of the languages of these countries than do English-speaking children living in the UK. On the other hand, there may be both surprise and value in finding that the same children demonstrate higher competence in mathematics than do children of similar ages in the UK. Though the standards required vary from one level of research to another students should satisfy themselves that the topic has sufficient potential along the dimensions of both scope and value.

DEVELOPING A RESEARCH PROPOSAL

At all levels of study considerable benefit can be gained by systematic planning. The aim must be to develop a realistic plan of action with clear objectives which, taking account of resources and constraints, has a high probability of being achieved. The planning process itself is discussed in the next chapter but at this point reference is made to certain documents which research students should be prepared to compile: topic analyses and the research proposal.

It is recommended that research degree students should undertake preparation of both types of document. Dissertation students can usually content themselves with preparing an abbreviated research proposal. Topic analyses and the research proposal will contribute to the achievement of the first major milestone, namely when both supervisor and student have agreed the study to be pursued.

Experience shows that the step of preparing and submitting views in writing for consideration by supervisors and others can be highly beneficial for students. Redirection of research can be accommodated much more readily at earlier rather than later stages and yet some students are reluctant to commit themselves to paper.

Both topic analyses and the research proposal are of similar structure and the latter is in fact an elaborated version of a topic analysis. The sections of each are shown in Table 2.1

The Topic Analysis

Topic analyses are convenient ways of summarising various aspects of one or more potentially acceptable topics. A topic analysis should not exceed a few pages in length. It should contain summaries, following careful consideration of each of the sections of Table 2.1, rather than a set of speculative observations.

Section	Topic analyses (2–5 pages)	Research proposal (20–50 pages for a research degree; 2–10 pages for a dissertation)
Summary		X
Research questions	X	X
Prior research in the area/literature review	X	X
Value in terms of possible outcomes	X	X
Research design or approach to the research	X	X
Tentative schedule	X	X
Provisional chapter details		X

Table 2.1 Content of topic analyses and the research proposal

The starting point for the topic analysis should be the formulation of a set of reasonably broad research questions that offer sufficient value and scope with, if possible, potentially high research symmetry. Experience shows that research questions are better suited to the early scoping of research. They tend to encourage wider thinking than the formulation of some hypothesis for testing as recommended by many traditional research texts. More importantly they are applicable to a wider range of doctoral research projects. Thus, examples might be:

1. What are the mechanisms underlying high temperature superconductors?
2. Is it possible to design approaches to metal cutting that use much less energy than conventional ones?
3. What is the impact of the UK Central Government's Best Value programme on the performance of local authorities?
4. What was the influence of the English Garden City movement outside the UK in the twentieth century?

The section of the topic analysis dealing with research value will be highly significant when research degrees are involved and will encompass the comments made above on social value, symmetry and scope of the research. It will be strengthened if evidence can be provided that authorities in the field agree that there is a need for the research proposed.

If more than one topic proves to be acceptable to both student and supervisor the final choice will most probably depend upon the weightings attached by the student to the value of the research and the approach likely to be adopted. Some students react positively to the challenge of higher value (but often higher risk) studies whereas others wish to maximise the chances of completing their research and hence select the topic most consistent with this.

Those students for whom the completion of a topic analysis is an essential part of the planning phase may wish to model their approach on the example which is presented at Appendix 1.

The Research Proposal

Whereas a topic analysis should contain just sufficient information for a decision to be reached on the line of research to be pursued, the research proposal should be seen as the document which finally establishes both the need for the study and that the researcher has or can acquire the skills and other resources required. Students should in fact imagine that they are tendering for a research contract through the medium of the research proposal. In reality it is highly probable that the latter will need to be refined, possibly more than once.

The final version of the research proposal for a research degree thesis might be 20 to 50 pages in length, whereas two to ten pages is usually enough for dissertation purposes. In those sections which are common to both the topic analysis and the research proposal the main elaboration in the latter case will be on prior research and probable methodology. Students working for higher degrees will accumulate many additional references during the course of their research and writing but before embarking on the execution phase they must be able to satisfy themselves and their advisors that they are wholly familiar with previous and current work in the area of their planned study. In addition to guaranteeing novelty this will be a major factor in assessing the value of possible outcomes. Thus, the account of prior research as indicated by the list of references and the bibliography contained within the research proposal should be comprehensive.

The proposal will need to describe in sufficient detail the approach which the student will use. In large measure this will indicate whether or not the line of study planned is feasible. The factors identified in the section labelled 'Feasibility of the research proposed' should be addressed. Thus, descriptions will need to be given of such matters as the sampling frame and method, any equipment needed, the data to be collected, the nature of the experiment, the methods of analysis to be employed, the resources and the time required to carry out the project.

This will probably be the most difficult section of the research proposal to write and there should be much resort to expert advice. Inevitably there will be questions still to be resolved. Students must, however, ask themselves the question: 'Dare I risk proceeding when significant uncertainty remains?' In some instances the answer must be 'No'. It would, for example, be foolish to write up a proposal which did not guarantee the opportunity to pursue a particular research design. On the other hand it would be reasonable for a student who is familiar with one statistical analysis package to assume that it would be possible to acquire the skills to use another.

Although only tentative, it is desirable that a schedule, along the lines of that described in Chapter 3, should be incorporated in a research proposal. It is important that, with limited time at their disposal, students should become used to thinking in terms of milestones and deadlines. Such a schedule will be beneficial to the research student when drawing up the research plan. Given the tight nature of the deadlines involved and the other calls on their time – the search for a job, for instance – a schedule of this nature is essential to the dissertation student.

Similarly, much is to be gained by including within the research proposal details of the chapters, in the form of, say, 6–12 main section headings per chapter. The chapters themselves will normally accord with a standard and logical structure. An example of such a structure (adapted from Howard, 1978) which relates to doctoral theses is as follows:

1. The introduction describing the general problem area, the specific problem, why the topic is important, prior research, approach of the thesis, limitations and key assumptions, and contribution to be made by the research.
2. A description of what has been done in the past, This is a complete survey of prior research which, if very nominal, might be combined with Chapter 1. If there is extensive prior research, the results might preferably be broken down into two or more chapters. It is normally an important section of the thesis because the description of what has been done provides background and also documents the fact that the candidate's research is unique as the thesis is not duplicating earlier work.
3. A description of the research methodology. One or more chapters may be used to describe the research method. For example, the chapter(s) might describe a simulation model, a data collection technique, a measurement technique, an experiment, or an historical method of analysis. In essence, this section describes how the research was conducted.
4. The research results. The results of the chosen methodology are reported: the data are presented, the conceptual framework is described, the historical analysis is defined, or the comparative studies are explained.
5. Analysis of the results. This may be included with earlier chapters depending upon the type of thesis. This is a key section because it explains the conclusions that can be drawn from the data, the implications of a theory and so on.

6. Summary and conclusions. The thesis is summarised with emphasis upon the results obtained and the contribution made by these results. Indication of the limits of, and reservations about, the chosen approach and an evaluation of the success of the project. Any suggestions for further research are also outlined.

> A RESEARCH PROPOSAL IS NOT A PROGRESS REPORT TO BE FILED AWAY, BUT A DOCUMENT FOR DECISION

The purpose of a research proposal should not be forgotten. It should not be seen as a progress report to be filed but as a document for decision. For the dissertation student it is essential to get the research proposal agreed by the supervisor as early as possible. In the case of a research degree student, the proposal is of sufficient importance for the student to arrange a formal presentation/seminar which preferably will be attended by other researchers as well as the supervisor. The result of this presentation should be general agreement that the researcher should now be able to proceed with some confidence. If such agreement does not materialise it is to be hoped that sufficient constructive criticism will have been obtained for a revised proposal to have a good chance of acceptance on the next round.

CHAPTER SUMMARY

TOPIC SELECTION: is a process which differs considerably for dissertation and research degree students.

Dissertation students with help from their academic institution will often select their topic without great difficulty but should always take into account potential value. Where a dissertation is carried out in an organisation care needs to be taken to ensure that the topic is of sufficient academic merit.

For a research degree student, topic selection can absorb a significant proportion of a research study. Certain steps can, however, be recognised which enable a systematic approach towards topic selection to be adopted; this should reduce the probability of excessive time being spent on this stage.

Research degree students are likely to find it useful to prepare one or more topic analyses before embarking on a fully fledged research proposal.

THE SUPERVISOR: Dissertation students normally only receive limited amounts of supervision directed to ensuring the research project is carried out competently. Detailed knowledge of the field is rarely needed by the supervisor and should not be expected.

For research degree students supervisor(s) should be appointed as soon as possible and should be heavily involved during the topic selection process.

THE GENERATION OF RESEARCH TOPICS: may be facilitated by a number of techniques which include analogy, relevance trees and morphological analysis.

FOR RESEARCH DEGREE STUDENTS THE ACCEPTABILITY OF A RESEARCH TOPIC: may be judged by giving consideration to its feasibility, value, symmetry and scope.

3

Planning the Research Project

There are a number of reasons why students experience difficulty in research. The most important of these are:

1. Difficulties in selecting a suitable topic.
2. The problem of selecting an appropriate analytical framework.
3. Inability to manage available resources, in particular, time.

The third reason is common at all levels of research, this inability being often symptomatic of the previous two. Where students experience problems in planning these often result in wasted time and lack of progress.

THE NEED TO PLAN

The aim of this chapter is very simple. It is to present students with a tool for planning their own research project which will enable them to realise when they have run into serious difficulties. More importantly, perhaps, this chapter is also intended to function as a motivational device by enabling students to see that they are achieving goals they have set themselves, since experience shows that the best way to successful completion of the research as a whole is through acquiring the habit of successful completion of intermediate stages.

Although the type of planning to be described is in itself a useful process, through which desirable courses of action are identified and potential pitfalls are anticipated, a major justification is that it serves as a basis for control. What is required is not a loose collection of estimates of what the research will involve but a comprehensively analysed schedule of activities against which research progress may be assessed. The planning referred to in this chapter is not that concerned with the nature of the research itself but with the management of the research project. This will be viewed as a number of distinct but interrelated stages or activities all of which must be completed before the study is finished. Although the activities will differ in importance each will be planned to the same degree to indicate when, ideally, they should take place.

The major purposes of such planning are to:

a) clarify the aims and objectives of the researcher;
b) define the activities required to attain these aims and the order in which they take place;
c) identify various critical points or 'milestones' in the research at which progress can be reviewed and the research plan reassessed;
d) produce estimates of times at which the various milestones will be reached so that progress can be clearly measured;
e) ensure that effective use is made of key resources;
f) define priorities once the research is underway;
g) serve as a guide for increasing the likelihood of successful completion on time.

If this list seems over-elaborate the reader should remember that the fewer the resources of time and money the greater the need for careful planning, and that in any research project the key resource is always the student's own time. Furthermore, planning is most necessary where the activities involved are non-routine so that possible difficulties can be anticipated.

A major difficulty in the planning of research is that the work content of the various stages cannot always be readily estimated. It is presumed, however, that students will have selected a topic which can be researched within the time available and that, although creative thought and deadlines conflict to some extent, the implied time constraints will be accepted.

At a minimum, the planning of a project requires that this is broken down into a fairly high-level list of activities in respect of which estimates of their durations are made. The researcher will have a view of the sequence in which these activities are to be undertaken and some sort of activity diagram such as a bar chart can then be drawn up. If the number of activities chosen is not great this will probably suffice. With increasing complexity and detail the probability that dependence will be overlooked increases rapidly and consideration should be given to a formal planning tool of the type described in the next section.

NETWORK PLANNING

In planning a research project, an approach should be adopted which will serve as a basis for control of projects of various lengths but will also be sufficiently flexible to accommodate the unpredictabilities of research. Given the success of network analysis techniques (notably Critical Path Analysis (CPA) and Programme Evaluation and Review Technique (PERT)) in planning and controlling industrial research projects as well as complex construction programmes, some form of network is indicated.

The development of the computer in the 1950s stimulated the application of network analysis particularly to construction projects in which thousands of activities may be involved. Much has subsequently been written about these techniques (see, for example, Lock, 2000). Their primary purpose is to assist in planning and control in situations in which the mind is unable to cope efficiently with the relationships among the numerous activities. The principles involved can be comprehended within an hour or two and application of the technique can be very beneficial to the completion of the study within the time available.

Thus, although the procedures outlined are rather formal they can be applied by students at any level. As elsewhere, it is argued that research students should employ them unless either they are sufficiently experienced in managing research projects to have their own system (which will inevitably be fairly similar), or they agree with their supervisor that these methods are inappropriate in their case.

Nevertheless, the methods have value in their own right as a model of the process of planning a research project and may therefore be so regarded, if desired.

AN EXAMPLE OF NETWORK PLANNING IN STUDENT RESEARCH

In this section an example will be employed drawing upon the research approach used by many students in the social sciences, namely the analysis of response to a questionnaire-based survey in order to test a hypothesis.

Whatever the level of research and whatever stage has been reached the process of network planning is always the same.

1. Determine the objectives.
2. Identify and list (in any order) the activities that need to be carried out.

3. Order the activities. Establish for every activity, those activities which precede it, those which follow it, and those which may be undertaken concurrently.
4. Draw the network.
5. Estimate the time needed to complete each activity.
6. Analyse the network using the completion times.
7. Check the resources and draw up the schedule.
8. Replan as necessary.

We now look at each of these eight activities in more detail.

Determine the Objectives

> AS A FIRST STEP, STUDENTS SHOULD ALWAYS DETERMINE THEIR OBJECTIVES

When a student first begins work on a project he or she should always determine their objectives since these may well influence many of the activities that appear in the list. In this case it is assumed that the student's primary objective is to pursue a career in social science research and that as a consequence during the first six months of study the following subsidiary aims have been defined:

a) work in an area with considerable research potential;
b) acquire familiarity with certain basic tools of social science research, such as the conduct of surveys and the role of statistics in survey analysis and the use of the computer for processing survey data;
c) successfully complete a PhD thesis in the 2.5 years (130 weeks) that the student expects to remain full-time.

Obviously, the points under b) are reflected in the number of activities on the list, whereas the requirement c) may well necessitate replanning if for some reason the analysis shows that the target cannot be met.

Listing the Activities

The student will next need to decide the level at which the activities should be listed. This depends on the length of the project and the stage which has been reached. In a research project for a taught master's course, there will usually be little difficulty in producing a list of activities at the level of detail shown in Table 3.1, which will probably suffice for the whole project. Indeed, students involved

Activity no.	Activity description	Abbreviation	Estimated duration (weeks)
1	Written statement of concepts and theories	Concepts and theories	3
2	First draft of questionnaire for pilot study	First draft QA	6
3	Finalising of questionnaire for pilot study	Finalise QA	1
4	Decide likely method of analysing response to survey	Decide analytical method	4
5	Select participants for pilot	Select pilot participants	4
6	Acquire statistical skills	Acquire statistical skills	8
7	Attend course on use of standard computer package	Attend computer course	6
8	Write (say, three) drafts of early thesis chapters	Draft early chapters	9
9	Carry out pilot study	Carry out pilot	4
10	Review pilot study	Review pilot study	3
11	Prepare questionnaire for survey	Prepare QA	4
12	Decide target population and sampling details	Decide target population	4
13	Carry out survey	Carry out survey	12
14	Process data for computer	Process data	6
15	Interpret computer output	Interpret output	6
16	Evaluate nature and extent of response to survey	Evaluate response	4
17	Write paper for presentation at conference	Write paper	4
18	Relate findings to concepts/theories/ hypothesis	Relate findings	6
19	Decide and carry out any further analysis or research	Decide further analysis	12
20	Complete writing of (say, five) draft chapters	Complete writing	15
21	Review and edit thesis	Review and edit	10
22	Correct thesis and obtain bound copies	Correct thesis	4
23	Prepare for oral examination	Prepare for oral	2
24	Allowance for holidays, job interviews, illness and general contingencies	Contingency allowance	24

Table 3.1 A list of activities for a student research project in the social science field

in projects as short as this are cautioned that, if they experience difficulties in drawing up a list of the activities or in assessing the time they will take, it may well mean that the project involves too much uncertainty and needs redefinition.

At the doctoral level however, it will normally be necessary to go through the planning process many times during the project and the level of detail appropriate at the beginning may be very different from that needed once a topic has been selected and the research is well underway. Thus at the very beginning a list of activities such as:

i)   attending Professor Brown's lectures,
ii)   participating in a 'spreadsheet analysis for beginners' course,
iii) selecting a topic,
iv)   drawing up a research proposal, and
v)   carrying out the research,

could well be quite adequate, in that it can serve as a basis for monitoring progress in the earlier stages, while not pretending to knowledge that the student does not have prior to topic selection.

Equally a slightly more complex model could be achieved by suitably adapting the stages of the research project shown in Figure 1.3. This would, for example, bring into more focus the time which could reasonably be allotted to the selection of the topic itself. In the present case, however, it is assumed that a research proposal has been submitted and accepted.

Several activities that have already taken place, for example, 'Topic selection', do not, therefore, appear in the network. Planning is about what has to be done and not about what has been done. This means that as the project progresses and activities are completed the network tends to shrink.

It should be noted that the activities listed in Table 3.1 are typical in that they involve a mix of motivational activities (for example, 'Write paper for presentation at conference'), preparatory activities ('Acquiring statistical skills'), activities specific to the research project ('Carry out survey') and, finally, those required for reasons of health and sanity and not directly related to the work itself, for example 'Allowance for holidays, etc.'. As far as the latter is concerned there is an element of flexibility in that it is part of the contingency allowance that is added to any time estimate. Thus, in this case the student has not scheduled any summer holiday during the research project proper, preferring to improve motivation to beat the schedule by earmarking some part of any time savings for holiday purposes.

It is sometimes the case that by slightly redefining the activity the student may considerably reduce the risk that the research will run into major problems. Thus, here, the student, though anticipating a high response rate, might well decide to despatch the questionnaire to a much larger sample in case the response proves to be far lower than expected and, in addition, to incorporate certain features in the questionnaire to make it possible to check for any bias in the eventual replies. Neither of these decisions is likely to have much effect on the time required for the activities involved. On the other hand, either or both of them considerably reduce the risk of failure through insufficient returns or returns with a serious but unrecognised bias.

Order the Activities

The basic method used for drawing the network is to represent the activities by boxes and the order in which activities must take place by linking the activity boxes by arrows. Thus the diagram is to be interpreted as:

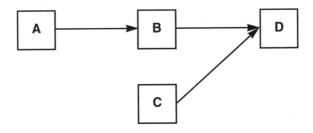

Activity A must be completed before Activity B can start
Activity C can run in parallel with Activities A and B but
Activity D cannot start until both Activity B and Activity C have been completed.

Draw the Network

The network of a research study represented at this level of detail can be drawn very quickly (for further details see, for example, Lock, 2000). The outcome is depicted in Figure 3.1 after consideration has been given to the ordering of activities. It will be noted that the project effectively divides into stages. Stage 1 comprises research design, data gathering and preliminary analysis. Stage 2 comprises final analysis and thesis preparation. (In the figure, the network has been split at Milestone M4 to reflect this.)

The virtue of such a presentation is that the interrelationship between activities can be clearly seen, particularly where the need for one activity to precede another is not immediately obvious. Furthermore, the first few times this approach is used it may well remind the researcher of activities that have been overlooked.

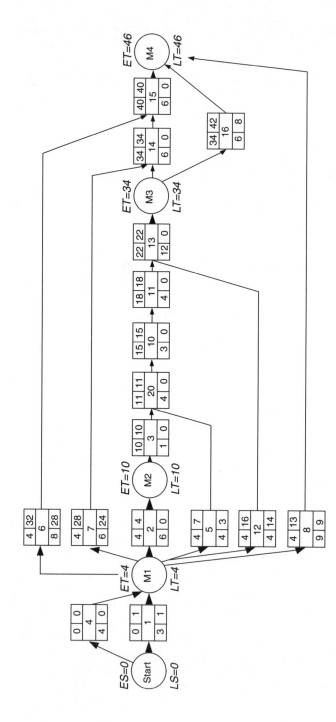

Figure 3.1 Network for a research study: Stage 1

58

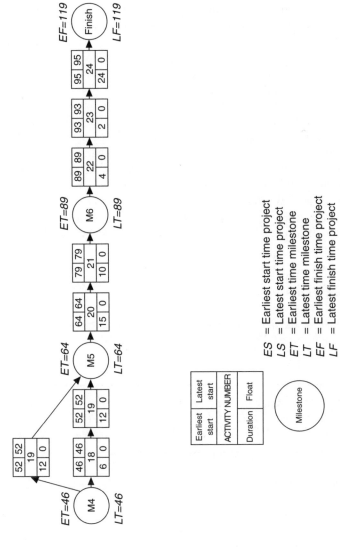

Figure 3.1 Network for a research study: Stage 2

59

Points in the project at which, in principle at least, the student can be working on several activities at once are indicated by parallel paths through the network – for example, 'Carry out pilot study' and 'Decide target population and sampling details'. These may well be helpful in fitting the project schedule to the resources available. In short, Figure 3.1 shows the 'logic' of the project on which planning must be based and is of very considerable value in itself. Indeed, some researchers use networks solely to indicate the way in which the project activities interact. It is customary to indicate the passage of time by ensuring that all arrows point in a forward (left to right) direction.

So far no reference has been made to activity duration as much value can be gained by drawing the network and thus appreciating the order in which work should be done. Furthermore, a network reduces the probability of overlooking an important stage of the research. There is, of course, no certainty that the study will in execution correspond exactly with the structure of the network. but it should represent the views of the student at the stage of the research reached. Thus, in Figure 3.1, activity number 19 ('Decide and carry out any further analysis or research') might be viewed at the time the network was drawn more as a contingency but in the event may involve several additional stages which need to be carefully planned.

Estimate Activity Times

A major advantage of the network approach is that by undertaking simple calculations a schedule of activities may be prepared and used for controlling the project.

IN ESTIMATING DURATION OF ACTIVITIES, STUDENTS WILL NEED ADVICE FROM THEIR SUPERVISOR AND, IDEALLY, FROM OTHER STUDENTS WHO HAVE COMPLETED RESEARCH IN SIMILAR AREAS

Included in Table 3.1 is an estimate of the number of weeks required to complete each of the 24 activities listed. It should be noted that 'Estimated duration' is the 'elapsed time' – that is, the period required to complete the activity. Usually this will be longer than the number of weeks of work entailed by the activity, because, say, the activity involves contacting individuals who are not immediately accessible; or, more importantly, when time is needed to integrate information that has been gained into the researcher's conceptual framework. The task of estimation is not an easy one and students will need advice from their supervisor and, ideally, from other students who have completed research in similar areas.

Thus, in the hypothetical example it may be possible to identify a researcher who has completed a questionnaire-based survey with considerable similarities to the study envisaged. These experiences would then be translated to assist in estimating the duration of activities 2, 3, 9, 10, 11 and 13 of Table 3.1. The student may be reasonably confident in estimating the time to allocate to activities 1, 5, 12, 17, 20, 21, 22 and 23. It is always necessary to take account of activities such as holidays and illness which will not further the project work. These are included in activity 24 which it will be seen extends the duration of the project by about 20 per cent. Although, as we have said, allowances need to be built into each activity it is sensible that further latitude is provided to cover activities which are not related to project progress.

This leaves activities 4, 6, 7, 8, 14, 15, 16, 18 and 19 which can be roughly apportioned between two groups:

a) those for which the work content may be reasonably estimated but which are undertaken intermittently (activities 7 and 8);

b) those for which there is considerable uncertainty about the work content (activities 4, 6, 14, 15, 16, 18 and 19).

The estimating problem raised by group a) is not too difficult to accommodate. A realistic minimum elapsed time equal to the content of the work should first be assigned to the activity. If after analysis the activity is found to be critical the student will need to establish whether parallel activities are involved and if so the extent to which the total period of the research must be extended. If the activity does not turn out to be critical there will then be scope for stretching it out over a longer period without jeopardising the completion of the project.

The preparation of schedules is made more difficult by the need to accommodate group b) type activities which by definition are incapable of precise estimation. A further complication is the recognition that in some instances the work will be carried out intermittently. Indeed, in the example, only activity 19 ('Decisions on further analysis') will continuously occupy the student's attention. The problem may best be resolved by the student attempting to incorporate work content within elapsed time. Thus, activity 6 ('Acquisition of statistical skills') will require that the student should read certain texts but in order to ensure that the concepts are fully understood an elapsed time of eight weeks may be allocated (as used in Table 3.1) for the comprehension of issues arising from an estimated 50 hours of reading (a standard time of ten hours is sometimes used for each book read but 'heavyweight' texts are likely to require much longer). In the example used, activity 7 ('Attend course on standard computer package') is placed in group a) as it is not envisaged that the student would need to gain competence in programming. If this were the case the activity would have been more appropriately placed in the group b) category.

A number of general points apply to estimating activity times. Firstly, standard times exist for some tasks – for example, reading books as cited above. Secondly, students can often reduce the time they require to carry out certain activities and incidentally improve their ability to estimate it by training and preparation – for instance, by taking a rapid reading course before embarking on a literature search. Thirdly, allowances may need to be built into all activity times to cope with the unexpected occurrences that always seem far more likely to extend the time required rather than reduce it. The need to do this can only be established in the light of the student's own performance on estimating. For this reason, for all except the short research project it is recommended that the student records on a control chart (see Figure 3.2) how long activities actually take as compared with the initial estimate. During the course of the longer research project it may then be realistic to derive a 'correction factor' to apply to the first guesses. Though apparently naive this can be surprisingly effective.

The difficulty of handling uncertainty is probably the major problem in planning. In general single figure estimates are employed (as in Table 3.1) and give a spurious indication of likely accuracy, but in some instances the ensuing errors of estimation are so great that the outcome of the project is prejudiced. An early application of the network approach, which gained a considerable measure of publicity, was to the Polaris programme of the US Navy. The network technique employed was described as PERT (Programme Evaluation and Review Technique) in which pessimistic, most likely and optimistic estimates were made of durations. Crude approximations of time variance may be computed by taking a weighted combination of the three estimates. Variances are then totalled through any path in the network to arrive at a rough approximation to a normal distribution of time. In this way, in addition to expected project completion times, it became possible to place probabilities upon particular events being completed by a certain date. A quick insight into the approach may be gained by accessing a US Navy website (h-w.ups.navy.mil) (2001), It is not suggested that the student should go to the lengths of using this addition to the basic approach but, even if this was done, the total time taken in this aspect of planning would still be only a very small part of the total study.

Analyse the Network using the Completion Times

Schedule control charts were used for many years prior to the introduction of networks and naturally took some account of the interdependence of activities, although the danger of overlooking a critical interrelationship in complex projects is obvious. The introduction of activity durations into a network enables analysis to be undertaken which leads to the scheduling of activities with an indication of spare time (float) associated with them.

A common convention is that used in Figure 3.1 where the duration of each activity is contained in the left-hand bottom subsection of each activity box. By working from left to right through the network, 'earliest start times' (the earliest times when activities can be started) are determined and are shown in the top left-hand subsection of each activity box. The latest times when activities may be started if the minimum project completion time is to be achieved (latest start times) are calculated by working backwards from the final project completion time and are shown here in the top right subsection of each activity box.

The computational procedure is simple and can be demonstrated by reference to a number of the activities included in Table 3.1. Assume that the student wishes to give consideration to the milestone which is achieved when the survey is completed (that is, at the end of activity 13). If, for simplicity, activities 6 and 8 are ignored the sub-network will include a total of 11 activities.

By taking account of activity durations it will be seen that the earliest time by which the survey will be completed is 34 weeks (remember that activity 2 cannot start until activity 4 has been completed). If 34 weeks is accepted by the student as the target towards which to work the latest event times can be determined by subtraction. Figure 3.1 also shows a complete analysis of earliest and latest start times.

Whether or not an activity carries float is of great interest to the researcher. Several types of this may be recognised but it is sufficient for our purposes to consider 'total float'. This is the amount of spare time available to an activity if the starting event occurs as early as possible and the finishing event is allowed to take place as late as possible (that is, without delaying the termination of the whole project). Several activities in Figure 3.1 possess total float:

Activity Number	Total Float (Weeks)
1	1
5	3
6	28
7	24
8	9
12	14
16	8
17	2

All of the remaining activities will be seen to have no total float and are said to be 'critical'. Information of this nature can be of the greatest help to students in scheduling their efforts. Of particular concern will be the path through the network which carries no total float (the 'critical path'). If any activities on the critical path take longer than planned the only way in which the project will be completed on time will be a reduction in the duration of a subsequent activity on the critical path. In Figure 3.1 the float for each activity is shown in the bottom right subsection of each box.

It will be seen that 119 weeks is the estimate of the total time needed to complete the project network shown in Figure 3.1, provided there are no resource problems (see next section, 'Checking the Resources and Scheduling'). Given the time required for topic selection and the preparation of a research proposal, this estimate falls comfortably within the requirement of our hypothetical student's third objective of completing the project in about three years from initial registration, given six months have already been spent on preparing the research proposal and so on.

A feature of student research which is frequently alluded to is the scarcity of resources. Thus, apparently parallel activities which would be feasible with freely available resources cannot be undertaken simultaneously. Full consideration must therefore be given to resource availability if realistic schedules are to be compiled.

Checking the Resources and Scheduling

In preparation for controlling the project a bar chart is prepared directly from the network diagram of Figure 3.1. This is shown here as Figure 3.2, merely presenting the information contained in Figure 3.1 in a different way.

Indeed, bar charts were used for project planning until the 1960s, after which network planning became the preferred method, as the scheduling of one activity before another that logically precedes it can be avoided. However, for a simple student project it is possible, with care, to proceed direct to the bar chart if that is what the student wishes.

The bar chart has time in weeks along the horizontal axis. Each activity is represented by a hatched bar starting at the earliest possible start time and with a length equal to its duration in weeks. Where activities have float its extent (being the difference between the latest finish time for the activity and its earliest finish time) is shown as a dashed area. Since critical activities do not have float they are shown as a simple hatched bar. In practice, the bar is labelled to identify the activity concerned. Because of space constraints the labels have been omitted in Figure 3.2.

It is likely that the bar chart will need to be revised at various points during the project. For that reason there is much to be said for producing the bar chart as a by-product of a computer analysis of the network plan. An alternative method where manual analysis of the network is preferred is to produce the bars as strips of card and either attach them to a steel-backed board magnetically or to pin them to a pinboard. In either case, it is then easy to move the bars around for purposes such as resource scheduling. Further details on bar charts and their uses can be found in a standard text on project planning, for example, Lock (2000).

Figure 3.2 permits a number of useful lessons to be drawn. Float is clearly

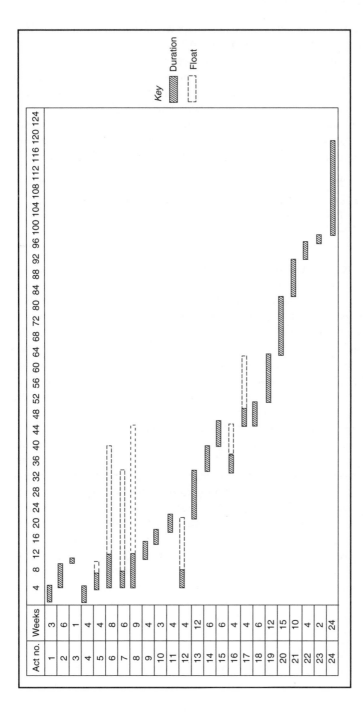

Figure 3.2 A bar chart based on the network analysis of Figure 3.1

indicated and provides an opportunity to smooth the demand for resources. Here the major resource is the student's time and although the student will, during the first year, be committed to attempting to complete the critical activities on schedule it will also be possible, if desired, to plan non-critical activities so that peak demands on the student's time are reduced. It would, for example, be possible to undertake activities 5, 6, 7, 8 and 12 sequentially. Thus, it might be decided first to select the participants for the pilot study and to follow this, in order, with the acquisition of statistical skills, decisions on target population and sampling procedures, drafting out three chapters and, finally, the acquisition of computing skills.

> EXCESSIVELY LONG HOURS OF WORK SHOULD BE CONFINED TO TIMES WHEN THEY ARE UNAVOIDABLE. LONG HOURS DO NOT NECESSARILY LEAD TO PRODUCTIVITY

Of course it may be that the demands on the student's time cannot be accommodated within the various activity floats available. Under those circumstances the project time will inevitably be extended. In assessing whether this is likely to happen it is important not to over-commit oneself. Experience shows that it is always a mistake to schedule 100 per cent of any resource on a project and this applies particularly to the student's own time during research. The project manager's usual rule of thumb would be to commit no more than 80 per cent of any resource leaving 20 per cent as a contingency margin. Obviously, in drawing up the research plan, each individual student must assess the implications of this idea for the length of the working day that will be assumed.

Over any length of time an average of 40 hours' effective research work a week would seem to be appropriate for most research projects, particularly since this can be increased if progress is slower than desired. Excessively long hours of work should be confined to times when they are unavoidable and should be restricted to a few weeks with appropriate periods of relaxation allowed afterwards.

Other resource considerations that may affect the project schedule relate to activities that are not under the student's control, such as times at which lecture courses run or to constraints on access to hardware – for example, certain equipment may only be available during university vacations. Only a few such factors should affect any particular research project and these can usually be accommodated by intelligent use of the bar chart.

Computer-aided planning

Network analysis as a means of planning and controlling projects involving thousands of activities was given a stimulus in the late 1950s with the advent of the computer.

It should be understood that as the computer cannot anticipate interdependencies it is not a means whereby the network logic can be drawn up. It takes over once the logic is in place and activity durations have been estimated. Thereafter it is able to print out the control charts which indicate critical and non-critical paths, together with the float attaching to the latter. It would be unrealistic to prepare the charts for large projects manually, particularly as replanning and revised networks will be needed as the project progresses. Although unlikely to be required by research students, computer software used in planning large projects has the very useful ability to handle resource constraints.

The student will have to decide whether or not to use network analysis and, subsequently, whether to employ one of the many PC-based packages for the purpose. The probability of continuing to use the technique through the execution phase is directly linked to the use of a package as with manual control there is less inclination to embark on a network revision and the ensuing recomputation of schedules.

Certain refinements to the basic approach become more feasible if packages are used. Reference has been made above to PERT, and most packages incorporate this facility. Again, students who are interested in examining the implications more closely could view PERT Chart EXPERT (an add-on to Microsoft Project) on the Web (Critical Tools, Inc. (2001)).

The point has been made that there are several levels at which networks may be drawn up, according to the level of detail at which the student wishes to work. As the research progresses and activities are completed, replanning may well necessitate changes to the list. Some activities may be dropped, but more likely, some will be broken down into finer detail as the relevant stage of the project approaches: for example, 'Review and edit thesis' might be expanded to include 'Get figures and tables produced'; 'Review and correct Chapter 1'; 'Review and correct Chapter 2' and so on.

The effect of this type of planning is that it is only activities in the near future that are elaborated in detail. As the project progresses the detailed section of the network advances like a wave and, of course, completed sections of the network disappear. This process has been referred to as 'rolling wave planning'. This is only necessary for activities which involve the coordination of several interlinked, lesser activities. The expansion process is compensated for by the completion of earlier activities so that the list is never much longer than shown here. Alternatively, it is possible to run two networks: a broad brush master network for the project as a whole and, where circumstances warrant it, a sub-network that breaks down a single master network activity into far finer detail, for example, where the analysis stage necessitates a set of interrelated computer runs. Most PC-based packages for network analysis make it very straightforward to carry out rolling wave planning. Thus, an activity such as 'Review and edit thesis' can at any time be broken down into more detail, if required.

67

Replanning

NORMALLY, ACTIVITY DURATIONS PROVE TO BE LONGER (RARELY SHORTER) THAN PLANNED AND THE PLANNED ORDERING OF ACTIVITIES WILL NEED TO BE AMENDED

The seven points dealt with so far relate to the planning of the research. As soon as the project gets underway the role of the network changes from that of being purely a planning tool to one in which it is primarily a control device. Experience indicates that if the project is of any complexity, two outcomes are inevitable. Firstly, activity durations prove to be longer (rarely shorter) than planned and, secondly, the ordering of activities still to be started needs to be amended. The former can be accommodated without too much difficulty, particularly if the basic schedule (that is, before resources are taken into account) is computer generated. The latter can, however, create problems.

Because of the full-time student's need to complete the project by a specific date it is always necessary to have in mind the extent of work yet to be completed. If the order in which activities need to be tackled changes (for example, access to data is delayed) then the student cannot be certain that the target date is still feasible. The only way to satisfy oneself that this is so is to undertake a careful replanning which will involve a revision of the network. As this has to be done manually and as pressure may have arisen because of an unanticipated change foisted upon the student the temptation may exist to put off the re-drawing. This can result in a situation arising in which there is little relationship between the network and the project work (this is often encountered outside the academic world). It is at these points that the student needs the self-discipline to spend some time on replanning, which does not immediately further the research but which in the longer term may make the difference between completing on time and failing to do so.

RENDERING PROGRESS EXPLICIT: RESEARCH MILESTONES

There is space on the control chart (see Figure 3.2) to enter progress, and the state of the study may be indicated by reference to a marker corresponding to the current week. This can be enhanced by filling in the duration allocated to each activity in a distinctive colour and marking the appropriate proportion of the bar below in the same colour as work progresses. This gives an immediate impression of which activities are ahead of schedule and which behind, provides a warning when dates begin to slip and, most importantly, provides a tangible measure of progress which can be very important in maintaining motivation as the project progresses. Alternatively, progress can be indicated by appropriately designed computer output.

A number of events in Figure 3.1 corresponding to the completion of a set of activities were designated as milestones by the student and depicted as circles in the diagram. These are particularly important events during a project where progress can be reviewed and will normally be at the end of activities whose outcome is to some extent uncertain. As such they form a natural point at which to assess progress and determine whether the research plan is still feasible or whether it needs modification. Usually, milestones will occur quite frequently but it is recommended that in a longer project no more than three months should be allowed between them (we have deviated from this in Figure 3.1 for reasons of space). In a shorter project – a dissertation for example – it is recommended that milestones be fixed at points which enable the feasibility of the project to be reviewed: for example, 'Topic is agreed with the supervisor'.

The achievement of a milestone should be marked by just such a review, involving at a minimum student and supervisor but quite possibly faculty members and students. This matter is discussed at greater length in Chapter 7.

THE ROLE OF NETWORK ANALYSIS DURING THE EXECUTION STAGE

The networks likely to be compiled by students will be much less complex than those used elsewhere and the task of re-drawing should not therefore be too great. Nevertheless, if networks are to be employed throughout the research they should reflect with reasonable accuracy the view which the student has of the sequence of activities likely to be followed until the end of the work. In other words, planning is not something that ceases once execution of the topic selected gets underway. Replanning may well need to be carried out several times in the light of appraisal of previous progress.

The Advantages of Network Analysis

Some students may not be attracted towards the idea of using network analysis. Before rejecting the idea as too complex or time-consuming, it is argued that consideration should be given to the following advantages.

1. The emphasis on rigorous planning, schedules and milestones is a notion to which students with limited time at their disposal should become accustomed.

2. If a network is used to plan a research study there is little likelihood that significant activities which need to be anticipated will be overlooked.

3. The levelling out of major peaks of demand on the researcher's time or the elimination of infeasible requirements for other resources may be possible.

4. In the event that planning indicates that, despite the rough estimates included within the research proposal, there would seem to be little prospect of achieving an acceptable completion date, major or minor changes to plan may be made.

5. The efforts of the student will be focused on the achievement of the next milestone, thus providing a way of regularly reviewing progress as the project unfolds and identifying situations in which replanning is needed.

6. Motivation is generated by visual evidence of tasks completed, together with an awareness of the extent to which endeavour should be increased.

7. The network and the associated charts provide an excellent basis for communicating to others what activities remain to be completed and how they are linked, achievement to date and the schedule the researcher proposes to follow. The very fact that the supervisor can be made aware of progress is a considerable aid to keeping on schedule. Moreover, the existence of a schedule makes it easier for student and supervisor to coordinate activities such as holidays, attendance at conferences, etc.

PLANNING PART-TIME RESEARCH

Most of the comments made so far in this chapter relate to full-time students. Part-time students have the added problem of planning their research so that it is managed in the context of other demands upon their time. If the research is to be part of a mixed course involving study and project, and if the student is in full-time employment, it is beneficial if the topic can be related to the nature of the student's occupation.

Research for higher degrees, with its need for extensive background reading, will need to be undertaken in the student's own time, even if data gathering may take place during full-time employment. In many instances, however, part-time students must confine the whole of their research to their nominal leisure time, accepting that their eventual completion time will be much longer than if they had been pursuing study full-time.

> THERE IS MUCH TO COMMEND THE USE OF NETWORK ANALYSIS BY PART-TIME STUDENTS

There is much to commend the use of network analysis by part-time students, the ordering of activities being at least as valuable an aid to planning as in the case of the full-time student. The major problem in constructing a control chart from an analysis based on activity durations is the sensible estimation of elapsed times (which include time spent on the study in addition to time needed to complete tasks unrelated to the study). Although the work content will be similar to that involved in full-time studies the often unpredictable effect of the student's occupation (including promotion, transfers, special projects, and so on) will render estimates of time much more uncertain. Indeed, it is worth pointing out that if research degree students encounter serious interruption to their plans they should consider requesting a suspension of their registration. Most institutions are prepared to accommodate requests for extensions with good cause. In some instances extensions of several years have featured in studies eventually completed. Successful outcomes in these circumstances are, however, far fewer than failures to complete. The distraction arising from whatever has caused the extension makes it increasingly difficult with the passage of time to return to study-mode. In addition the time-dependency of research work may well make it impossible to pick up and continue with the original topic.

If students are single-minded about their research though, and the nature of their job permits, control through schedule charts compiled from network analysis can be both realistic and effective. In other cases it may be more sensible to adopt an approach in which progress is simply marked up on the network. This will enable the part-time student to either take stock periodically or to consider the extent to which milestones are, or (more importantly) are not, being achieved.

If, during the conduct of the research, there is a total disaster in the sense that it becomes impossible (for example, if facilities for fieldwork are withdrawn because of relocation or redundancy) or pointless (for example, if it is discovered that the work has been done before, or if logical errors come to light) it becomes even more essential that the student is able to assess what may be achieved during what time may still be available. The potential value, to the part-time student, of network analysis in these circumstances is obvious.

CHAPTER SUMMARY

PLANNING: can demonstrate the feasibility of student research within the time available by helping to identify all the activities which will be involved.

NETWORK ANALYSIS: although an additional task for the student, can be of great benefit in showing the interrelationships among activities and in providing the basis for a realistic control chart.

CONTROL CHARTS: enable students to smooth out their efforts when a number of tasks may be addressed in parallel.

NETWORKS AND CHARTS: which reflect progress can act as motivational devices as completed work is recorded.

PLANNING IS A CONTINUOUS PROCESS: and is much facilitated by the network analysis approach. It should continue throughout the research to ensure that the work develops logically towards satisfying the aims of the researcher, whether full- or part-time.

4

Literature Searching

Most research work involves substantial use of published literature. Indeed, the ability to seek relevant facts is often seen as the primary activity of the researcher, and the regulations for research degrees always contain a requirement that the candidate should demonstrate the ability to make proper critical use of relevant literature. Accordingly, the successful researcher needs to be able to do just this. More importantly, for ordinary students, the growth of information searching via the Internet has meant that they are now expected to demonstrate that they can successfully undertake research on a topic by electronic means. Indeed, this is one of the 'Key Transferable Skills' now expected of graduates from the UK higher education system. It should be noted that carrying out research by electronic means does not mean use only of websites; these remain just part of what we mean by this term. Students must be able to show that they can identify by electronic means the full range of sources relevant to their study. These are largely journal articles and books, albeit some may be held in electronic rather than paper form.

This chapter will, accordingly, address literature searching by electronic means and it will, therefore, be assumed that the student is familiar with the use of Web browsers and the Web itself.

THE ACADEMIC LIBRARY

Although the logic of electronic publication would seem to be that most academic libraries will eventually be replaced by large central facilities serving many HE institutions there are too many obstacles to this change for it to happen in the near future. These range from payment to publishers for access to electronically held material through to obtaining agreement among institutions on what such a central facility should comprise. Academic libraries will remain, then, an important resource for students.

It is assumed that the reader is reasonably familiar with the use of academic and specialist libraries. For our purposes the key features of such libraries are:

1. The existence of comprehensive catalogues (usually computer based). The catalogue of book stocks will be classified by author and class number. The latter, in academic Anglo-Saxon libraries, is often based on the Dewey Decimal Classification System together with a classified subject index that allows the class number corresponding to a particular topic to be determined. In addition, many libraries now catalogue books by title. Catalogues of periodical material will normally consist of lists of journals and so on held, and information on which issues are available. Subject catalogues (including those of other academic libraries) will, of course, be available in electronic form.

2. Substantial collections of:
   a) primary sources – essentially the first publication of a piece of work;
   b) secondary sources – involving the indexing and classification of primary sources and the organisation of the information they contain into the general body of knowledge;
   c) tertiary sources – intended to facilitate the location of primary and secondary sources.

It is important to note that the nature of these sources is changing: electronic sources, especially of secondary and tertiary material, are becoming ever more important.

The sources that a researcher can use to carry out a literature search are listed in Table 4.1. Researchers should familiarise themselves with all the sources likely to be useful at the outset of their research. Academic libraries usually provide excellent guides within their websites to their facilities and the way they are organised.

MAJOR PRIMARY, SECONDARY AND TERTIARY SOURCES

Some of the sources in Table 4.1 are more important than others. We shall therefore provide a quick review of them.

Primary sources	Secondary sources	Tertiary sources
Academic (refereed) journal articles	Monographs (specialist texts on particular subjects)	Subject indexes and bibliographies
Conference proceedings	Textbooks	*Web of Science*
Theses and dissertations	Abstracts	Encyclopaedias, dictionaries and thesauruses
Reports/occasional papers	News groups and bulletin boards	Online journal indexes
Government publications	Review series (annals)	Handbooks
Standards	Review papers in primary journals	Guides to specific literatures
Codes of practice	Journals covering a specific literature	Specialist websites
Patents	Online journals	General bibliographies
Trade/professional/ specialist journals	Indexes of publications	
Newspapers	Current awareness/alerting services	
Ephemera		
Catalogues, specifications, directories		

Table 4.1 Some literature sources

Academic (Refereed) Journals

This is the source with which researchers in most fields will need to become familiar. Articles in such journals will have been subject to peer review by experts in the field to which they relate. Most errors of fact will, therefore, have been eliminated and the authors will need to have adduced evidence in favour of their arguments and conclusions. Such claims cannot always be made with respect to, say, newspaper articles or consultants' reports.

Monographs

A monograph contains an in-depth treatment of a particular topic by an authority in the field of study. It is likely to embody considerable original research and may well have been peer reviewed, that is, reviewed by other specialists in the field.

Therefore, monographs as a reference source tend to rank close to refereed journal articles.

Textbooks

In any reasonably rapidly changing field, researchers should expect that most of their references will be to articles rather than books, which are usually less up to date. For this reason, a literature search that relies solely on textbooks is likely to be considered seriously inadequate in most student research.

Recent years have seen the emergence of the 'textbook website', which contains supplementary material, readers' questions, authors' comments, etc. Since they are more up to date and more comprehensive than the paper textbook they may constitute a worthwhile source in their own right.

A more modest version of the same idea is the textbook that is available in pre-publication form on the Web.

Theses and Dissertations

Theses and dissertations completed recently may be a useful source of ideas and even possible collaboration. Also at the doctoral level it is necessary to establish that the researcher has made an original contribution to knowledge. Accordingly, it will normally be necessary to check that no theses on the lines the researcher proposes have been completed.

> MANY ACADEMIC LIBRARIES CARRY LISTS OF THESES ACCEPTED FOR HIGHER DEGREES IN VARIOUS COUNTRIES

Major academic libraries carry lists of theses accepted for higher degrees in various countries, in particular Britain and the USA. For example, the *BRTT* (British Reports, Translations and Theses) *Bulletin*, as well as listing reports, translations, theses and so on produced by British government organisations, industry and academic institutions, also lists most doctoral theses produced at British universities. The *ASLIB Index* covers theses produced as a result of a research study and is an index to theses with abstracts accepted for higher degrees by the universities of Great Britain and Ireland plus certain others. The *BRITS Index*, published by the British Theses Service, provides another source for theses in the period 1971–87, being last published in 1989. Since the *ASLIB Index* tends to be one or two years behind, it is useful to be able to supplement this by information from *CRIB* (Current Research in Britain) which covers most types of research. For theses published in the USA similar information can be obtained from Dissertation Abstracts International.

In most, if not all, fields of research the risk of exact duplication of research topic and outcomes is low (see Chapter 7).

Reports/Occasional Papers

In many fields, technical reports can be a major source of information. It may well be, therefore, that the more complete account given in a technical report will be of greater use to the researcher than journal articles on the subject. Furthermore, the reports of certain research bodies, such as the World Bank, are sufficiently prestigious for the researchers concerned to favour them as a method of disseminating their results. The upshot is that, as well as being more comprehensive, research reports are often more up to date. Similar remarks apply to the occasional papers which tend to be published by many research units particularly in the social sciences. Again, in certain fields, such as the commercial applications of IT, the reports of specialist consultants like Forrester Research are generally regarded as authoritative (they are, however, expensive!). Obviously, this is a special category of material and details of it are usually best obtained through special guides such as those produced by the British Library (www.blpc.bl.uk), in the UK. In many cases these guides also provide information on how a copy of the report can be obtained.

The easiest way of accessing most reports, however, rather than making use of these individual services, is by the use of a search engine as discussed later.

Government Publications

The amount of material published on behalf of governments, and the EU, is enormous and forms an important reference source for many types of research. Indeed, for much UK research this material is a major data source. For this reason it will be considered in more detail in Chapter 6.

Because of the sheer volume of material produced, most academic libraries classify government publications separately, very often outside the normal subject index system. Accordingly, researchers need to ascertain whether important material is to be found in this area and, if so, how to obtain it in the libraries they use. In the UK, for instance, this will mean consulting the annual, monthly or daily lists of material published by HMSO (Her Majesty's Stationery Office) or the *Catalogue of British Official Publications not published by HMSO.* Nowadays, however, UK government reports are usually most easily accessed by reference to the appropriate departmental homepage in the UK Central Government website (www.gov.uk).

Similarly, EU reports, directives, etc. can be readily accessed via the European Union website (www.europa.eu.int).

In the USA, monthly lists of the US Government Publications Office provide similar information or via the guide to US Federal and State Government web-sites (www.firstgov.gov).

Standards, Codes of Practice and Patents

> STANDARDS CAN BE AN IMPORTANT SOURCE OF INFORMATION, ESPECIALLY IN TECHNOLOGICAL FIELDS

In technological fields standards can be an important source of information since the introduction of new standards may well spawn considerable development activity and in some markets is a major determinant of product performance. For the latter reason, standards and the similar codes of practice may also be impor-tant as a data source for the researcher interested in the history of some aspect of technology. In the UK, the most important source of standards is the British Standards Institution (BSI), with similar roles in the USA being fulfilled by the American National Standards Institute, in Germany by DIN standards, in the European Union by EN standards and, internationally, by ISO standards.

Outside science and engineering most professional bodies also publish stand-ards or codes of practice with which their members must comply. In the account-ing field in the UK, for example, the Institute of Chartered Accountants plays a major role in determining accounting standards.

In many types of applied research in technology, patents are important either because they indicate new techniques and methods to solve particular problems or because they suggest further inventions that did not occur to the originator of the patent. They also provide an important data source for researchers interested in the history or economics of invention and innovation.

Information on patents appears in a number of indexing and abstracting services. Copies of British patents are available in the UK from regional patent deposit libraries or members of the British Library Patents Information Network. Ideas are usually patented in more than one country, so using a concordance of patents which gives the number assigned to the application for the same patent in different countries makes it possible to find, say, the British application corresponding to a patent that was first taken out in Japan.

Trade/Professional/Specialist Journals and Newspapers

To many student researchers, this is an important and up-to-date group of material. In certain types of research, especially in rapidly changing fields such as information technology, trade journals and newspapers can be important data sources. This is particularly true of the former which often carry information that is not recorded elsewhere.

In the past, few UK libraries stored these types of material. The situation is now much better. Trade and professional journals normally have associated websites and subscription is free to those involved in the industry concerned. There will usually be access to the contents of the journals extending back several years together with additional material for which there was no space in the printed version.

Specialist journals, such as *The Economist*, will normally be available in electronic form to subscribers. Newspapers will usually have websites which contain abstracts of the day's articles plus supporting material that could not be published in the newspaper. Some newspapers, such as the *Financial Times*, maintain archives of previously published articles that can be accessed for a small charge. Although it can, at best, be described as an 'honorary newspaper' the BBC website (www.bbc.co.uk) is worthy of note as a rich source of contemporary comment.

Practice with regard to the storage of trade journals varies widely in the UK. Few libraries, save the Copyright Libraries*, take more than a small fraction of those published reflecting the fact that many of them are most unlikely to be used again once they cease to be current. Furthermore, many of those that are taken are not bound, with the result that individual issues may disappear. For these reasons such material is often not all that easy to access and the researcher may well find it worthwhile going to a specialist library for it.

The position is somewhat better as far as UK national newspapers are concerned as there are a number of commercial indexing services available for the quality press at least. For example, *NEWSPLAN* (formerly the *British Newspaper Index*) provides an index to materials contained in *The Times*, the *Sunday Times*, the *Financial Times*, the *Independent* and the *Independent on Sunday*. The Clover Newspaper Index covers besides these newspapers, the *Daily Telegraph*, the *Sunday Telegraph*, the *Guardian*, the *Observer*, *The Economist* and the *European*. Microfilm or microfiche copies of major newspapers are available which, though somewhat inconvenient to use, do ensure that copies of fairly recent material are available. Increasingly, abstracts of the text of newspapers are available through

*The Copyright Libraries are those libraries entitled under UK law to a copy of every book published in the UK. They are: the British Library; the libraries of Oxford University and Cambridge University; the library of Trinity College, Dublin; the National Library of Scotland. In addition, for some books, the National Library of Wales, Aberystwyth.

online computer services such as Profile or Lexis-Nexis. The text of a number of newspapers (the *Guardian*, *The Times*, the *Independent*, etc.) has been available in machine-readable form for some time.

Where local newspapers are concerned matters are more complex. It is unlikely that any formal index is available and therefore it may be necessary to work through them systematically for the period of interest if that was some time ago. For relatively current material, however, excellent advice may well be available from the newspapers' own libraries.

Ephemera

> *SIGLE*, THE SYSTEM FOR INFORMATION ON GREY LITERATURE IN EUROPE, IS AN IMPORTANT SOURCE OF INFORMATION FOR EPHEMERA

Much material is not stored in a library in the usual way and, indeed, may not be catalogued. Examples are company reports, specifications of products, catalogues, price lists, opera programmes, notices of forthcoming sales, applications for planning consents, and so on. Such items are not published in the formal sense and are generally referred to by librarians as ephemera, or 'grey literature', because they are normally useful only for a brief period. Libraries generally have no obligation to stock ephemera and individual items are likely to be traceable only if they are of sufficient interest to collectors for a catalogue to have been published – for example, Victorian Christmas cards – or they form part of a recognised collection of historical material that has been properly catalogued. However, there is a very large European project called *SIGLE* (System for Information on Grey Literature in Europe) available online and on CD-ROM. The only useful counsel that can be offered to all but the very experienced researcher is that, if circumstances warrant, an attempt should be made to solicit the support of an expert on ephemera in the field of interest.

Abstracts

Contributors to academic journals are almost invariably required to submit an abstract of their articles to be published at the head of the full text. In many fields one or more abstracting services exist that give summaries of the contents of journal articles and/or patents. Such services are reasonably up to date since they tend to be compiled electronically and cover a wider range of journals in the field than are available in all except the very largest libraries.

An example of how this type of service might be enhanced is provided by the Emerald Independent Reviews service in the field of management, delivered in both hard copy and electronically. Independent abstractors, with subject expertise, compile the abstracts and add comments thus providing researchers with an opportunity to narrow the search. A similar facility is offered by abstracting services in other fields.

Traditionally, abstracts served as a quick way for researchers to appraise recent contributions to their field of study. Their principal use, nowadays, is to judge whether a paper identified through some bibliographic search service, such as the *Web of Science* (http://wos.mimas.ac.uk), which will be discussed later, would be worth obtaining.

Subject Indexes and Bibliographies

Although subject indexes and bibliographies are still of interest in tightly defined fields (such as law or Middle English) their use has been superseded for most student researchers by sources such as the *Web of Science*, which cover a wider range of fields and are very up to date. In fields where important sources are books published long ago, however, such as social history, electronic bibliographies such as the *International Bibliography of Social Science* (www.lse.ac.uk/IBSS/) are very important.

Encyclopaedias, Dictionaries and Thesauruses

These sources are mainly useful as a way of identifying search terms to carry out a literature search electronically.

Encyclopaedias provide an excellent method of getting a quick feel for a subject and a picture of knowledge in that field and related areas. It should be remembered that as well as general encyclopaedias, such as the *Encyclopaedia Britannica*, a variety of more specialist guides and handbooks exist on particular subjects. Nowadays, many of these sources are available online or on CD-ROM and are, therefore, extremely convenient to search.

Where a topic cannot be found in an encyclopaedia or guide, dictionaries are useful for suggesting terms having a similar meaning which can be looked up instead. Note that some fields – for example, social science – have their own dictionaries. A further possibility is to use a thesaurus – that is, a list of alternative terms for the same concept. As well as general thesauruses, such as *Roget's Thesaurus*, certain specialist libraries maintain ones specific to the field they cover. The researcher with more time to spare can often profitably make use of additional sources of ideas as discussed later.

News Groups and Bulletin Boards

There are many thousand specialist Internet news groups/bulletin boards where the student researcher is likely to find bibliographies and references related to the subject of the news group or bulletin board.

News groups or bulletin boards often have a relatively short existence while a new subject is developing. At such times, however, they can often host lively debates on contentious issues. In a way, the student researcher becomes party to something like an international conference to which their contributions will be welcomed provided they help to foster debate.

WHY SCAN THE LITERATURE?

There are two major reasons for carrying out a survey of the literature:

1. As part of the process of topic selection.
2. As part of the research project proper.

In addition, students are reminded of the point made in the introduction to this chapter; they must, nowadays, be able to demonstrate they can carry out effective searches of the literature by electronic means.

Reference has been made in Chapter 2 to a variety of questions that need to be taken into account when selecting a topic. Thus, there is the broad review of reported work in a field in the hope that previous authors will have suggested fruitful studies to be pursued by others. Equally, assessing the novelty of promising ideas will normally involve researchers checking the literature to ensure that the proposed topic has not been tackled before and to define an area of study that they can consider their own.

Having selected their topic, researchers will normally need to carry out several surveys of relevant published literature(s) in rather greater depth. The preparation of a detailed research proposal will require the researcher to define previous work in the proposed field and in those allied to it. Thus, for example, a study of the use of hovercraft in cross-Channel transport in the 1970s and 1980s would certainly not confine itself to that mode of transport alone. It would be necessary to examine other means of crossing the Channel so as to clarify the unique features of a hovercraft-based service. Again, it would probably be necessary to look at whether hovercraft were in use in ferry services elsewhere in the world to ascertain whether they were particularly well suited to cross-Channel operations as compared to other means of crossing water. In assembling this wider picture, researchers would be able when presenting the research findings to make proper acknowledgement of the work of previous authors and to delineate their own contributions to the field.

As well as scanning the literatures of their chosen fields and related ones, most researchers find it necessary to familiarise themselves with a rather different literature dealing with research tools appropriate to their topic. Thus, geophysicists may well find it necessary to employ Fourier Transform methods in analysing and interpreting data signals. A social scientist on the other hand may need to attain a reasonable proficiency in the use of statistical methods.

MOST RESEARCHERS HAVE TWO TYPES OF LITERATURE SEARCH TO DO: ONE ON THE SPECIFIC SUBJECT, THE OTHER ON RESEARCH METHODOLOGY

The line of research having been selected, most researchers, have two broad types of literature search to do: firstly, on the specific subject – closely related to the topic of interest – and, secondly, that on research methodology. Usually the former will need to be pursued to considerably greater depth than the latter. It should be noted that some research projects involve the translation of methods devised in one field into another and normally require that an in-depth literature search be carried out for both fields.

A number of different phases can be expected in the course of a literature search in accordance with the various stages of the research plan. Whatever the purpose of a particular phase, only limited resources are available for its execution. Almost always, the restricted time that the researcher can devote to the task is the major constraint.

Often there will be the additional problem that there are insufficient funds to borrow all the desired references from a central library such as the BLDSC (British Library Document Supply Centre), to pay for unlimited visits to a relevant specialist library or to pay for electronic copies of the documents required. For these reasons, we shall consider how to conduct a literature search efficiently and successfully by electronic means.

LITERATURE SEARCHES AND RELEVANCE TREES

A useful model of the literature searching process is to regard it as an exercise in the construction of a relevance tree of the type described in Chapter 2. At the topic level an initial keyword or subject, selected as a basis for searching, will lead to the discovery of further keywords derived from the early books and journals scanned. Some of these will lead to new literatures not directly related to that dealing with the initial subject. Each of these will in turn suggest further subject headings under which to search.

As an example of a relevance tree, Figure 4.1 shows one set of subjects that

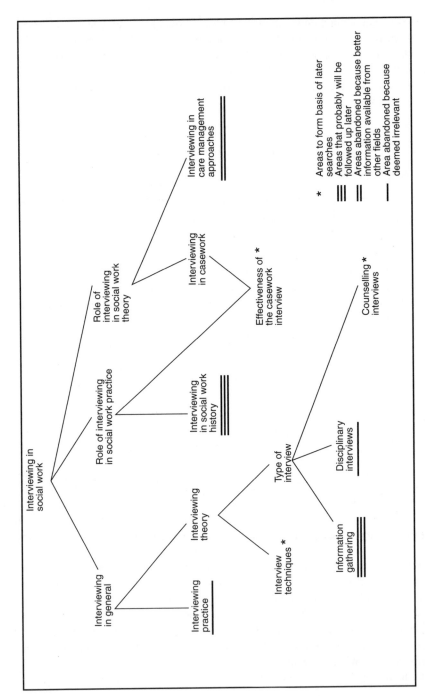

Figure 4.1 A relevance tree for the subject 'Interviewing in social work'

Interviewing in
social work

Role of
interviewing
in social work
theory

Interviewing in
care management
approaches

Interviewing in casework

Effectiveness of *
the casework
interview

Role of interviewing
in social work practice

Interviewing
in social work
history |||

Counselling *
interviews

Type of
interview

Disciplinary
interviews ——

Interviewing theory

Interview
techniques *
——

Information
gathering |||

Interviewing
in general

Interviewing
practice ——

* Areas to form basis of later
   searches
||| Areas that probably will be
     followed up later
|| Areas abandoned because better
    information available from
    other fields
— Area abandoned because
   deemed irrelevant

might be scanned in defining a topic within the broad framework 'Interviewing in social work'. The figure shows how, starting from the subject 'Interviewing in social work', three broad subject areas have been selected, namely: 'Interviewing in general'; 'The role of interviewing in social work practice'; and 'The role of interviewing in social work theory'. These three have in turn been used to suggest further subjects.

Though at this stage it is not necessary to pursue any of the subjects in depth it will be assumed that, having advanced the search as shown in Figure 4.1, the researcher has gained sufficient feel for the literature of each to decide that the research will focus on the 'Effectiveness of the casework interview' and that important related subjects will be 'Interview techniques and counselling interviews'. At a later stage each of these subjects will probably form the starting point for another phase of the literature search. This example is, however, typical in that it involves four activities.

1.   The generation of a number of alternative subjects/keywords.
2.   Deciding which subjects to pursue.
3.   Deciding which subjects to abandon.
4.   Deciding when sufficient effort has been put in for the purpose in hand so that the process can be (temporarily) halted.

To carry out these four activities effectively we need ways of generating new subjects since without an initial touch of inventiveness our search is likely to be fairly superficial. Conversely without criteria for abandoning lines of enquiry the literature search rapidly gets out of hand.

The Generation of Alternative Subjects

Once the literature search is successfully underway, finding new, related subjects ceases to be a problem. In practice, the difficulty of getting started can vary enormously from one subject to another. Thus, researchers who have only a few weeks available to conduct their work should stick to the rule that if they cannot get their literature search beyond the stage of looking for new subject areas within a couple of hours, they should select another topic.

The alphabetical subject index provides a quick and convenient way of finding related subject areas or alternative terms for the same keyword. It also provides a rough and ready guide to the volume of literature in a particular area, since, broadly speaking, a subject area is extensively subdivided only if a substantial amount has been written on it. Once a subject has been identified the subject index will provide its class number. The classified catalogue can then be consulted to provide a list of all books that belong to that particular classification.

A useful trick is, therefore, to find one relevant book, ascertain its subject classification and then consult the classified catalogue for other similar books.

Deciding Which Subjects to Abandon

Given our broad interest in effective management of student research a word of caution is appropriate at this point. Though many research projects may involve areas that are developing rapidly (for example, e-business in the early 21st century) researchers must limit the time they spend scanning the literature if they are not to prejudice other activities. Without mechanisms for deciding which lines of enquiry not to pursue, most literature searches soon get completely out of control. For this reason many researchers adopt the often somewhat arbitrary rule of scanning only 'the literature of the subject'. In some well-defined fields (for example, particle physics) such a strategy is very sensible. In other less clear areas, such as economics, this may be detrimental to the quality of the literature survey. Thus, as well as examining the literature of industrial relations the researcher in the field of wage bargaining might well be advised to consider the literature of conflict theory which might not necessarily be considered relevant to the industrial relations specialist. If the literature search is not to be confined within the straitjacket of 'the literature', other ways must be found to decide which avenues not to explore.

In practice this means applying one of three rules.

1. Abandon it because it is irrelevant to the area of interest.
2. Ignore it because the literature of some other subject (to be) studied covers the ideas better.
3. Do not pursue it any further for the present since sufficient information has been obtained for that purpose for which the search is being carried out.

Thus, in the example of Figure 4.1, our researcher has not further subdivided the asterisked items because though all will need to be examined further, enough work has been done on them for the present. Similarly, the triply underlined items, though probably relevant in a later phase of the literature search, do not require further elaboration at this stage.

As an example of Rule 2 above, the researcher's decision not to follow up the role of interviewing in care management (doubly underlined) is noted. This is because interviewing plays a far more central role in casework and as such it is unlikely that the literature of care management will provide insights not available from the casework literature. Finally, the singly underlined subjects have been excluded from further study on the grounds that they are probably irrelevant to the subject of interest.

The literature searching strategy embodied in Figure 4.1, whereby the search commences with a very specific subject and is gradually extended into related areas, is of general applicability. The search should always start with the most specific subject definition the researcher is able to supply. Where there is a copious literature the researcher may never need to go beyond this initial subject to amass sufficient references. Where less has been published the relevance tree approach provides a systematic way of expanding the search.

CITATION INDEXES

Most articles of a research nature cite previous work and in doing so tend to reference seminal books and articles in the field of interest. Major articles in that field not only provide a useful way into past literature but also with the help of the citation indexes, into journal articles published at a later date. The principle of the *Science Citation Index*, the *Social Science Citation Index*, and the *Arts and Humanities Citation Index* is a simple one. For each article by a particular author, the citation index lists articles that have cited it in a particular interval of time. Originally, this provided a way of picking up subsequent articles on the same subject. By reference to the citation index it was then possible to produce a list of papers cited by those authors. Besides covering articles in academic journals, the citation indexes also cover book reviews in such journals and conference proceedings.

CITATION INDEXES PROVIDE AN EFFECTIVE WAY OF CARRYING OUT A LITERATURE SEARCH IN MANY FIELDS

Citation indexes provide an effective way of carrying out a literature search in many fields. Because they deal with recent journal articles, book reviews in academic journals and conference proceedings, they are most useful for subjects that are evolving rapidly. In such fields, most publications of relevance to the researcher are likely to be found in journal articles published in the past few years. Conversely, in fields such as history where articles published several decades ago may well be extremely relevant or in fields where most important reference material is to be found in books, the citation indexes are less useful. Nevertheless, in most fields they provide at a very minimum an important check that no major articles have been overlooked and the reader who is unfamiliar with them is advised to consult the citation indexes themselves for further information on their use.

The Classic Use of a Citation Index

Originally citation indexes were intended mainly to identify much cited papers, which were presumed to be key papers. To give a feel for this use, Figure 4.2 shows an example of a forward literature search using the *Science Citation Index* in the classic way as it might have been conducted in 1995. The general field of interest of the researcher is the topic of computer security. From an article by Landwehr, published in 1983, it is possible to construct a relevance tree extending forward in time. As will be seen later, the citation indexes (as embodied in the *Web of Science*), and similar indexes, provide the main tool for electronic literature searching but are now used for backward rather than forward searches.

Closing Off the Citation Tree

Just as it is necessary to restrict the growth of a subject relevance tree so too the researcher needs to find ways of halting the growth of the citation tree. Two ideas are particularly useful here. Firstly, the notion of core books. In any reasonably established field, certain books embody the key ideas of the subject and this is evidenced by the frequency with which they are cited by other authors in journal articles. Similarly, any particular field of research will have core journals in which any major work in the area is most likely to be published. Defining core books and journals restricts the citation tree by limiting the citations that will be followed up to those publications. Armed with the names of core journals the researcher can rapidly extend the list by using the volume to identify those journals that carry most of the references cited by authors of papers in the journals already known.

The notion of core journals is used by librarians in many subject areas as a basis for bibliographic services such as lists of current contents of journals or for deciding which journal articles should be abstracted. Accordingly, examination of the journals that crop up frequently in the course of a bibliographic search provides one quick way of establishing the core journals. The scope of a search may be reduced by setting a publication date prior to which references will not be followed up. In rapidly changing fields such as particle physics it may be only a few years ago, whereas in fields such as economics or social history, publications dating back fifty years or more may well be very useful.

It should be remembered that for a preliminary search in a field the cut-off date need not be set very far back since most authors refer to and summarise the work of their predecessors. The literature of the past ten or twenty years will therefore usually provide a reasonable outline of the field for fifty years or more. If at a later stage of searching it appears that significant work on the subject was published before the cut-off date an earlier date must obviously be chosen.

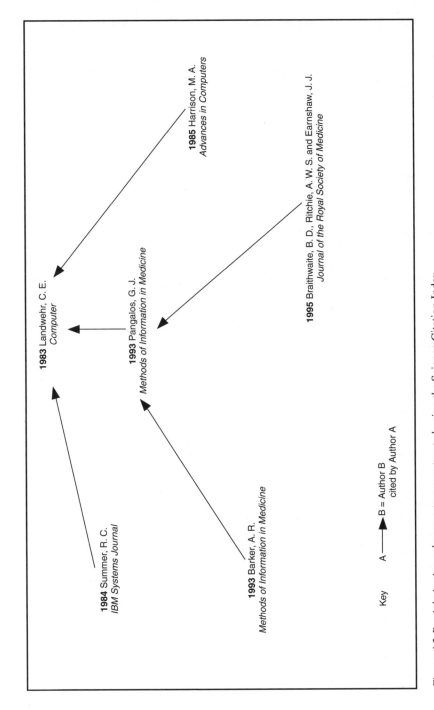

1985 Harrison, M. A.
Advances in Computers

1983 Landwehr, C. E.
Computer

1993 Pangalos, G. J.
Methods of Information in Medicine

1995 Braithwaite, B. D., Ritchie, A. W. S. and Earnshaw, J. J.
Journal of the Royal Society of Medicine

1984 Summer, R. C.
IBM Systems Journal

1993 Barker, A. R.
Methods of Information in Medicine

Key   A ——▶ B = Author B
                          cited by Author A

Figure 4.2 Partial citation relevance tree constructed using the Science Citation Index

CARRYING OUT A LITERATURE SEARCH ELECTRONICALLY

There are five main tools of electronic literature searching:

1. Electronic bibliographies used to identify books.
2. The *Web of Science** (citation indexes) used to identify academic journal articles, conference proceedings and book reviews.
3. Online journal collections used for searching up-to-date articles from the professional and trade press and for obtaining an electronic copy of articles identified using the *Web of Science*.
4. Newspaper and specialist journal websites mainly used for identifying up-to-date comment in the quality press.
5. Search engines used for Web searches.

The ways in which 1, 2, 3 and 4 are applied are very similar. Because most student researchers need to become familiar with the use of the *Web of Science*, we shall use it to illustrate how the first four tools can be used.

Search engines are in many ways complementary to the first four search methods. We shall, therefore, consider them in more detail too.

Electronic Searching and Boolean Logic – A Note

The researcher faces two potential problems in conducting a literature research:

a) not finding enough useful references (remedied by using **OR**)
b) finding too many references (remedied by using **AND**).

Most electronic searching tools allow these problems to be addressed by judicious use of **OR** and **AND**. Thus the descriptor:

Sewer* AND (Maintenance OR Repair)

where the * stands for any set of characters which will result in all articles whose titles (or keywords) contain the words (Sewers, Sewerage) and Maintenance in any order, or the words (Sewers, Sewerage) and Repair in any order being selected. As can be seen, the effect of **OR** is to increase the number of relevant papers (both those dealing with Repair and those dealing with Maintenance are selected), while the effect of **AND** is to reduce the number (unless they deal with either Repair or Maintenance as well as Sewer(s) etc., they will not be selected).

*The *Web of Science* is maintained by the Institute for Scientific Information (the producer of the citation indexes). It is available through a number of Internet servers. Some users, for example those in UK higher education institutions, may access it via an intranet. However it is accessed, the outputs will be as depicted here save that some intranets provide access only to references from, say the past five years rather than back to 1981 as in the examples below.

AN EXAMPLE OF AN ELECTRONIC LITERATURE SEARCH

To illustrate the process of electronic literature searching we consider the case of a student who has to complete a dissertation project for a degree with a specialism in biology. The student has come across reports that North Sea Cod numbers are declining. Because of an interest in environmental biology and with an eye to future biology teaching the student decides to write a dissertation on this topic. For expository reasons we will assume rather less initial knowledge on the part of the student than would normally be the case.

THE *WEB OF SCIENCE* SEARCH

The student considers that books are not likely to be a particularly important source. It is necessary to demonstrate the ability to use the *Web of Science* (WoS) so this is the natural starting point, especially since this will enable reviews of books published in the last ten years to be picked up.

The process of the Web of Science *search*

The student starts by consulting the help screens for guidance on how to use WoS, and determines from these that the *Arts and Humanities Citation Index* is not likely to be relevant. The *Science Citation Index* (SCI) certainly is, however, as is the *Social Science Citation Index* (SSCI) since there are clearly political aspects to the problem.

Web of Science search stage 1

Because papers on the topic could potentially be found in both science and social science journals, the student decides to search both the SCI and SSCI using the **Easy Search** topic search facility of the *Web of Science*. The search topic is identified as:

North Sea Cod Fish*

This term will find all papers, for the entire period (1981–) covered by the citation indexes, which have the phrases: North Sea Cod Fishing; North Sea Cod Fisheries etc. in either their title, the list of keywords supplied with most papers, or the abstract (if there is one).

Although it is always a good idea to start with a very specific topic, as here, the result in this case is **No papers found**. This is a common result of a specific topic search. It is necessary to broaden the search.

Web of Science search stage 2

The search topic is identified as:

(North Sea) AND Cod AND Fish*

This term will find all papers which have the phrase North Sea and the words Cod and Fishing, Fisheries, etc. in either their title, the list of keywords supplied with most papers, or the abstract (if there is one). Note that the words and the phrase may appear in any order, not necessarily that shown, and be separated by very considerable numbers of words.

This search produces 169 papers. A quick glance at the first few, however, show that few of them look relevant to the issue of North Sea Cod population.

Web of Science search stage 3

A new search term is identified with the aim of picking up material on cod populations:

(North Sea) AND Cod AND Population

This produces 48 papers, about a third of which appear relevant (an extract of which is shown in Figure 4.3). Note that papers deemed possibly relevant have been marked by the student by 'ticking' the left-hand box. These marks for each web page will be used to build up a list of papers that can be e-mailed to the student later.

The student derives some further conclusions from this search:

1.   A core journal appears to be that abbreviated as **ICES J MAR SCI**. This is identified by clicking on a relevant article title as the *ICES Journal of Marine Science* (see below for an explanation of ICES)
2.   The Latin name for cod is *Gadus Morhua*. There is an associated technical English word *Gadoid*.
3.   Other terms used for population are: **stock(s)** and **biomass** (this term is not shown in the example extract. It appears on another page of the output).
4.   The relatively small proportion of relevant articles seems in part to be due to the search terms being pulled out from different parts of abstracts, so a more specific search is in order.

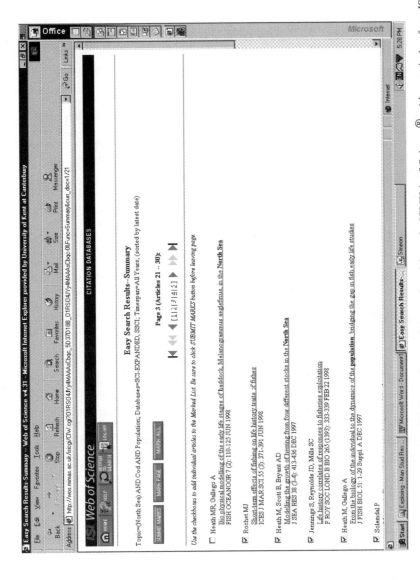

Figure 4.3 Extract from results of WoS search stage 3 (reproduced from the ISI Web of Science® with permission from ISI)

93

Web of Science title only search stage 4

A more specific search is next generated by searching on Title only. The rationale for this is that papers dealing with the North Sea Cod population are likely to reflect this in their title. Such a search is carried out using the Full Search facility of WoS. The search term used is:

(North Sea) AND Cod AND (Population* OR Stock* OR Biomass*)

This produces no papers at all!

Web of Science search stage 5

The student decides that the problem may be that relevant articles may focus on a number of cod populations rather than just that of the North Sea. The **Title** search is therefore repeated with the broader search term:

Cod AND (Population* OR Stock* OR Biomass*)

This search identifies 100+ articles but many relate to cod fisheries far from the UK.

Web of Science search stage 6

The student, therefore, decides to repeat the Title search with a more specific search term restricting consideration to only cod fisheries fairly close to the UK:

(North Sea OR Irish Sea OR Atlantic OR Baltic) AND Cod AND (Population* OR Stock* OR Biomass*)

This search produces 60 documents, quite a number of which are relevant (see Figure 4.4). The student notices, however, that none of the papers identified so far have appeared in other than scientific journals. This suggests that a search be conducted on the *Social Science Citation Index* alone.

Web of Science search stages 7 and 8

Search 7 involves a search on titles on the SSCI only. A narrow search term such as those used in searches 4–6 is not appropriate since those searches did not identify any journal articles from the SSCI. Instead the single broad term:

94

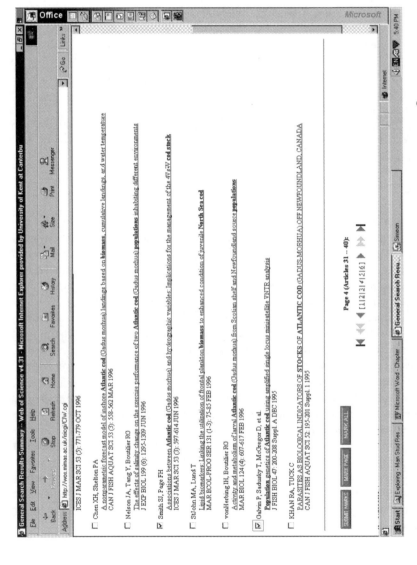

Figure 4.4 *Extract from results of WoS search stage 5 (reproduced from the ISI Web of Science® with permission from ISI)*

Cod

is used. This identifies 84 documents but a number of these relate to what is obviously the abbreviation, **COD**. Reference to the appropriate abstracts shows that this is a term used by the US Internal Revenue Service that has nothing to do with fishing!

This problem is known to information scientists as the *false drop problem*. To overcome it the student repeats the title search with:

Cod AND Fish*

This search generates 23 references to articles on fishing policy most of which are relevant (see Figure 4.5).

Examination of the abstract of article 3 to determine whether it is relevant (it is) produces two abbreviations ITQs and IVQs that could clearly serve as search terms. IVQs are Individual Vessel Quotas – that is clear from the title – but what are ITQs? (see p. 101).

Web of Science search stage 9

As a final search the student carries out a title search on **Cod AND Fish*** using the WoS database of scientific proceedings. This produces 20 references, most of which do not look relevant. However, it turns up a 1993 *Symposium on Cod and Climate Change* and a 1994 *International Symposium on the Sea Ranching of Cod and Other Species*. These suggest two dimensions of the problem, climate change and fish farming, that the student may wish to take further.

The process outlined here took less than an hour. No pretence is made that it represents the best approach. Indeed student researchers could benefit from reflecting on how they would have improved it. Nonetheless the process has pro-duced 59 relevant references that the student can now proceed to obtain and use in the preparation of the dissertation.

It should be noted that it is important to the success of the process that the student capitalise on new search terms, new related fields, etc. thrown up during the course of the search. Equally the student needs to review progress critically; to decide whether searches are to be conducted on title, keyword and abstract or on title alone; which WoS databases should be searched; and how the search terms should be varied to increase or decrease the number of relevant papers identified. Although it was not explored in this example, it may sometimes be worth confining the search to only part of the period (from 1981) covered by the citation indexes,

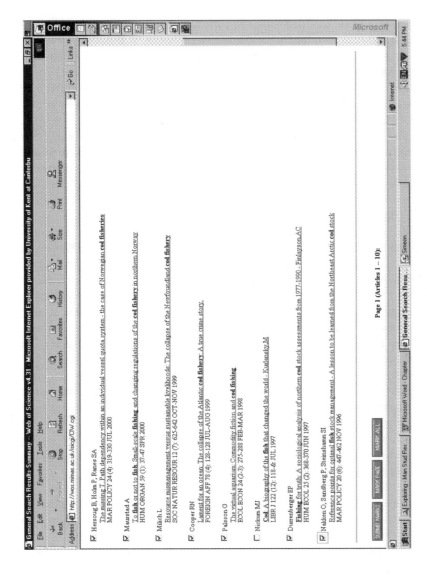

Figure 4.5 Extract from results of WoS search stage 8 (reproduced from the ISI Web of Science® with permission from ISI)

97

THE *WEB OF SCIENCE* HOLDS ONLY ABSTRACTS, NOT THE FULL TEXT OF PAPERS

Once the researcher has identified a suitable list of references and has verified through the abstract that they are potentially useful, there is then the problem of obtaining the articles. This cannot be done from WoS itself since it does not hold the full text of articles. Students should first check their own library's stock, since the journal may well be held in either paper or electronic form. Again their own library may well subscribe to one of the increasing number of online journal collections which may provide a copy. If this fails then the usual method, in the UK, is to order a paper copy from the British Library Document Supply Centre: this will normally be done through the student's own library. It will be appreciated that this is an area that is rapidly changing; there is a clear trend to electronic document delivery which is far faster than sending paper documents by post. The student needs to check on a regular basis, therefore, as to which ways are available to obtain the references identified.

A different issue with WoS is what happens if there are important references that predate the start of the citation indexes in electronic form (1981). These can, of course, be picked up through the use of a suitable electronic bibliography. Indeed, as pointed out earlier, if all important references are likely to be earlier than 1981, there is no point in using WoS. In the normal case where WoS is relevant but where there may be important references prior to 1981, the student needs to exploit the basic principle of the citation indexes. Study of the cited references in papers identified through the WoS search will soon reveal any key references from before 1981.

WoS deals essentially with the academic literature. The reader is reminded that searches on newspapers, specialist journals and trade and professional journals need to be undertaken on different databases but follow similar principles to those outlined here.

USING A SEARCH ENGINE

We turn now to the use of a Web search engine. As indicated earlier, this is a useful complement to a WoS or similar search. A variety of search engines exist on the Web. Perhaps the best known is that provided by www.yahoo.com. A very useful one for more academic purposes, and the one we shall use here, is www.google.com. There are a number of 'meta search engines' that set other search engines such as Yahoo and Google to work to deal with a query as well as searching their own database. One such search engine is www.Askjeeves.co.uk and the interested reader may like to experiment with this.

Search engines classify websites and documents available through the Web using markers (tags and metatags) that identify their content. A huge effort is required to maintain the search engine's database, since new websites and documents need to have their details inserted, obsolete information needs to be removed and the relative popularity of different items of reference material needs continually to be assessed. The maintenance of a search engine is, accordingly, expensive. Since most, and certainly the ones mentioned here, are operated by private sector companies they need to generate revenue to cover these costs. Most search engines do so by carrying advertising. Some generate money by other methods such as taking a commission on commercial transactions conducted via the search engine too. This means that most search engines inevitably have a bias towards business use.

The Example Search Continued

We continue with our example on North Sea Cod examined earlier. After selecting the website www.google.com, the search term:

North Sea Cod

is entered. A large number of references is immediately generated, the first page of which is given as Figure 4.6.

It is clear from this extract that there has been comment in *The Guardian* newspaper's website and in the ENN (Environmental News Network) website, that the Ministry of Agriculture Food and Fisheries is working on the problem and that it has received attention from the European Commission. The article by Dr John Casey reveals another important acronym (CEFAS) with which is associated a laboratory. The article (which can be accessed immediately) provides detailed data on the decline of North Sea Cod; the student will clearly want to pursue other publications of this laboratory (which could be done through WoS).

Later pages reveal considerable activity by those EU governments whose countries abut the North Sea together with Norway, which though a non-EU nation has a clear interest in the problem. The student is able to identify a (European) Commission Regulation (EC) No 259/2001 which sets out measures to allow North Sea Cod stocks to recover.

This search, has, therefore, produced in just a few minutes a mass of material that very usefully complements the WoS search. Moreover, most of the material has been obtained in full text rather than abstract form.

Guardian Unlimited | Special reports | Ban on **North sea cod ...**
... Ban on **North sea cod** fishing Special report: Global crisis in fishing Paul Brown
and Andrew Osborn in Brussels Thursday January 25, 2001 The Guardian A 40,000 ...
www.guardian.co.uk/fish/story/0,7369,427764,00.html – 37k – <u>Cached</u> – <u>Similar pages</u>
North Sea warming puts the heat on diminishing **cod** – 3/9/ ...
... In December 1999, the allowed catch of **North Sea cod** was reduced 39 percent from
145,640 tons to 89,100 tons by the European Union Fisheries Ministers. ...
www.enn.com/enn-news-archive/2000/03/03092000/cod_10861.asp – 20k – <u>Cached</u> – <u>Similar pages</u>
BBC News | SCI/TECH | Warm water threat to **North Sea cod**
... Wednesday, 8 March, 2000, 22:37 GMT Warm water threat to **North Sea cod** A large **cod**
landed at Lowestoft in 1991 (Photo: Greenpeace) By environment correspond-ent ...
news.bbc.co.uk/hi/english/sci/tech/newsid_670000/670248.stm – 26k – <u>Cached</u> – <u>Similar pages</u>
The **North Sea**
... in the **North Sea** to ensure that this vibrant ecosystem and vitally important industry does not suffer the same fate as Canada's east coast **cod** fishery ...
www.greenpeace.org/~comms/cbio/nsea.html – 7k – <u>Cached</u> – <u>Similar pages</u>
FID – **North Sea Cod** Crisis – Norway and the EU Agree on ...
... 81 522. **North Sea Cod** Crisis – Norway and the EU Agree
on New Measures. At a meeting ...
odin.dep.no/fid/engelsk/p10001957/pressem/008041-070046/ index-dok000-b-n-a.html – 14k – <u>Cached</u> – <u>Similar pages</u>
COD STOCKS IN THE **NORTH SEA** 2001
File Format: PDF/Adobe Acrobat – <u>View as Text</u>
... the Council of Ministers decided that the international Total Allowable Catch for
North Sea cod should be reduced to 48,600 tonnes. The UK quota has initially ...
www.marlab.ac.uk/InfoPDF/07RCode.pdf – <u>Similar pages</u>
The Commission adopts emergency measures to help the recovery ...
... The Commission adopts emergency measures to help the
recovery of **North Sea cod** stocks. ...
europa.eu.int/comm/fisheries/news_corner/press/inf01_08_en.htm – 20k – <u>Cached</u> – <u>Similar pages</u>
Prospects poor for **North Sea cod**
... Prospects poor for **North Sea cod**. Dr John Casey from CEFAS's Lowestoft Laboratory
outlines the preliminary results of the assessment of **North Sea** fish stocks ...
www.cefas.co.uk/fisheries/nscod.htm – 28k – <u>Cached</u> – <u>Similar pages</u>

Figure 4.6 Extract from results of Google search

During the course of the searches, we have identified a number of acronyms that we require a meaning for. A search engine is a good way of sorting these out. By entering the acronyms into Google, the student rapidly finds

> **ICES International Council for the Exploration of the Sea**
> **ITQ Individual Transferable Quota**
> **CEFAS The Centre for Environment Fisheries and Aquaculture**

Problems With Web Search Engines

> A KEY SKILL IN USING THE WEB FOR RESEARCH IS THE DEMONSTRABLE EXERCISE OF JUDGEMENT IN REJECTING DUBIOUS MATERIAL AND USING WORTHWHILE SOURCES CRITICALLY

Given the success of the Web search in our example, it might be wondered why we have ascribed Web searches a complementary role. Although the ultimate logic of the Internet may well be that all searches could be conducted solely by means of a Web search engine, there are a number of reasons why, for the foreseeable future, students will need to base their searches on Methods 1–4 listed above and, in particular, to be familiar with WoS.

1. Because of the commercial orientation of Web search engines, it is common for searches to turn up several thousand items that, though they have an obvious business relevance, are of little use to the researcher (cf. Appendix 1). It can be extremely difficult to refine such a list to contain just those references that are of interest. Thus, although we were fortunate here, it is frequently not possible to turn up any useful references.
2. It is often the case that material uncovered by a Web search is only available for a fee. In some cases, for example consulting firm reports, this fee may be substantial. For the student researcher with a limited budget this can be frustrating.
3. Little control is exerted on the content of material uncovered by search engines. This means that references turned up may reflect a very partial view of a topic, for example of a pressure group, or may be of very dubious quality. Higher education departments of all types urge their students to exercise judgement in using the Web. Among the skills that students have to demonstrate are those of being able to reject dubious or worthless sources

and being able to identify worthwhile sources and to use them critically. Calvert (2001) discusses a number of ways in which misinformation can get onto the Web, including fabrication (invention of data); falsification (deliberate distortion); and plagiarism (passing off another's words as one's own); plus the main cause, human error.

SETTING UP ONE'S OWN BIBLIOGRAPHY

The citation indexes embody a principle that is important for the individual researcher – the results of a literature search need to be incorporated in the researcher's own bibliography. Sooner or later some or all of the references will have to be compiled into a list for a dissertation or a thesis or an article in an academic journal. They must, therefore, be recorded in sufficient detail to facilitate this process and preferably in such a way that the multiplicity of different referencing standards – for example, numbered in order of appearance, listed in alphabetical order – are readily accommodated. Furthermore, a good bibliography in any new field is a very tradeable commodity and researchers who possess one are likely to find that if they make it available to other researchers, those researchers will in turn make their data available to them. In fact, nowadays many mail groups encourage the compilation of composite bibliographies on new research areas derived from submissions from individual members, provided that the results are made available to all members of the mail group. It is obviously helpful, if one wishes to compile such a list, to use such composite bibliographies as a starting point. Certainly, for students who come after them (including perhaps their own subsequent research students), an up-to-date and comprehensive bibliography is invaluable.

For these reasons we shall now discuss how students can set up their own computer bibliography. Using a word-processing package, a spreadsheet, or even a simple communications package, the effort involved in developing such a database is little different from that required to record the necessary information manually. Indeed, there are a number of PC-based packages that are specifically available for this purpose.

Increasingly commercial bibliographic database systems such as EndNote are becoming available to the student researcher. However, we will assume that the student does not have such a database available. A bibliographic database can only be set up if certain standards are adopted. It should be remembered that a system intended for use mainly by one or few researchers need not have the sophistication of a commercial system; the user needs only to adopt a suitable set of conventions. This will usually involve carrying the following information for each reference:

Author(s)/editor(s)

Type of work: book, paper, thesis, for instance and

For a book	*For a journal article*
title	title of paper
edition	name of journal
number of volumes	volume
publisher	issue
place of publication	page numbers
date of publication	year

Research students may well find it useful to produce further information, such as:

A set of *keywords* describing the contents of the work
Supplementary information

For obvious reasons, the student is advised to make sure before setting up their own database that the details from it are compatible with any commercial system to which they may eventually gain access.

Given that a comprehensive set of details are recorded, the biggest problems likely to be encountered are:

a) spelling errors which can easily be removed if each reference is checked after entry;
b) the transliteration of certain foreign names, where different publishers and writers adopt different conventions – for instance, 'Dostoevsky', 'Dostoevski'.

> **A STUDENT SHOULD ADOPT ONE STANDARD FOR A BIBLIOGRAPHY AND STICK TO IT**

The remedy for the latter problem is for researchers to adopt one standard and stick to it. Provided they are consistent all occurrences of this name can be edited to some other form at a later date, if desired.

There are bibliographic standards; for example, for referencing, there is in the UK, BS 4821: Recommendations for the Presentation of Theses, published in 1982 by the BSI.

The practice adopted by the major international databases, for example the citation indexes referred to earlier, themselves constitute a set of de facto standards. It is sensible for student researchers to bear such standards and quasi-standards in mind when selecting a format for their own bibliographies, since this greatly facilitates downloading of information from international databases directly into the student's own bibliographic database.

It is suggested that in the second section of the reference, keywords are included describing the work in question. The individual researcher should give them serious consideration, since their use makes possible much more effective searches within the database. Given the restricted amount of information that can be incorporated in a title (particularly in the case of books), and the fact that titles can mislead as to contents, if searches are based on title alone, a number of relevant references will be missed.

To implement a keyword system the researcher needs to set up a thesaurus of keywords for indexing purposes. This must be sufficiently detailed for a precise description of the contents of any work to be given but should remain reasonably small. It should be remembered that there will often be synonymous terms. In such cases one should be chosen as the thesaurus term and a note should be made under the synonyms of the term actually adopted. In general, for one researcher a thesaurus of a few hundred terms should suffice. Nevertheless, maintenance of the thesaurus is made easier by keeping that on the computer also. Again, it should be borne in mind that international databases may well contain relevant terms and, for obvious reasons, it is useful for the student to conform with these, where possible.

The use of keywords means that the researcher needs to provide a list for each of the references read. This is a useful discipline and is a way of making at least brief notes on a reference and is a check on whether the researcher has understood it. The number of terms used need not be particularly large; the aim, after all, is to categorise the article or book, not reproduce it. In fact, in most fields, a dozen or so terms seems quite adequate for all save the exceptional work. The third section of the record allowing supplementary information to be recorded is usually also worthwhile. It normally causes little trouble to design such a feature into the system from the outset even if, initially, it is not used. To incorporate it later, however, may well be more difficult. This type of facility is useful because most researchers need to record additional information about some references: for example, which libraries hold it, or the researcher's opinion of the work, or quotations from it that may be useful for eventual incorporation into the thesis. If the work is deemed potentially useful then the student should also provide a brief summary.

Electronic Copies and Plagiarism

Since many articles can now be downloaded from the Web in electronic form it might be thought that the third section might also contain a downloaded electronic copy of the reference. We would strongly counsel students who choose to do this to exercise great care. If the entire document is available in electronic form the student runs the risk of unwittingly incorporating substantial chunks of it into the finished dissertation or thesis as their own work. The student has then committed, in the eyes of HE institutions, the extremely serious offence of plagiarism – passing off as one's own the work of others. The penalties for plagiarism are severe, often amounting to failing the entire qualification. Moreover, much research has gone into enabling it to be detected automatically. To avoid the danger of inadvertent plagiarism the student may prefer to work only from paper copies of reference documents. The production of a summary of useful references, as recommended above, is a great aid in this. Where the student does make use of electronic copies of texts, all quotations from them must, of course, be scrupulously acknowledged.

SERENDIPITY IN LITERATURE SEARCHING

The preceding sections have been concerned with the execution of a formal literature search. While at this point the importance of mastering the procedures involved is re-emphasised, it is worth reminding the student that there are also benefits to be gained from relatively unplanned, intermittent and informal searching activities. For the student with easy physical access to an academic library, browsing in sections of the library where books related to the field of study are stocked provides one such method. Regular inspection of the new titles shelf to be found in most libraries provides another. Casual observation of the books and journals that other researchers, perhaps in very different fields, are using is a third way. For the student without easy access to a library who must perforce conduct the literature search entirely electronically, pursuing search terms and new research dimensions thrown up by the electronic literature search in the ways outlined above fulfils the same role. For both groups, a lively curiosity about and a good general knowledge of one's own field of study are also very useful and can be promoted by regular reading of book reviews in the quality press and in specialist journals. In the short term, it is unlikely that such activities will lead to a marked benefit in conducting a specific literature search. Most researchers would agree, however, that in the long term they do substantially enhance the quality of their literature searches, and reduce the time required to carry them out.

THE ROLES OF SUPERVISOR AND LIBRARIAN

For doctoral students, the help they receive both from their supervisors and from specialist librarians may well be greater in the early stages of research than that they obtain from pursuing the formal literature search discussed above. Usually, however, a supervisor will know the key references in a field and the most prominent people working in it, so that the research student is saved much preliminary spadework. Similarly, the subject-specialist librarian can be relied on for information about core references and core journals as well as information about pertinent abstracting services. Nonetheless, being able to use the literature effectively is an important part of the researcher's craft. Research students should therefore demonstrate that they have mastered it to the extent that they can pay their way by helping newcomers to their subject to carry out literature searches electronically and by finding references that are useful to their colleagues and their supervisor. If they can do this they need feel no qualms in turn in asking for assistance in those cases where they genuinely need it. As we have made clear above, students at lower levels will be required to demonstrate that they have mastered the art of literature searching by electronic means.

USING THE REFERENCES

Finally, it should be remembered that successful identification of relevant references is only part of the story. Unless the information they contain can be purposefully used, as detailed in the next chapters, the researcher is left with little more than an impressive bibliography – which may well prove counterproductive if the researcher cannot demonstrate the ability to use it competently. It may well be, therefore, that the study of a book such as Fairbairn and Winch (1991) on reading skills – including the improvement of comprehension as well as reading speed – may prove to be a worthwhile investment.

CHAPTER SUMMARY

LITERATURE SEARCHES ARE NECESSARY: for topic selection and as part of the research proper.

LITERATURE SEARCHES SHOULD BE CONDUCTED ELECTRONICALLY: students at all levels must demonstrate that they can conduct such searches effectively.

THERE ARE TWO MAIN APPROACHES TO CARRYING OUT LITERATURE SEARCHES ELECTRONICALLY: these are by searching online databases, such as *Web of Science*, and by carrying out a Web search.

ABSTRACTS OF ARTICLES AND KEYWORDS ARE USEFUL: to determine whether the full text is worth obtaining.

ONCE POTENTIAL REFERENCES HAVE BEEN IDENTIFIED THEY MUST BE OBTAINED: increasingly the documents are available in electronic form.

INDIVIDUAL BIBLIOGRAPHIES: set up and maintained by the research student are much to be commended. They are the precursor to gaining real insight into the topic being researched.

CARE MUST BE TAKEN TO AVOID PLAGIARISM: it is easy to pass off a section of an electronic document as one's own work. Students should take care not to do this.

Part B

Data Analysis and Gathering

5

Analysing the Data

THE ROLE OF ANALYSIS

As pointed out in Chapter 2, until a feasible outline of the type of analysis to be undertaken has been determined, the research plan must be considered incomplete. Many students are tempted to embark on literature searches and massive programmes of data gathering before thinking about how the results are to be analysed. All too often this leads to considerable wasted effort. Essential items of data are not collected, or the first attempts at analysis are too trivial so that a complete rethink is necessary.

We argue strongly that time should be spent, consistent with the level of study to be undertaken, on planning. At all levels topic analysis should feature and at the higher levels the rigours of completing a project proposal should pay off in recognising some of the challenges that lie ahead. In particular the research design will indicate which analytical approaches could well be relevant and an unwillingness to make use of some of these will have a bearing on the methodology selected.

If for example there is something of an antipathy towards the application of multivariate statistical analysis the student may well decide that the collection of rich data relating to a limited number of subjects, for example through in-depth interviews, will be the approach to be preferred rather than conducting a postal survey seeking responses.

We considered the analysis of data before addressing issues involved in their collection (Chapter 6) so that the student will gain some idea of the implications of adopting a particular methodology.

We suggest that after having read this chapter the student refers to the ANALYSIS AND ANALYTICAL TECHNIQUES section of the select bibliography which forms Appendix 2.

One key function of analysis is to communicate the value (whether academic, social or scientific) of the findings. An even more important purpose is to convince the reader that, through the innate value of the knowledge gained, the research report makes a sufficient contribution for the level of research in question and that the research measures up to the necessary standards of academic worth. For this reason at the doctoral level there is a flavour of the legal process about analysis. It should be seen that it was done for good cause and that it was properly carried out. At the lower levels of a research project, of course, such exalted standards may not come into play. Rather, given the crucial role of analysis in the research process, the primary aim of requiring students to carry out a research project may well be to enable them to develop the ability to evaluate the analysis of other researchers.

Such requirements are usually evident, for example, in university regulations for dissertations produced as part of a master's degree, with their emphasis on 'an ordered presentation of knowledge in a particular field' or 'a critical exposition of previous work'. At undergraduate level the requirements are on the whole more modest but are likely to require students to demonstrate both an ability to use the literature and to evaluate the work of others.

RESEARCHERS WITH OUTSTANDING GIFTS AND SKILLS ARE RELATIVELY FEW IN NUMBER

Of all the stages of research, the related activities of data gathering and analysis (and particularly the latter) demand most intellectual input. Student researchers should recognise this and accept that those with greater skills and insights will be able to achieve a higher standard of work. Researchers with outstanding gifts and skills are relatively few in number. It should therefore be accepted that research into a particular topic will lead to a very different outcome according to who is undertaking the work.

Thus, an economics undergraduate may choose to develop a national energy policy model as a final year project. It will, nevertheless, be recognised by both student and supervisor that the output of the research will, in all probability, fall well short of what an experienced econometrician would achieve. We argue that, provided the student is prepared to seek to acquire the skills appropriate to the level of research being undertaken and to identify the depth of analysis needed to satisfy requirements for the programme being followed, successful completion is in prospect. Guidance from the supervisor at this stage is of great importance.

DEFINITION OF ANALYSIS

> ANALYSIS IS THE ORDERING AND STRUCTURING OF DATA TO PRODUCE KNOWLEDGE

For the purposes of this chapter analysis will be assumed to involve the ordering and structuring of data to produce knowledge. Structuring will be taken to include summarising and categorising the work of others, which is often the main form of analysis in lower level research projects. Data will be interpreted broadly as information gathered by observation, through books or pictures, field surveys, laboratory experiments, etc. The chapter will cover approaches to analysis that can be applied in a variety of different fields. As such it addresses two topics often separated in texts on research methodology, namely research design and data analysis. In practice, these are closely interlinked – at least in principle – since the design determines the data and what can be done with it, whereas the end purposes of the data analysis are the major determinants of the research design. For this reason we deal here with both aspects.

The definition of analysis proposed is a broad one and it will be presumed to embrace a whole range of activities of both the qualitative and the quantitative type. From the 1960s through to the beginning of the 1990s there was a discernible tendency for research to make increasing use of quantitative analysis and in particular statistical methods, for example in attempting to quantify notions such as culture. Statistical methods enjoy a special position in research because they grew up through attempts by mathematicians to provide solutions to problems of defining and building knowledge noted by philosophers. They therefore provide a very useful model of many of the processes of data analysis. Furthermore, they reflect the structure of the analysis process in many different fields. Inevitably, then, the bias of this chapter is towards statistical methods. Rather than give a detailed account of some techniques, which would inevitably involve arbitrary selection, we provide here a brief outline of a rather greater number, indicating in particular where they fit into the overall picture, and follow this outline with detailed references in the bibliography at Appendix 2. To avoid pointless repetition in what follows it will be assumed that researchers will consult the bibliography for further details of techniques of interest to them.

Despite the bias towards statistical methods we shall pay some attention to the considerable proliferation of readily available computer analysis packages that has taken place in the past fifteen years. These range from packages used by engineers to analyse and synthesise designs, through to packages designed to facilitate the analysis of qualitative data, such as interview notes.

The Qualitative Dimension of Analysis

Any data analysis, whether quantitative or not, needs to be discussed in writing. This is a crucial aspect of good analysis that is often neglected. For that reason we shall attempt to consider it in this chapter.

In the last twenty years, there has been a growing interest in the analysis of qualitative data. This is partly because of the convergence of interest between students of humanities and those of social science, for example in fields such as cultural studies. It is also because such data can be considerably richer than quantitative data and their use can therefore lead to deeper understanding. As always with such reactions, there have been those, such as French sociologists, who reject previous modes of research, such as quantitatively based research, entirely. We shall not take this view. Quantitative analysis, in general, and statistical analysis, in particular, provide an excellent model of much research. Also as much student research will involve a quantitative dimension as well as a qualitative one, especially in fields concerned with the practical application of ideas, both types of data are needed.

An overview of some common purposes of analysis is provided in Figure 5.1, which shows particular aims consonant with those purposes and certain 'techniques' for meeting those aims.

TYPES OF DATA AND THEIR PLACE IN ANALYSIS

Before commenting on each of the purposes listed in Figure 5.1 it is useful to review the data typology that will be adopted – namely textual, nominal or categorical, ordinal or ranked, interval and ratio.

> TEXTUAL DATA ARE RICH AND FLEXIBLE BUT MUCH ATTENTION NEEDS TO BE PAID TO THEIR CONTENT AND MEANING IF THEY ARE TO BE PROPERLY UNDERSTOOD

The description *textual data* is given to that which records a written or spoken description. Most books and papers are principally composed of material of this

Purpose of analysis	Aim of the analysis	Applicable quantitative techniques	Applicable quantitative techniques
Description	Concept formulation Classification Critical review	Content analysis Factor analysis Cluster analysis Discriminant analysis	Critical analysis Data interrelationship depiction Causal mapping
Construction of measurement scales	Multi-attribute scale construction	Unidimensional scaling Multidimensional scaling	
Application of a methodology	Demonstrate ability to apply the methodology	Engineering design techniques	Methods of enquiry, e.g. Checkland methodology
Design	Design of some real world object Design of systems	Most general quantitative techniques Engineering design models	Multimedia databases Practitioner reflection
Generation of empirical relationships	Pattern recognition Derivation of empirical laws	Correlation methods Graphical techniques	Theories of history
Explanation and prediction	Comparative analysis Policy analysis theory generation/Construction of a shared language	Loglinear analysis Experimental design model Regression models	Theories of history

NB. 1. Columns 2–4 represent aims and techniques that are relevant to the purpose defined in column 1, that is, no meaning should be attributed to the fact that items in Columns 2, 3 and 4 are in the same row.
2. The bibliography of Appendix 2 gives further reference material relating to this table.

Figure 5.1 Some common tasks of analysis and some techniques applicable to them

kind. Textual data are rich and flexible but much attention needs to be paid to their content and meaning if they are to be properly understood. Usually, they appear in an analysis in summary form as either a precis or as selected quotes. While in some fields – for example, biblical studies – concordances exist so that occurrences of particular words or ideas are easily traced, this is not usually the case and hence data of this type can pose particular problems. Although textual data cannot be used directly for quantitative analysis they may form a basis for it. Such analysis is usually referred to as 'content analysis'.

The use of the term(s) *nominal* or *categorical data* allow classification, for example, 'male', or 'an item of foreign origin'. Such data can be counted and cross-tabulated and hence are frequently used. Purely nominal data cannot be effectively compared but it is often desirable to be able to do this. The first type of data that allows comparison is *ordinal* or *ranked* data. Thus, hardness of materials is defined as such a scale by saying material A is harder than material

B if it can scratch B. All solid materials can then be ranked in order of increasing hardness on this scale. Note, however, the characteristic feature of such scales in that though A may be harder than B it does not make sense to say A is 1.3 times harder.

A type of scale that enables measurement of the differences between individual values on the scale is' provided by *interval data* where an actual numerical value can be given to each point on the scale. Such scales are used for purposes such as the measurement of sound intensity where values are assigned to the difference in intensity of two sounds rather than the absolute intensity of either. Interval scales do not have a meaningful zero although one may be arbitrarily assigned as in, for example, the Fahrenheit temperature scale.

To obtain *ratio data* by which individual items can be evaluated on a scale it is necessary for the measurement scale to have a meaningful zero. Many engineering measurements are of this type, for example, length. In the social sciences, too, they occur frequently, for example, national average wage on a particular date. Any method of quantitative analysis can be applied to ratio data. Most methods can be used with interval data (basically any technique that uses only differences in values).

The range of methods that can be applied to ordinal data is considerably smaller whereas with nominal data little can be done besides basic enumeration. As far as quantitative analysis is concerned, as we move up the hierarchy from nominal to ratio scales, we can extract progressively more from the data. Usually then it is best to obtain the highest level of data one can for analysis.

THE PURPOSE OF ANALYSIS

Having defined the broad framework within which analysis is located the remainder of this chapter will examine each of the major purposes of analysis in turn. The assumption will be that the purpose of the analysis should be a major determinant of the approach used. In general, the nearer any technique of quantitative analysis is to the bottom of the list in Figure 5.1 the more conditions have to be fulfilled before it can be applied. Many research projects that are concerned with quantitative analysis of data are therefore likely to be concerned with purposes nearer the top of Figure 5.1, particularly those in fields that are relatively little developed; that is research is likely to be exploratory rather than explanatory in nature. Furthermore, many of the approaches require extended effort and are not suitable for the shorter type of research project. In principle, the type of analysis would be decided taking into account these various factors, but in practice there is an additional significant determinant of the approach, namely the field in which the research is being conducted.

Any subject with a reasonably established tradition will place particular emphasis on certain approaches to analysis. It is hard, for instance, to conceive of research in physics that would involve purely descriptive analysis based on the use of textual data. In addition, it must be remembered that students will normally need to draw on their supervisor for guidance as to how to conduct their analysis. Obviously, this should have some bearing on their choice of approach since otherwise not only may that guidance not be forthcoming but also communication may break down because supervisor and student have no shared language in which to discuss the analysis stage of the project.

Of recent years, there has been a notable increase, particularly in the social sciences, in the view that even at the doctoral level research should be viewed as merely exploratory in nature because of the lack of knowledge in the area of study. Given the explosion that has taken place in the academic literature and the much greater ease with which that literature can now be accessed, this is a somewhat dubious contention. The standards by which analysis is judged will vary by level of research and the subject under study. Students should beware, however, of not considering carefully what is an appropriate depth of analysis no matter how new their subject. We can only urge students to consider how the field in which they are working should affect their approach to analysis, supplemented by the comments made below about general criteria which must be satisfied if logical inferences are to be drawn from analysis.

PROPER ARGUMENT AND ANALYSIS

Whether quantitative techniques of analysis are employed or not, proper development of an argument, is essential. Moreover, this is often an area where many student researchers fall down. The key principles are:

1. The argument must have a clear sense of direction. The reader must know what the researcher is trying to achieve and be able to follow the route by which the researcher's conclusions must be reached.
2. The argument must be based on the presentation of evidence, not mere assertion. Of course, what constitutes evidence will differ – for a physicist it may be reference to data; for someone writing on the influences on the writings of a famous author it will be accounts, textual or otherwise, of key influences on that author.

Research and Logical Inference

We believe that for the majority of student research that is not concerned with the interpretation of texts or discourse, the laws of logic constitute 'the rules of the game' that must be observed if the researcher's quantitative analysis is to persuade others. Although this has become an unfashionable view in some circles it remains important to understand certain basic principles in the presentation of research findings. For this reason, we would certainly advise the doctoral student to consult some of the texts cited in the bibliography in Appendix 2. Brief comments will be made on some of the more important principles.

Falsifiability

> NO PROPOSITION HAS VALUE AS A BASIS FOR RESEARCH IF IT CANNOT BE DISPROVED BY SOME DATA OR OTHER

It must be possible to disprove a proposition if it is to have value as a basis for research. Thus, though the suggestion that Sirius is circled by a planet on which intelligent life exists is interesting, it is quite unfalsifiable with our existing technology and therefore is not a valid subject for research.

The need to search for alternative interpretations

Alternative interpretations of data are not normally difficult to find. In a statistical analysis, for example, one that is often very plausible is that the results apparently obtained are 'data artefacts' – merely a function of the particular set of data collected – which would disappear were other data gathered. On the other hand, research students cannot consider every possible alternative. Rather, what is required is that they deal with one or two highly plausible ones (especially those that may have been advanced by other researchers). By its very nature research work tends to lead to quite a narrow perspective and to find this overturned by a rather obvious oversight at the external examination would be a disaster.

In fields where the potential for application is evident (engineering and the social sciences are examples) researchers should recognise that there are a number of options as to the focus of their research. Different options will probably require the gathering of different data. Failure to recognise this in the study design could lead to the frustrating experiences of realisation at an advanced stage that more data are needed. Thus, a student undertaking a master's dissertation may recommend to an organisation facing considerable pressures on space that it should sub-contract some of its activities rather than move to a two-site operation, having completely overlooked that home-working for some of the staff may have been a better solution to the problem. Limited time available for the research might well preclude the subsequent evaluation of this option and severely reduce the value of the findings.

Simplicity of explanation

Simple explanations are to be preferred to complex ones; valid explanations that involve few variables are superior to those that involve many. Some research fields lend themselves to powerful theories involving only a few basic concepts whereas in others (for example, the social sciences) this is often not the case. However, even in the latter circumstances it is often possible to find one explanation that involves distinctly fewer variables than another. This is frequently a worthwhile aim since, though an explanation involving very many variables will usually be better for a specific phenomenon, it will usually be of far less general applicability.

The impossibility of proving relationships

Outside mathematics, the researcher cannot prove explanations or predictions completely, merely render them more probable. For the student, the practical implication is that a research project with a demonstrable outcome is often a safer bet than one that attempts to predict or to explain some phenomenon; such projects (in the terminology of Chapter 2) may prove to be highly asymmetrical.

The need for variables to take on more than one value

> VARIABLES MUST BE ALLOWED TO TAKE ON MORE THAN ONE VALUE

If explanation and prediction are to be based on the value of a group of variables, it is necessary that those variables be allowed to take on more than one value to demonstrate their effects. The practical implications of this are that what can be extracted from the analysis of a particular set of research data depends critically on what variables have taken on more than one value. If it is required to use the value of a particular variable for predictive or explanatory purposes, information about its value must be obtained at the data gathering stage.

Though the need for variables to vary if anything is to be said about their influence may appear self-evident, it is very common to find unwarranted conclusions being drawn about the influence of variables given the values they have taken.

These principles discussed above show that the conclusions that can legitimately be derived from an analysis depend critically on the data on which it is based. Any piece of research other than that involving the construction of pure deductive theory, as in mathematics, can be viewed as being based on some type of sample from some notional population. It is often difficult to determine just how the results of a particular study can be generalised if sufficient thought is not given to sample selection prior to data gathering. Accordingly, the likelihood of generalising from the results needs to be considered before undertaking the research: a conclusion that will be met again when the problem is examined in the light of the statistical experimental design model which is considered later in the chapter.

A REVIEW OF SOME COMMON PURPOSES OF ANALYSIS AND APPLICABLE TECHNIQUES

This section explores in rather more depth the diagram of Figure 5.1. Under each of the main purposes we consider some common aims related to a particular purpose and discuss quantitative and qualitative techniques applicable to those aims.

Description

Description involves a set of activities that are an essential first step in the development of most fields. Students who can identify a topic about which little is known, of whose importance others can be convinced and for which data can be collected may need to do little other than record them to have their work adjudged satisfactory. Usually, however, knowledge is not so rudimentary and structure must be put on the data by developing or inventing concepts or methods of classification.

Concept formulation

A CONCEPT IS A USEFUL IDEA WITH A NAME

In order to make any sense of data we need concepts that enable us to focus on those factors and measurements that are relevant to the field of study. In essence, a concept is a useful idea with a name, and concept formulation is thus intimately associated with the idea of language. A concept, to be useful, must ideally satisfy a number of criteria. It must be unambiguous so that it is possible for different workers to agree whether or not it applies in any given case. Other workers should find it natural to use, and it should be unique and not merely a new name for a concept that already exists in some other field.

Relatively little work seems to have been done on how to effectively formulate concepts from textual data (Bolton, 1977). It seems likely, however, that an

120

important method is the use of analogy; for example, the application of the notion of 'half-life', derived from atomic physics, to the declining usefulness of subject-specific journals over time.

Another very powerful way of developing concepts is the use of pictorial data. The need for the concept of 'crater' in discussing the moon is obvious. In general, seeing provides a very powerful way of getting at concepts, for which reasons many statistical approaches present the results in pictorial as well as numerical form.

It is often the case that the researcher wishes to identify concepts in textual data derived from journal articles or transcripts of interviews or transcripts of the discussion of a 'focus group' on the area of interest. Traditionally this has been done by reviewing the different documents and attempting to find common concepts. This may mean allowing for the fact that different authors or interviewees use different terms for the same concept: for example, some may talk of 'new technology monitoring' while others talk of 'identifying technological opportunities' while the researcher is happy that for the purposes of the research these can be considered identical. This process has recently been facilitated by the introduction of PC-based packages for *data interrelationship depiction*. These depict interrelationships in different items of textual data – for example, mind maps, NUD·IST, N-VIVO.

A variety of statistical methods are available as aids to concept formation. These are all based on the underlying notion that good concepts are those which enable us to find differences among the objects under study. They accordingly attempt to tease out the major sources of differences in the data to form prototypes, at least, of useful concepts.

One of the oldest sets of statistical techniques are those of *factor analysis*. These take a number of measurements for each object, for example psychological test scores, and attempt to select from them a few combinations of these measurements that explain most of the differences between individuals – the so-called 'factors', which can then be named. This approach is applied, for example in intelligence testing, to identify the factors of spatial ability and verbal ability.

Another approach is to compare objects according to how similar they are and then group them in descending order of similarity. This is the basis of *cluster analysis*. Thus, we might consider grouping people in the light of similarities in educational qualifications. A number of groups would then be expected to emerge naturally: for example, in the UK, those educated to postgraduate level, to graduate level, to A level, and so on.

Classification

The successful development of concepts results in a number of 'pigeon holes' into which individual objects can be classified.

The easiest type of classification procedure to adopt is one that assesses each of the objects to be classified in the light of the concepts to be applied and then assigns it to the category which it most nearly fits. Thus, someone who spends five hours a week playing football for a payment of £50 to cover travel expenses might be assigned to the category 'amateur footballer' rather than 'professional footballer' if the concepts relevant to this classification decision are 'hours spent playing or practising football' and 'amount of income derived from playing football'. An obvious refinement of this idea is to weight the different concepts according to their importance. Thus, we might assign a weight of 100 to hours per week played and a weight of 5 to amount of money received and then classify as a professional footballer anyone scoring more than 4000. With this weighting scheme our footballer would receive a weighted score of

$$100 \times 5 \text{ (hours/week)} + 5 \times 50 \text{ (£/week)} = 750$$

and therefore be classified as an amateur footballer.

Rather than derive the weightings subjectively it is often useful to calculate them using the statistical technique known as *discriminant analysis*. The essence of the approach is simple: a number of objects that have already been classified are taken. Measurements of a number of variables for each of them are used to set up a set of predictor functions that will enable future cases to be classified by using a weighted combination of the relevant measurements.

Critical review

We have already noted the importance of critical review to students at all levels. The ability to evaluate literature is a skill which has to be developed as students progress through any field of study. Students pursuing studies in humanities or fine arts will in addition be able to draw on the apparatus of *critical analysis* to which they will almost certainly be exposed during their studies.

The aim of *content analysis* is to put qualitative data into a more quantitative framework. It was originally devised by political scientists for the interpretation of official texts but it can also be used for, say, the analysis of tape recordings from discussion groups.

The essence of content analysis is to:

a) identify the target communications;
b) identify a number of dimensions of the subject in hand;
c) go through each communication assigning statements to it to one or other of the dimensions;
d) count the number of times each dimension is addressed in each communication.

Thus, for a study of the impact of the concept of global warming on, say, the public consciousness in the UK, the target communications might be decided to be the quality newspapers over a specified period of time. A number of dimensions would suggest themselves from the literature, discussion with experts and so on, including issues like the impact on agricultural yields; the impact on biodiversity; the impact on low-lying countries, etc. It is then a straightforward matter to examine the newspapers concerned.

It will nevertheless be appreciated that, firstly, such a process can be very time consuming and, secondly, that it is likely to be expedited considerably by confining attention to those newspapers to which access in electronic form can be obtained. In the latter case, analysis can be considerably expedited by the use of PC-based packages for qualitative data analysis such as NUD·IST.

Often students may wish to describe how different individuals or organisations view a particular situation, for example in the field of Conflict Studies. The technique of *causal mapping* allows their views to be described pictorially in terms of the cause and effects seen as operating by them. Software such as Ethnograph and Decision Explorer has been available for this purpose for a number of years.

Construction of Measurement Scales

A frequent purpose of analysis is the construction of a measurement scale of the interval or ratio type; such a need occurs surprisingly often. For example, a host of different variables such as height and weight can be measured for a building but none of them provides a direct measurement of the attribute 'earthquake-proofness'.

Traditionally, the approach to the problem of constructing scales has been to adopt surrogate measures: for example, the use of performance on standard flame tests, as a measure of fire resistance. Scales based on the weighting of a number of different attributes or values (as discussed in our footballer example above) have become an increasingly popular alternative: for example, in assessing the fire risk of buildings in the UK.

At a more sophisticated level during the past thirty years, however, a host of techniques have been developed, by psychologists in particular, for constructing scales for which no 'obvious' measurement exists. These may be single (*uni-dimensional*) scales which measure a variable along a single dimension, for example, the measurement of an 'intelligence quotient'. On the other hand, *multidimensional* scaling techniques apply to situations where more than one concept, or dimension, is relevant. In the case of two, or more dimensions, such techniques result in a 'perceptual map'. To revert to our earlier example of the footballer, it might well be that in this case it may be sensible to measure interest in football along two dimensions: firstly, the average hours per week spent playing football; and, secondly, the proportion of the individual's income derived from football. Such a representation would obviously provide a richer measure of the variable of interest than a unidimensional scale.

Of recent years, the *analytic hierarchy process* of Saaty (1980) has attracted considerable interest as an approach to the construction of scales representing subjective judgements as to the relative importance of objects of interest: for example, the benefits from investments in different computer systems, or the preferred locations of businesses.

Application of a Methodology

INCREASINGLY, STUDENTS ARE REQUIRED TO DEMONSTRATE THAT THEY CAN APPLY SOME RESEARCH METHODOLOGY SUCCESSFULLY

A type of research project that has grown in importance of recent years is one that requires students to demonstrate that they can apply some methodology successfully. A major reason for this is that the assessment of such an ability is done more easily through a project rather than a conventional examination.

Such projects are common in engineering or technology; the methodology is likely to be underpinned by a computer package, for example for integrated circuit design. In many areas of social science students are more likely to find themselves applying some problem-solving methodology, such as that of Checkland (1999).

Analysis in the context of applying a methodology requires the student to do two things:

1. To explain the application of the methodology clearly.
2. To make it clear they understand the conceptual and theoretical bases of the methodology.

In many cases there will be added a third purpose, to evaluate the methodology. It is by no means easy to achieve these aims. Many student engineering projects, for instance, consist of little other than a series of printouts that reflect a mechanical application of the methodology rather than any deeper understanding of it.

Design

Many student research projects involve the design of something. Engineers may design test apparatus or prototype new products, architects a building complex, while health administration students may design new appointments systems. Like the application of a methodology this is a category of research project that has grown in importance over the past twenty years because of the unsuitability of conventional written examinations for assessing design knowledge.

The placement of design in Figure 5.1 is appropriate for student researchers at undergraduate and taught postgraduate levels; the techniques appropriate to the research activities above it in the diagram all apply to design, as well as analysis. Design involves a creative element. Traditionally-inclined research students are unlikely to find themselves involved in design. With the growth of new forms of doctorate, for example in the visual arts, however, even doctoral students may find that a major purpose of their research is design.

Design research tends to be eclectic in the techniques it applies. Depending on the type of design the various techniques listed higher up in Figure 5.1 are likely to be useful. To these we can add two others: multimedia databases are of great utility to designers of physical artefacts; while the notions of the *Reflective Practitioner* (Schön, 1984) are very valuable to designers of items that embody a social element, ranging from buildings to social welfare systems.

Generation of Empirical Relationships

This section is concerned with the identification of regularities and relationships among them. This is an area in which research students can often expect the major results of their analysis to fall. While the sciences and engineering pay considerable attention to the derivation of empirical laws this is less so in the social sciences and humanities. Relatively little seems to have been published on suitable techniques. All in all this area seems underrepresented in texts on research methodology, given its importance in much student research, and for this reason will be explored at some length here.

The essence of the problems dealt with in this section is that there is usually no obvious idea of what relationship will be found, and the richness of the data needs to be displayed in such a way as to suggest fruitful avenues to explore; pictures often provide a good way of doing this. It may well be worth the student exploring the use of a suitable computer graphics or spreadsheet package (see Chapter 8).

Pattern recognition

The recognition of pattern and order in data is a fundamental step in the development of theories to explain them. The commonest quantitative approach to such pattern recognition is by the use of *correlation methods*. Patterns may conveniently be broken down into three basic types:

1. Those showing association among variables.
2. Those showing groupings.
3. Those showing order or precedence relationships between variables.

Association between two variables is very easily detected using a scatter diagram in which one variable is plotted against another. The quantitative equivalent of a scatter diagram is, in many cases, the correlation coefficient, for which there is an extensive statistical theory.

Equivalents of the simple correlation coefficient exist for the case where there are more than two variables. A useful measure is the partial correlation coefficient that measures the strength of association between two variables when the effects of another variable on both of them are allowed for. This is useful, for instance, in cases of spurious correlation such as the relationship between the number of pigs in the USA and the US output of cars, both of which are substantially associated with the third variable, US gross national product per head. Partial correlation methods are in turn closely related to those of path analysis, discussed later.

Obviously, *grouping* techniques are closely related to the classification problem discussed earlier. In the present case, however, our interest is in situations in which the number of classifications (if any) is unknown. For this reason, methods such as cluster analysis are appropriate whereas discriminant analysis is not.

Precedence relationships are a type of pattern that occurs in many different contexts. They show order, precedence or priority. Perhaps the simplest instance is one where we search for a pattern in some sequence of activities, for example, in detecting a 'typical' pattern of community growth from hamlet to city.

The quantitative approach to detecting sequences of this type is by the use of cross-correlation coefficients that measure the strength of the relationship between one variable and another a specified number of time units later. They are much used in econometrics and in control engineering for detecting the lag between a change in one variable and the corresponding change in another – for example, an upsurge in orders and the consequent upsurge in deliveries.

In qualitative analysis, pattern recognition is far more likely to be achieved through the application of some suitable theory. The obvious examples here are various theories of history that seek to explain the evolution of societies, of technologies, of movements, etc. A further area of application is in tracking the influence of, say, one artist on other artists. There are two broad patterns here. The first is where one artist influences another, for example Le Corbusier's influence on later architects (here we are concerned with tracing links that go only one way); the second is where artists influence each other, for example the members of the Cubist movement in the early 20th century (where the links run both ways).

> THE SCIENCES AND ENGINEERING PAY CONSIDERABLE ATTENTION
> TO THE DERIVATION OF EMPIRICAL LAWS; THIS IS LESS SO IN THE
> SOCIAL SCIENCES AND HUMANITIES

In many fields of technology it is possible to develop empirical laws in the form of simple equations relating one interval or ratio-scaled variable to a few others. Since it is generally possible to find simple relationships between variables there is a long tradition of using graphical methods for their determination, particularly where detailed theoretical knowledge is lacking. Such laws are of considerable practical use in engineering and for researchers in associated fields. To them the methods described may well be very familiar. In the main, however, the picture has been very different in the social sciences. The general belief has been that there is no reason to expect that relationships between variables will be simple and, therefore, there is scant point in trying to establish them using graphical techniques. Accordingly this section is primarily intended for researchers in this field.

It is perhaps worth beginning by suggesting why simple laws can be found in the physical sciences and the circumstances under which it might be worthwhile looking for them in the social sciences. Basically simple relationships seem attainable in the physical sciences because they typically describe the behaviour of many millions of entities: for example, where we relate the maximum safe load on an embankment, comprising billions of molecules, to the angle its sides make with the horizontal. This suggests that success in finding simple empirical laws in the social sciences is most likely in fields where the behaviour of a very large number of objects is being described. Thus, as an example, in a number of countries the proportion of companies above a certain size, as measured by turnover or manpower, can be well described by a standard statistical distribution known as the Pareto distribution.

Searching for empirical relationships is best done using certain tricks of the trade. By far the most important is the use of various types of scale that lead to straight-line graphs, since a straight-line relationship is much easier to fit by eye and lends itself to unambiguous extrapolation.

The starting point of any study of relationships between two variables will be, then, the graphing of variable A against variable B on simple linear scales, that is, the construction of a scatter diagram. If a reasonable straight-line fit is found, no more need be done. Otherwise the next step must be to apply non-linear scales to one or both variables. Graph papers are available with a variety of different scales. Indeed, a glance at the catalogue of a specialist supplier can in itself be a useful way of deciding possible non-linear relationships to explore. Similarly, the

127

manuals for computer spreadsheet packages contain a variety of examples of the different scales provided and examples of their use.

Explanation and Prediction in Quantitative Analysis

TRADITIONALLY, KNOWLEDGE AND RESEARCH HAVE BEEN EQUATED WITH THE IDENTIFICATION OF CAUSAL RELATIONSHIPS

Traditionally in the Anglo-Saxon world, knowledge and research have been equated with the identification of causal relationships, and research directed to this end has been accorded the highest esteem. Many fields have not yet been developed to the level where causal explanation is possible or valid predictions can be made. These offer their own special research opportunities, as has already been discussed. Nonetheless, in science and technology where sufficient knowledge exists to make explanation or prediction possible it is not easy to see what benefits would be attained if they were not attempted. In this sense causal explanation and prediction must be seen as involving a higher level of knowledge – though, of course, not necessarily a higher level of research skill.

The meaning of the notions of 'cause' and 'causality' have exercised philosophers for at least three centuries and continue to be the subject of lively debate. Experience suggests that, whereas epistemological considerations of this type are usually too time consuming for the researcher involved in a short project, students undertaking a research degree will often find it necessary to give thought to these matters at some stage in their work. Since the space required to adequately rehearse the philosophical arguments would be substantial the interested reader is referred to the bibliography at Appendix 2. For the purpose of discussion, however, it is necessary to give a more concrete interpretation to the idea of establishing causal relationships.

In practice, this involves the interrelated activities of causal explanation and prediction which are often couched in terms of hypotheses: for example, 'the existence of a close-knit Quaker community was an important factor in the early development of the iron industry' (implicit explanation); or, 'the falling costs of computer hardware have made software costs a more important factor in developing a computer system' (implicit prediction). Since most tests of hypotheses appear to fall into one or other of these categories and the logical and statistical methods required are the same as those needed for explanation and prediction, they will not be discussed independently.

In what follows, explanation and prediction will be construed as enabling the values of one set of variables to be derived given the values of another. Thus biochemists may direct their efforts to explaining why the body rejects certain types of foreign tissue. Better explanations of tissue rejection in turn enable better predictions to be made about the likelihood of rejection given various forms of treatment. Equally, an important test of a theory is that it makes predictions which can be confirmed by observation or experiment. In pure science, then, explanation and prediction are intermingled. In fields such as engineering this may also be the case but the fact that research is often directed towards the formulation of empirical laws on which predictions can be based means that there also exists the possibility of successful prediction for which no satisfactory explanation can be given. Thus, in hydraulics it is possible to apply standard formulae to relate the flow of a river to its gradient and depth but to give a satisfactory explanation of the basis of the formulae may not be possible. This type of situation illustrates another facet of the interrelationship between explanation and prediction; that is, in practice, we often use the same method for testing out whether we can satisfactorily predict a phenomenon as we do to establish whether we can successfully explain it.

In many social sciences, explanation is often deemed impossible because of the complexity of the systems involved. Frequently, the task of social sciences is, therefore, presented as finding associations between variables that can be generalised to various situations, for example, that urbanisation leads to a growth in reported crimes. Though a variety of explanations of this phenomenon have been offered by criminologists, sociologists and so forth, none can be said to command general acceptance. Nonetheless, such an association is useful, if it can be established, because it forms the basis of prediction.

Quantitative techniques for explanation and prediction

Several techniques which are relevant to explanation and prediction will be examined briefly. As indicated in Figure 5.1 these are loglinear analysis, experimental design and regression.

The technique of *loglinear analysis* explains the variations in probabilities of class membership. For example, in the UK, the probability of a person being convicted of a crime before the age of 25 might be explained in terms of variables such as sex, socioeconomic status of the individual's family, highest educational level attained, etc.

The *experimental design* model has, as well as its applicability in analysing many different types of research data, considerable virtues as a conceptual model of quantitative research directed towards explanation and prediction.

Fundamental to the model is the notion that the variable of interest can be measured on a ratio or interval scale and that the values of the variable to be explained or predicted are affected by a number of other variables usually referred to as factors. Each factor takes on more than one value and each value is called a factor level. Factors may often, however, be measured on nominal scales, for example, fertiliser A, fertiliser B or represent fairly crude groupings – for example, application of less than 100 grams of fertiliser per square metre, application of more than 100 grams per square metre, and so on. Finally, we assume that for each combination of factor levels we have at least one measurement of the variable whose value is to be explained or predicted. The model assumes this value is made up of a number of components: a base value plus various additive effects due to each of the factor levels and also due to interactions between factor levels, plus finally a random term representing errors in measurements, the effects of factors not considered directly, and so on.

The virtues of the experimental design model as a conceptual model of the processes involved in explanation and prediction are very considerable even if, for whatever reason, no attempt is made to carry out a statistical analysis. It offers an explanatory framework which is capable of handling complex relationships between the respondent variables and factor levels along with predictions of the effect of any particular set of factor levels. The factor levels can be recognised as independent variables and the implicit requirement of the model that there be at least two levels of each factor enables their effects to be isolated. The experimental design model assumes that the researcher can control the experiment to the extent of selecting the factors and factor levels whose effects are to be examined. This is, of course, not always the case in the social sciences but it may still be possible to approximate to an experimental design by using the fact that particular variables vary between one organisation or country and another or over time. Such applications of the model are usually referred to as 'quasi-experiments' (Cook and Campbell, 1979). The idea of quasi-experiments was originally developed in the context of education research because in investigating the efficacy of, for instance, different reading schemes teachers have only partial control of the classroom situation. The ideas have, however, proved invaluable in a host of organisational and social situations in which it is desired to examine systematically the impact of different policies.

The *regression* model has the attraction that it deals with situations where there is no control over the selection of factor levels. In principle, it expresses a dependent variable y in terms of various independent variables $x1$, $x2$ on which the value of y is supposed to depend, and so on, the precise form of the relationship being derived from the data. Obviously, this model represents a generalisation of the experimental design model since $x1$, $x2$ etc. can represent combinations of factor levels/treatments and may be nominal, interval or ratio data. The particular advantage of the regression model is that it does not require observations to be available for specific factor combinations and to a large extent, then, it is capable of utilising the data 'as they are'. On the other hand, this usually means that the rigorous control implicit in experimental design is lost and so the researcher cannot always have the same faith in the results as when an experimental design approach is feasible.

A useful extension of the regression model is that of *path analysis*. In essence, this attempts to select the set of relationships between variables that is most consistent with the available data. As such it has an obvious bearing on the problem of distinguishing independent, dependent and intermediate variables. As a typical example we might consider two possible explanations for the strong correlation between father's social status and son's social status that is observed in many Western countries. The simple explanation is that the father's status determines the son's status directly. A less obvious explanation is that the father's status determines the level to which the son is educated and the level of the son's education determines his status. Path analysis enables a choice to be made between such competing hypotheses.

Explanation and Prediction in Qualitative Analysis

By comparison with quantitative analysis, explanation and prediction in qualitative analysis are clearly different. They typically involve the close analysis of textual and other material, such as multimedia databases in graphic design, using theoretical constructs and frameworks derived from the humanities and social sciences.

Very often, for example in studying political systems, explanation and prediction are most easily approached through *comparative analysis*. For example, if we find that a particular industry is dominated by large companies in both a developed country and in a developing country, this suggests that ownership has little to do with average incomes or other variables that differ between the countries. On the other hand, if both countries have stockmarkets on which company shares are traded internationally, it remains a possibility, to be investigated further, that the structure of the industry may be affected by its ownership. In effect, this enables the student to have many of the benefits of the experimental design model discussed below.

Some research students find themselves working in the broad area of *policy analysis*. The aim of their research is either to carry out an evaluation of the effects of past policies and draw lessons from it (evaluation research) or to formulate, and argue the case for, new policies. Much social science research is of this type as, less obviously, is a considerable amount of research in technology. What differentiates this type of research from those discussed hitherto is that it is primarily aimed at non-academic audiences. Nevertheless, though it has an obvious 'political' dimension it must still meet academic standards, and since such research clearly involves explanation and prediction, the relevant standards are those pertaining to those topics.

> GOOD THEORIES PROVIDE A COMMON LANGUAGE WHICH CAN BE USED TO DISCUSS A PARTICULAR FIELD

The highest level of explanation and prediction is that of *theory generation/construction of a shared language*. As such, it is most likely to be undertaken by research students. Theories have an important characteristic that we wish to emphasise because it is important to student researchers at all levels. Good theories provide a common language which can be used to discuss a particular field. They therefore offer an important aid to researchers both in formulating their research questions and in carrying out their analysis.

TESTING A QUANTITATIVE ANALYSIS

Until now this chapter has been concerned with statistical methods mainly as models of particular types of analysis. For statistical methods of analysis it is, of course, possible to specify procedures for testing results derived from them. Since there are very considerable overlaps in testing procedures for different statistical methods discussion of this question has been delayed to this point. The most common reasons for the rejection of a piece of quantitative research are:

a)   lack of depth;
b)   faulty analysis.

Through our review of common types of analysis we have already covered lack of depth. Faulty analysis relates to inadequate testing of the conclusions by the researcher. Two common reasons for this are:

a)   an optimistic assessment of the degree to which the data and analysis support the hypotheses advanced, or
b)   an erroneous assumption that because of the 'exploratory' nature of the research, only very limited testing is possible or, indeed, required.

Whatever the reason, it reflects insufficient attention to the quality of the results, which in turn shows ineffective management of a key aspect of the research project. For this reason, and because this subject is not so well covered in the literature as are statistical methods, this topic is now examined further.

Most statistical techniques embody methods of testing the results they give for statistical significance. In practice, however, such tests often give an overly rosy picture of the results obtained from them. Basically this is because the test must be based on the notion that some statistical model or other describes reality perfectly, whereas it describes reality only imperfectly. It is therefore useful, particularly where more complex models are concerned, to supplement the statistical tests with other ways of evaluating the results of an analysis. A number of strategies for testing an analysis, namely complete enumeration, checking for representativeness, random split half methods, hold-out methods, and checking for missing explanatory variables, will be discussed.

Complete Enumeration

As observed earlier, most research involves (notional) sampling and hence is prone to sampling error. One strategy available to some researchers however is that of complete enumeration – a census. Thus, many studies of UK companies are restricted to those that are listed on the Stock Exchange since, as far as published accounting data are concerned, complete enumeration of the few thousand companies involved is perfectly realistic where it would not be if the study were also to cover over a million unlisted companies.

Checking for Representativeness

As is evident from any textbook, statistical theory relies heavily on the notion of random samples. A frequently adopted procedure for assessing the randomness of a sample is to check how representative it is by comparison with information known about the population being sampled from other sources. Thus, in a UK study of corrosion problems in cars the number of cars of each make and year in the sample could be compared with what might be expected on the basis of information about the actual numbers of cars in each category as recorded at the Vehicle Licensing Agency. Often, several characteristics can be checked in this way. Thus, it would also be possible to check the number of vehicle owners in each social class in the sample against the Register General's estimates for the UK population as a whole.

This type of approach has obvious links with the device of quota sampling much used in market research.

Scale Reliability/Split Half Testing

Scale construction can often run into significant problems of reproduction, in that aspects of the scales are very much a figment of the data used and disappear if other data are studied. In essence, this problem is due to an attempt to over-explain the preferences or attitudes being scaled. A useful way of detecting the problem is to split the data randomly into two halves and to carry out the scaling operations on each completely separately. If the two samples give similar results they are combined and the analysis carried out again on the total sample. Where they give different results, attempts should be made to eliminate the problem by simplification; for example, by reducing the number of dimensions in multi-dimensional scaling.

Usually, data can be split randomly several times and the procedure repeated with a consequent increase in the reliability of the results. Random split half methods are well suited to tests of factor analyses, measurement scales and cluster analyses, and to the evaluation of discriminant functions and regression models. Their biggest drawback is that large amounts of data are required. The sample size usually recommended for cluster analysis, for example, is of the order of several hundred if split half techniques are to be used.

Split half analysis is built into many statistical routines in common use, for example, those for measurement scale reliability testing in SPSS (the Statistical Package for Social Scientists).

Hold-out Methods

Where fewer data are available hold-out methods are often attractive. The essence of such a method is to remove the data from one (or a few) object(s) or respondent(s) and derive the scale, discriminant function, and so on, using the remaining data and then with the model obtained compute the relevant values for the held-out data and use these to evaluate the performance of the function in question. Thus, in testing a regression model to be based on n observations, one is removed at random and the model computed on the basis of the other $n - 1$. This model is then used to predict the value of the dependent variable for the held-out data point from the values of its independent variables.

Hold-out methods are, obviously, closely related to testing through prediction (the connection in many cases between prediction and satisfactory explanation has already been discussed). In practice, the hold-out process is repeated a number of times and each of the resulting models are compared. Where the removal of one or a few data points causes a marked change in the model it is a clear sign that the analysis is far from satisfactory. Again, simplification may often resolve the problem: for example, reduction of the number of independent variables on which a discriminant function is based. For small data sets in particular, hold-out methods are an excellent safeguard against an apparent, though in fact spurious, high degree of success in fitting the model in question.

Again, commonly available statistical packages like SPSS make it easy to use hold-out techniques in conjunction with statistical methods such as regression or discriminant analysis.

In certain fields, such as econometrics, a slightly different approach is possible. Thus, a regression model can be constructed using data for the period 1980–2000 and tested on data for 2001. This reflects the fact that extrapolation (prediction for values of the independent variable outside the data set) is always a more powerful test than interpolation where the prediction is made for a value within the original data set.

Checking for Missing Explanatory Variables

Sometimes bias may be introduced into the analysis because important explanatory variables have been omitted. Thus, a study aimed at increasing the amount of time certain equipment is productive where the users were recruited on a voluntary basis might well result in a preponderance of users whose equipment spends an above average proportion of time out of service. In this case the relevant measure of bias would be the average proportion of time the user's equipment is out of service. In such cases the bias can either be reduced or removed by using this variable as a factor in an experimental design model or by formally accounting for its effects through a regression equation. This latter approach is often used, for example, in the assessment of training programmes where participants are given a pre-test and a post-test on a relevant area of knowledge so that the impact of prior learning on the effect of the training can be established.

Another approach to this problem that is useful in longitudinal studies conducted over a period of time is to use time itself as one of the dependent variables. Where it turns out to be an important explanatory variable this is usually a sign that other important dependent variables that have changed in a systemic way with time have been omitted from the study. A similar approach often adopted in studies of organisations is to use some measure of size as an additional variable of the same type.

THE USE OF THE COMPUTER IN ANALYSIS

If researchers wish to use many of the techniques discussed here, as distinct from merely viewing them as providing a conceptual model of some type of analysis, then they will not only need to be familiar with the underlying theory of these methods but also will need to use a computer program to carry out the analysis. There is no doubt that the advent of specialist computer packages aimed at carrying out particular types of analysis, for example, statistical packages such as SPSS or engineering design packages, has made a considerable difference to what student researchers are expected to do by way of quantitative analysis, compared with what was feasible for many of their supervisors. In our view and, more importantly, in the view of those such as the Quality Assurance Agency in the United Kingdom which is responsible for undergraduate degree syllabuses, or those responsible for research student training, such as the Economic and Social Research Council, this is a fact to be taken into account when deciding on the worth of the analysis contained in a research report or thesis. What might previously have been regarded as desirable but infeasible, such as the detailed computation of the characteristics of the flow round an obstacle in a water channel, is now straightforward for the student who has mastered the use of the appropriate software.

ENSURING THE ANALYSIS IS OF AN APPROPRIATE STANDARD

There are many aspects to analysis and even the somewhat cursory discussion here has necessarily been fairly long. It is worth, therefore, recapitulating the opening remarks. An acceptable analysis is in many ways the key aspect of any research study and students who wish to manage their research effectively must accordingly ensure that their analysis is adequate. Of course, what constitutes an adequate level of analysis depends on both the field of research and the level of the qualification being pursued. Even undergraduate projects in scientific fields are likely to be accompanied by a statistical analysis. Whereas this was not necessarily the case in humanities or social sciences, in the past, where the emphasis might rather have been on the critical analysis of the work of previous authors, the advent of computer packages such as NUD·IST for handling qualitative data means that increasingly a quantitative element may be expected in their analyses too.

INADEQUATE ANALYSIS IS ONE OF THE COMMONEST CAUSES OF UNACCEPTABILITY OF A RESEARCH REPORT AT ANY LEVEL OF STUDY

Students should be aware that inadequate analysis is one of the commonest causes of unacceptability of a research report at any level of study. It may be helpful to bear the following points in mind:

1. Plan the analysis early in the project so that data gathering can be organised around it and any necessary skills can be acquired.
2. Make sure that you are thoroughly familiar with the methods of analysis

136

usually employed in your field of study, particularly if you wish to deviate from them.

3. Decide on the methods to be used and master the relevant literature, particularly that dealing with the snags and pitfalls.

4. Do not avoid employing an appropriate method, for example, a software package, just because it will require time to learn it. Do not, on the other hand, lavish sophisticated techniques on data of dubious quality. Data can be poor and no amount of analysis can put that right.

5. Make sure that you provide suitable evidence to support your arguments. Argument by assertion without the presentation of any supporting evidence is a frequent cause for the rejection of student research by the examiners.

6. Make sure that the analysis respects the rules of logical inference given above.

7. Test your conclusions wherever possible, using the methods suggested in the literature and in this chapter.

8. Write down conclusions as you go so it is clear what you are claiming. Expose them to the scrutiny of your supervisor and your friends. If you are pursuing a research degree, review them every month or so as the analysis progresses to make sure they stand the test of time.

9. Where doubts are expressed about either the logic of your conclusions, or whether the analysis has the necessary depth for your level of research, heed them. If nothing more, they show that there is at least one person who is unconvinced about an important aspect of your research.

10. Try to do rather more than is necessary. An analysis that aims at minimum standards all the way through not only runs a considerable risk of rejection by the examiners, it is also unsatisfying to the researcher and means that much of the benefit that should have been derived from carrying out the research is lost.

CHAPTER SUMMARY

THE ROLE OF ANALYSIS: is to supply evidence which justifies claims that the research changes belief or knowledge and is of sufficient value. This is done through the ordering or structuring of data.

THE DIRECT PURPOSES OF ANALYSIS: are description, construction of measurement scales, application of a methodology, design, generation of empirical relationships, and explanation and prediction.

FOR ANALYSIS TO BE CONVINCING: it must develop an argument based on evidence that respects the principles of logic.

QUANTITATIVE ANALYSIS MAY BE TESTED: by a number of techniques besides those usually given in statistics texts.

THE TECHNIQUES OF ANALYSIS THAT NEED TO BE USED: are related to both the field of study and the level of qualification being pursued. Whatever the level, however, inadequate analysis is a common cause of lack of success.

6

Gathering the Data

Almost all research projects involve the gathering of data, both quantitative and qualitative. Indeed, as remarked earlier, that process is often equated with research itself. Managing this key activity has two aspects. There is a technical component concerned with why data are collected and how to do so; and there is a variety of tasks connected with successful data gathering which must be carried out effectively.

As discussed in Chapter 5, the type of analysis employed and its purpose substantially dictate the nature of the data needed. In practice, however, many types of analysis (and, therefore, of research project) are difficult or impossible to carry out because suitable data gathering techniques are not available. The invention of new methods of collecting data or the improvement of existing ones can therefore have a substantial impact on the research done in a particular field, as witness the impact of the Web on the ease with which government reports or company information can be obtained. At the higher levels of research, just as the development of new methods of analysis is often a good route to success so, too, is introduction of novel approaches to data gathering or of major refinements to techniques already in use. There are two categories: primary data that the researcher collects through observation, experiment, and so on; and secondary data that have been collected by others.

The gathering of secondary data can have much in common with literature searching and many of the techniques discussed in Chapter 4 apply here. Furthermore, the literature search – whether it consists of measurements by other workers or statements of opinions and theories – is often the major source of data for fields such as theoretical physics or philosophy where at first sight research can be conducted without data.

Whether the researcher is concerned with primary or secondary data there are a number of general points that apply to either type and these will be discussed before considering the individual types of data in more detail.

ACTIVITIES INVOLVED IN DATA GATHERING

However the researcher chooses to collect the data certain activities will be common. The data must first be located and then arrangements made for their collection. They must be recorded in a form suitable for the intended analysis and checked. Adjustments may then need to be made for errors and omissions or data that for some reason are unusable.

> THE IMPLICATIONS OF GATHERING DATA MUST BE FULLY COMPREHENDED BY THE STUDENT

The location of data may often be very difficult and at higher levels the researcher is, at the outset, often unsure as to what the sources will be. Against that, data for the short-term research project need to be fairly accessible if the data gathering stage of the project is not to get out of hand. Students undertaking short projects must avoid situations where a great deal of effort is involved in arranging the data collection because, for example, laboratory rigs have to be set up and commissioned, or because considerable training is needed before a particular data collection method can be used.

The gathering of data requires time and there are relatively few fields in which it does not also involve substantial effort. On occasions it may be necessary to await rather infrequent events, as in a study of volcanic eruptions, or the actual process of obtaining the measurements may be long drawn out, as in certain bio-medical tests. Whatever is involved in gathering the data, the process by which they are recorded often sets a definite limit on the rate at which they can be gathered and the ease with which they can be analysed. It is no accident that the fields in which most data are gathered, such as radio astronomy, are almost totally dependent on computer methods for gathering and recording data.

In short, data gathering requires time – for acquiring skills and for making the necessary arrangements for collection and to ensure adequate quality – and time is usually the researcher's major resource. Furthermore, it is affected by technology which may place definite restrictions on what can be done in collecting and recording data.

ACCESS TO DATA

Gaining access to data is often a problem for student researchers. They may need to employ special facilities where application to use them must be made long in advance and which may be rationed in other ways. Social scientists often find that the organisations or groups that they wish to study are unwilling for reasons of confidentiality or lack of time to provide them with data.

The student who is involved in a short research project cannot afford such problems and, if access to data is difficult, should find another project. In the longer project, however, where the student is willing to contemplate a period of negotiation, it is worth bearing in mind a number of devices for improving the chances of getting access to the data needed.

Firstly, the sponsorship of a prestigious institution and/or of some individual of distinction is extremely useful. Research students are fortunate in that educational institutions do still enjoy high prestige and if the student is sponsored or supported by an official body this may well be of great benefit in obtaining access.

In broad terms co-operation is most likely where the providers of access gain something in return. If the results of the work are of interest to them, the promise of a copy of any papers that emerge from it may help to secure collaboration. Also, as observed in Chapter 4, many types of data are a tradeable commodity and the researcher may be able to gain access on condition that the data are made available once collected. Researchers have, of course, a responsibility to later researchers. They should observe the elementary politenesses and as far as possible adhere to any bargains that may be struck so that, for example, if a copy of the research report is promised this should be provided.

GATHERING DATA TO AN ADEQUATE STANDARD

It is important that the researcher demonstrates that the data were properly collected. Ideally this means that others working at the same level would have been able to arrive at the same readings or observations. Where primary data are concerned this is usually not feasible. Instead, researchers must settle for following a procedure that will be adjudged adequate in the light of the level of their research; in particular by the examiners to whom the research report will be sent for assessment. This question is taken up later in the broader context of the assessment of the research report. The following checklist of points can be used to secure adequate data gathering standards for both secondary and primary data. These are that:

1. The data actually measure what they purport to measure.
2. Proper attention was paid to measurement error and the reduction of its effects.
3. A suitable sample was used; in particular that
   a) it provided a basis for generalisation; and that
   b) it was large enough for the effects of interest to be detected.
4. Data were properly recorded; in particular that
   a) the conditions under which the data were gathered were properly noted; and that
   b) suitable data recording methods were used and efforts were made to detect and eliminate errors arising during recording.

Not all of these points apply in every situation, and the full list is perhaps only appropriate in the situation where data are to be gathered in some systematic way and are of the nominal, ordinal, interval or ratio type. The researcher's own notes, which we view as textual data and an important data source, would probably need to be judged only against standard 4 above. Nonetheless, the list will now be reviewed point by point, with the greatest emphasis being placed on data recording.

Ensuring the Data Measure what they Purport to Measure

In the last chapter it was noted that very often it is difficult to measure the actual variable of interest and instead surrogate measures may be adopted. This is particularly likely to be a problem in secondary data gathering where the researcher may not know just how the data were derived. For instance, there is at least one country whose smooth upward growth in recorded consumption data over the 1970s owed more to the predilections of the civil servants who calculated them than to the behaviour of consumption itself.

Errors in Measurement

Quantitative data are often subject to measurement error and the size of that error may have important implications for both the way the data are used and for the scale of the data gathering effort.

Aside from errors due to malfunction of measuring equipment which are of no interest in this context, error may take the form of bias: as in the under-reporting of small company activities in many official statistics; deliberate or instinctive falsehood, as in many answers to questionnaire surveys; or distortion of one form or another, as in the response of a laboratory amplifier to a high-frequency signal.

The practical implication of all three possibilities is the same: information is lost and the data do not fully represent the phenomenon under study. Though it is often easier for the engineer to overcome such difficulties by employing more sophisticated measuring devices, similar opportunities may well arise in the social sciences. Webb et al. (1966) made a number of creative suggestions for methods of coping with this problem in the social sciences, by the device of 'unobtrusive measurement': for example, measuring the popularity of paintings in art galleries by wear on carpets in their vicinity.

Another form of measurement error that is relevant to quantitative data is pure random error that is supposed on average to fluctuate about zero. Since this is relatively easy to cope with statistically, it is the usual (though not always the most accurate) model of error adopted.

In practice we can attempt to deal with measurement error in one of two ways. The first is to measure the phenomenon of interest by several different methods. Where each gives rise to random measurement error, a combination of the measurements can be expected to give a better estimate of the true value, provided the methods are not subject to the same error. Obviously this approach requires more data gathering effort but has much to commend it in fields where accurate measurements are difficult. It is thus much used in social science research, often under the term of 'triangulation'.

The second way of dealing with measurement error that is more or less random is to increase the size of the sample, and this is discussed below.

Choosing the Sample

Data gathering normally involves some kind of sampling. The conclusions that can validly be drawn from the sample depend critically on both the population sampled and the procedures used for generating the sample. The first step in choosing the sample is, accordingly, to choose a target population to be sampled that permits interesting conclusions to be drawn and to select a sample in such a way that the conclusions are valid. Though this is unlikely to be a problem for the physical scientist it certainly is in many other fields, particularly the social sciences. Very often, the sheer cost of data gathering pushes the student in the direction of some 'convenience sample' that meets neither of these criteria.

> ANY STATISTICAL METHOD REQUIRES A CERTAIN SIZE OF SAMPLE TO BE COLLECTED TO SATISFY REQUISITE LEVELS OF CONFIDENCE

Any statistical method requires a certain size of sample to have a reasonable probability of detecting an effect of interest and in these circumstances the collection of enough data may be quite beyond the resources available to the student researcher. Some social science projects, for example, are very unlikely to produce the hoped-for results because they are not based on enough observations. In such cases a large sample is needed if the effects are to be revealed. A crude rule of thumb applicable in a number of situations is that the sample size needed is proportional to the square of the accuracy of the estimates derived from the sample. Thus, to double the accuracy it is necessary to increase the sample size fourfold. It follows that the ideas of statistical power testing that enable the necessary sample size to be inferred before carrying out the data gathering are potentially of interest to many student researchers (Kraemer, 1987).

There are many different procedures that can be used for sampling and the reader should consult a specialist text for further details.

Recording the Data

In Chapter 5 the relevance of the experimental design model to many types of research was discussed. An important aspect of that model is the idea of factors and, by implication at least, the values of all factor levels should be recorded along with the actual measurements of interest. This provides protection against the discovery that further variables, and therefore measurements, are relevant to the phenomenon in question. Equally, notes on the sources of data and time and date of collection can be extremely useful when, many months later, the researcher is attempting to correct an error or to decide whether a set of figures whose origin has long since been forgotten can be used in analysis. In both cases the recording of adequate additional information will help to ensure that few data that have been collected will prove to be unusable. Experience suggests, however, that this is by no means always the case. As stated in Chapter 5, researchers do waste effort by having to repeat data gathering activities because certain information was omitted originally. In practice, it is almost always straightforward to collect additional measurements, when the initial data gathering takes place. In further discussions of data recording it will, therefore, be assumed that consideration has been given to exactly what data are to be recorded and the focus now will be on how to record them.

In primary data gathering, recording may involve two processes. Firstly, data must be captured in some way that is feasible in the context in which they are to be gathered, following which it is often necessary to transcribe or convert the data into a form suited to computer input.

The main concern here is the reduction of data to a form suitable for computer analysis. Ratio and interval scaled data are already in this form and present no problem. Ordinal data can either be input as ranks, or equivalently, using letter codes – for example, A=1, B=2. Pictorial data need to be converted into numbers in some way or other; the most usual method nowadays being by the use of a digital scanner. We note though that digitised picture data, although numeric, is not suitable for most analytical purposes; a picture generates too much numeric data. Nominal data may be recorded by using the number 1 to denote the presence of some attribute (for example, the item is green), or zero if it does not possess it. For pure textual data there is little choice but to input them as they stand.

Transcription may also be the major process involved when secondary data are being used. This two-stage process is at best somewhat inefficient and at worst may introduce errors at the transcription stage, so automatic data gathering methods that collect the data directly in a form suitable for computer analysis have obvious attractions. To that end it is normal to use a digital scanner in conjunction with a text-reading package to transcribe secondary data that exist only on paper, such as tables in books. When this is done, however, it is rare that transcription will be completely accurate especially with older documents produced using non-computer typefaces. It is, therefore, necessary to undertake a careful correction process (which is much facilitated for prose by running the electronic text through a spellchecker). Such processes do not, however, find all the errors without considerable effort. If the text is one that is useful to other researchers it may well be worth putting it on the Web. Such scholarly generosity has been the source of much material on the Web, especially in the arts and humanities.

DATA CAPTURE INVOLVES BOTH VALIDATION AND VERIFICATION

The detection of errors at the data capture stage may, by analogy with data processing terminology, be dubbed validation. The ensuring of accurate transcription will similarly be referred to as verification.

Validation is primarily based on identifying implausible data: for example, a questionnaire that records a pregnant man or more typically, but more subtly, one anomalous liberal response from an individual amidst a host of authoritarian ones. Not all anomalies will, in fact, be errors and, conversely, such procedures will not identify data that could be correct but in fact are not. Successful validation is heavily dependent on experience and this is one reason why training in the use of data gathering techniques is necessary.

Verification lends itself to more mechanical methods. The traditional approach in data processing, for example, is for two different people to enter the same data into the computer system and then accept the two sets of data if they are the same but otherwise to examine them for transcription error. This approach relies on the reasonable assumption that the same mistake is unlikely to be made by two different individuals. However, the student researcher is unlikely to be able to afford to pay for this type of verification which is increasingly confined to large-scale professional surveys so needs to think of ways either of approximating to it, or better, improving the quality of data entry.

The rejection of data at the validation or verification stage is a somewhat negative process. Though transcription errors are usually remediable, validation errors will not be unless thought is given to making them so. The only way in which this can be done is to introduce redundancy – that is, extra information – into the data gathered so that incorrect or missing data can be reconstructed. If, for instance, the aim is to measure a length, one way is to measure it in millimetres and record it. If this is done incorrectly, however, the complete set of measurements related to this length will have to be thrown away. On the other hand, if it is also measured in inches, any error will be evident when that measurement is converted to millimetres. This example also throws light on the role of 'feel' in validation. Many people in the UK have a far better intrinsic concept of imperial measurements than metric ones and a check of this sort will accordingly have a good chance of detecting the error at the time when the measurement is made.

A related issue is the need to check what units a variable is measured in. The loss of a Mars Lander because NASA produced measurements in feet and inches which were assumed by European collaborators to be metric illustrates the point neatly. However, more subtle versions of this problem exist: time series of, say, office space construction may have switched from being recorded in square feet to square metres.

In many social science applications it may well be possible to approach the respondents again; and in science and engineering studies the measurements can, in principle, be repeated. Nonetheless, both of these approaches require effort and in some cases may for all practical purposes be impossible. Therefore, if the researcher is to avoid throwing away hard-won data it is advisable to devote a little thought to how errors in them can be detected and eliminated.

Though the avoidance of error is a common theme in all types of data capture or transcription there are many different methods that can be used for either or both of these purposes. These differ in the amount of equipment and preparation required to use them, in their costs and in their suitability for dealing with large volumes of data. Though the division is far from being clear cut it is useful to distinguish between methods that are primarily suited to data capture and those that are mainly used for transcription, and that approach will be followed here.

Data Capture

In Figure 6.1 some common methods of data capture are listed. As noted in Chapter 5, it is very likely that the data will be subjected to computer analysis and

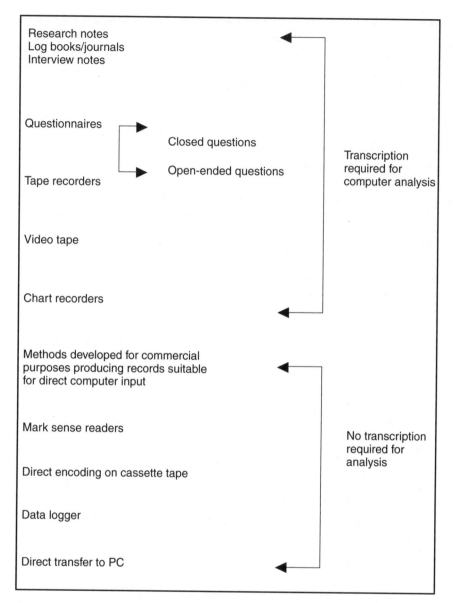

Figure 6.1 Some common methods of data capture

the methods are divided into two groups according to whether transcription is needed. They range from 'traditional' methods requiring subsequent transcription through to sophisticated ones that cut out this latter process at the cost of much greater dependence on equipment. The initial discussion will be confined to the data recording aspects of these methods, though certain of them, for example questionnaires, will be considered more broadly later.

The one form of data that will be gathered by all researchers is their own research notes which are worthy of more attention than they are often afforded. Though the researcher who has pursued an almost uninterrupted academic career should have developed effective notetaking practice, this may need amendment when, as is often the case, the research is concerned with a new field of study. The problems of the part-time researcher or of someone returning to academic study after a number of years are likely to be greater.

The basic problem with research notes is that they arise from a variety of activities, from the researcher's own reading through to occasional flashes of inspiration. Usually, they eventually comprise a huge mass of data of many different types. Furthermore, there is no simple way of ensuring that two different pieces of data that should be juxtaposed will be.

As far as notes on books are concerned the most effective practice is probably to make them as the books are read and to produce photocopies of selected passages of particular interest that can be annotated as the student wishes. The selections should rarely amount to more than a small percentage of the work in question unless some form of textual study is being undertaken, so there should be no problem with copyright law. Certainly it is usually a sign that the researcher has not digested the contents of a work if it is found necessary to copy most of it, and proper cross-referencing soon becomes impossible if the practice is repeated wholesale. Moreover, under such circumstances as discussed in Chapter 4, problems of copyright law and – even more importantly as far as academic institutions are concerned – plagiarism, are likely to arise. An alternative approach that avoids these difficulties is for the researcher to compile notes as the text is read.

In normal circumstances, researchers will want to produce substantial notes of their own relating to projected analyses, organisation of the research report and so on. These are usually easier to deal with. For the unexpected insight it is worth carrying a pocketbook, notebook PC or electronic organiser in which sufficient information can be jotted down to enable the idea to be properly worked up later into notes.

Logbooks and journals are the simplest method of data recording available to the experimental scientist or the researcher conducting a field study. Their use is relatively straightforward and is often facilitated by employing a standard layout for each type of observation to be made. Appropriate blanks can be photocopied to be filled in and filed in a binder as required. It should be noted that, nowadays, the logbook will frequently be on a PC, since even in the field, notebook and sub-notebook computers provide a more convenient and flexible way of recording notes and observations. As research is a learning process some students find benefit in viewing the logbook as a chronological record; not a day-to-day diary but a record of key incidents. Examples of such would be: opinions expressed by others during the study; sudden insights gained; and more effective ways of conducting the research. Notes of this type could trigger action and, in some fields of study, assist in the production of the research report.

Interview notes and similar materials are rather more difficult to structure because it is hard to predetermine the course of an interview. Nevertheless, there will in most cases be an interview schedule listing those topics to be covered and this may well serve as the basis of a data gathering instrument with half a page, say, being allocated to each subject heading.

With a little experience it is usually possible for researchers to generate their own 'shorthand' for recording, thus enabling them to come nearer to a verbatim record. In view of the high information content of pictorial data it makes obvious sense for the researcher to record data in that form, where possible.

Questionnaires provide a more structured approach to gathering data of this type. Where closed questions (those which provide for only a limited list of responses) are used, subsequent transcription is particularly easy. It pays to design them from the outset with processing in mind if it is intended that they should be analysed by computer eventually.

Tape recorders are generally acceptable in most interviewing situations, subject perhaps to certain parts of the interview being 'off the record'. Cassette recorders are sufficiently portable for two to be used, preferably with tapes of different playing time to allow for continuity during changeovers and a measure of back-up. It may well be worth carrying both 'narrow' and 'wide angle' microphones so that the most appropriate type can be selected.

ONE ASPECT OF TAPE RECORDING INTERVIEWS WHICH IS OFTEN OVERLOOKED IS THE TIME AND COST OF TRANSCRIPTION

One aspect of tape recording which is frequently overlooked by student researchers is the cost of transcription. Six to eight hours' transcription per hour of tape recording may well be needed. Moreover, it needs special equipment and is best carried out by experienced staff.

For these reasons, and to cope with the situations where recording is not acceptable, the student still needs other methods of recording. Though the act of taking notes can be useful in pacing an interview, the ideal method is one that the student can carry out while still looking at the interviewee. At a minimum this will usually require some sort of shorthand or code with the ideal being the ability to recall every detail of the interview (remembering that non-verbal behaviour is often very important) an hour afterwards. It is useful to write notes on the interview as soon as possible after it has taken place.

149

Lightweight video cameras are easy to use and it is a straightforward matter to produce digital video that can be stored on a hard disk. Given the advent of data compression formats such as JPEG for video and the size of modern hard drives, substantial amounts of video material can easily be stored on a PC. As noted above, however, applying computer analysis to such video images remains, in general, a difficult task.

A special type of video image that is useful to many researchers, especially those involved in information systems research, is the image of PC screens. These can be stored as a video image or in the case of Web browser screens as hypertext markup language (html). This type of data has the further advantage that software packages exist that enable the interaction of a user with a website to be analysed.

Chart recorders were, in the past, used in conjunction with many types of measuring equipment, for example, temperature recording. Since they lent themselves to online connection to the computer they have mainly been replaced by datalogging equipment (that is, equipment which records measurements that can be fed directly into a computer analysis). It should be remembered though that chart records of, say, seismograph readings from past earthquakes may well continue to be important data sources.

Another method is one that enables the data to be transmitted directly to a computer file with the obvious attractions noted earlier. The first group of such methods are those that were developed for commercial purposes, for example, the tally-roll printouts produced by the older type of cash register. Perhaps the most neglected one from the point of view of student research is the mark sense reader capable of recording the presence or absence of a pencil tick in a box in a specified position on a sheet of paper. These are widely used for, amongst other purposes, providing automatic marking of multiple choice examinations and scoring student course evaluations in academic institutions.

One commercial data recording method that finds some application in research is direct encoding on to cassette tape. Such recorders were originally developed for stock control in supermarkets where the item code number and a count of the number actually on the shelves were entered on to the tape along, perhaps, with the time at which the data were entered. Similar devices may be used in observation of human behaviour to record the type of behaviour, the time of its onset and the time of its completion.

Finally, for the scientist or engineer there are the modern equivalent of the 'dataloggers' referred to above. PCs have long been used for this purpose, for example, together with laser rangefinders in field archaeology. However, the user of datalogging data that were gathered some time ago and input to an obsolete computer system may sometimes be faced with a somewhat unexpected transcription problem. The ease with which data can be transferred to a PC for analysis varies markedly depending on the computers involved. The researcher is accordingly well advised to explore how best to transfer the data before carrying out the experiments.

Transcription Methods

The standard method of transcribing data for computer input is by entering them using a spreadsheet or word processing package. The process of verification by duplication has already been described and for data sets larger than a few dozen numbers it is advisable to get data verified in this way if possible. Many student researchers are not, however, able to afford this process. The alternative is to employ a variety of checks already discussed in the context of validation. A further useful device is to require that the data be input in a rigid format. For example, if the numbers are up to four digits long it is possible to fit 16 of them on to the usual 80 character input line leaving a space between each. Provided that where necessary leading zeros are supplied so that '32' is typed as '0032', the fifth, tenth, and fifteenth character positions and so forth should be blank. This can be verified on input, and any input lines that fail the test are then corrected. Such a test detects, for example, accidental double keying, for example, '00322' for '0032'. It will not, however, detect the other common form of transcription error, namely, transposition: for example, '0023' for '0032' which the student researcher will still have to guard against. Many computer packages, for example SPSS, make it easy to apply such checks. There should be no trouble in getting data entered into the computer directly from well-designed questionnaires or similar documents as long as these have been correctly completed. Pictorial information can be reduced to numbers by using a digitiser. Line information can similarly be converted to numbers by using a light pen.

There are also many circumstances in which the student wishes to analyse textual data. An obvious example is in the production of concordances and another is the content analysis of a set of interviews where it is required to find all instances where two or more ideas or variables appear together. As noted in Chapter 5, computer packages such as NUD·IST have made this latter task much easier than it used to be. However, the reader is reminded that text data can be most easily transcribed into electronic form by the use of a suitable digital scanner and text reader rather than requiring someone to type the text into a word processing package.

PREPARING FOR DATA GATHERING

Though in certain parts of the social sciences, in particular, the view is sometimes expressed that all data are inevitably partly subjective, we do not feel that such a view is generally helpful to student researchers whose aim is to complete their research successfully in a reasonable time. Accordingly, we would see the demonstration that researchers have gathered their data in a fashion that could have been repeated by themselves or others at the same time and would have led (allowing for measurement error) to the same results as a matter of practical as well as philosophical importance. Usually, this is not a trivial matter. Measuring instruments must be calibrated and the researcher must become sufficiently familiar with the techniques being used to be able to obtain satisfactory results. Even an apparently simple task such as the accurate determination of the relative proportions of salt and sand in a mixture can require a lot of practice before it can be carried out successfully. In more complex situations, such as the observation of the interactions of two different groups within an organisation, the researcher may well find that perceptions of what, say, constitutes aggressive behaviour changes as the context becomes more familiar. In both cases it is clearly important that researchers allow enough time to 'calibrate' themselves as well as any equipment they may need, and this has obvious implications for planning the research project as discussed in Chapter 3.

Earlier we pointed out that many student researchers, particularly part-time students, find themselves involved in *action research*. Though this may provide ready access to past data, for example, minutes of meetings, it is easy for such researchers to neglect the need to record data about their own interactions with the organisation concerned.

ORGANISING THE DATA

Whichever of the above methods is used to gather data it will normally be necessary to maintain an extensive set of supplementary notes on the sources of the data, the conditions under which they were gathered, their relationships to other sets of data, and so on. These need to be stored in such a way as to offer some reasonable prospect of retrieval when required. In practice, the type of data with which they will be concerned is textual data: numeric data are readily dealt with by whatever database management tools are provided in the quantitative computer analysis package being used. The easiest way to do this is on a PC. In many cases it will be obvious that notes could usefully be filed under more than one heading. Where they are brief this is perhaps most easily accommodated by inserting a copy of the document concerned in each of the relevant PC files. Where the material is more bulky, the best way is to make use of a suitable computer package, such as ENDNOTE or NUD·IST, to organise the textual data. Such concerns are perhaps particularly relevant where data are subject to computer analysis. It is often possible to find students repeating a computer run because insufficient information was kept about the original one for its results to be located. Nevertheless, this is an illustration of a far more general point. Effective management of data gathering requires that thought be given to the organisation of the data early in this phase of the project before any retrospective attempt to impose some system and order upon them becomes infeasible. As in many other situations the important thing is to have a workable rather than a perfect system.

COLLECTING PRIMARY DATA

Most research students will be expected to collect primary data. Even in the arts and humanities, where much of the data may take the form of documents, these may be so difficult to access as effectively to constitute primary data. The other group of students who are very likely to be expected to collect primary data are undergraduates. For them, an important learning objective of a research project is that they become familiar with primary data collection methods. In order to discuss the practical aspects of the collection of primary data it is necessary to break them down into a number of categories, namely: laboratory measurements; field observation; archives/collections; questionnaires; and interviews. Whilst this list is not exhaustive there are important differences between the various categories listed.

Laboratory Measurement

Laboratory measurements typically offer researchers the greatest control over their data gathering activities and therefore lend themselves to careful planning The most important considerations are usually to design the apparatus or experiment to collect and record the necessary data as efficiently as possible, to construct it and to ensure it is working correctly. This can take a great deal of time.

Efficient design is primarily a matter of considering the way in which the data will be used in analysis. To verify that gravity attracts objects towards the earth rather than repelling them needs only very simple apparatus and few observations. To determine the law governing that attraction, however, requires much better equipment and many more measurements. Beyond that it is worth remembering, since extreme measurements always provide a better test of theories, there is much to be said for attempting to design apparatus to cope with a wider range of measurements than it is believed will be needed.

Building a test rig or organising an experimental situation can often be speeded up by formal methods of planning of the type described in Chapter 3. Ensuring that the experiment is functioning as intended and that data are being properly recorded is often harder to plan. The researcher can at least, though, give proper consideration to the things that might be wrong with the data and ways in which they could be detected at an early stage, for example by using a duplicate measuring device from time to time to provide a spot check on the main instrument.

Though it is obviously important to detect erroneous data and situations where the experiment is not functioning as planned, the opposite problem also exists of being too willing to abandon data because they are 'not right', or because something must have been wrong with the experiment when they were collected. This can lead to important behaviour being rejected in the name of consistency. All experimenters recognise that there are situations under which data must be rejected for these reasons. Against this, some scientific data are often suspiciously tidy with much less error than might have been expected on a statistical basis.

Field Observation

Many types of research, for example, geophysical and ecological, make heavy use of field observation. Where possible it is better to use simple, familiar, measuring equipment capable of operating reliably under field conditions for carrying out measurements of this nature.

IN ACTION RESEARCH, THE RESEARCHER IS AN IMPORTANT PART OF THE SITUATION, AND THE RESEARCHER'S BEHAVIOUR IS PART OF THE EXPERIMENTAL DATA THAT SHOULD BE GATHERED

Field observations of human behaviour are of so many different types that it is hardly possible to do more than state some of their major advantages and disadvantages. Where the observations cannot be carried out without the knowledge of the subjects as, say, in anthropological data gathering, researchers may well cause unrepresentative behaviour repertoires to be displayed in their presence. Again, there are types of research like action research where the researcher's explicit aim is to bring about a change in the situation under study. It follows here that the researcher is an important part of the situation and the researcher's behaviour is part of the experimental data that should be gathered.

For the student interested in this type of observation it is worthwhile consulting the obvious sources of expertise, namely, the cultural anthropologists or sociologists interested in deviant groups. One of the issues here is that the researcher's perceptions and therefore the basis of data collection can change as the field observations progress. The ideas of the Grounded Theory approach of Glaser and Strauss (1967), and in particular their emphasis on continual restatement of the theory on which data gathering is based, are also of considerable interest in this context.

Field observation need not always be completely passive. Substantial experimental manipulation may be possible even though the complete control of the laboratory situation is not possible. This is traditionally the case in 'double blind' tests of drugs in which participants are randomly assigned to receive the drug or a placebo without either the participant or the researcher knowing which is the case.

Situations of this type can often lend themselves to analysis by the statistical experimental design model discussed in Chapter 5. Interpretation of the results is not usually, however, anywhere near as simple as in the laboratory situation and generalisability is often more difficult to assess because of doubts about how typical the field situation is.

Archival Data

Many subjects make extensive use of data available in some type of archive or collection. In many countries, locally maintained records and the minutes of learned societies are important data sources for the historian. The archaeologist is likely to make extensive use of museum collections of artefacts. For example the accurate astronomical records kept by certain ancient civilisations are of importance in some branches of astronomy.

Public funding for research is often conditional on the data generated being eventually deposited in some publicly accessible collection or, nowadays, online database. In the social sciences in the UK, for instance, such a role is fulfilled by the ESRC Data Archive. Similar bodies exist in other countries.

Less well recognised is the existence of private archives or collections of data. Many private collections of paintings or drawings, for example, are not publicised for insurance reasons. On the other hand, there is a mass of material available to the researcher arising from records of normal day-to-day business for which this problem does not exist, for example the records of 19th-century hospitals. If the student can discover the existence of such a collection and obtain access to it then the prospects of producing interesting research findings are well above average.

For recognised collections it is often possible to obtain access for the purpose of bona fide research. The problems for the researcher interested in archives of this sort are to obtain sufficient resources to visit them (since there is little prospect of borrowing the material) and then to find some satisfactory way of recording (since the data involved are rarely intrinsically easy to record and there may well be limitations on, say, the photographing of old documents). Some archives of this kind are available as facsimiles – for example photographs of drawings or microfiches of company accounts – and for these it should usually be possible to find sufficient money to pay for copies of major items of interest. Increasingly, as discussed later, such material is to be found on the Web.

Academic bodies have traditionally looked favourably on the provision of travel grants and scholarships specifically for visiting archives and similarly there may be some possibility of obtaining funds from the sponsor of the student's research.

As private collections are rarely compiled for research purposes, obtaining access can be difficult. As was stated earlier, students may obtain access more easily if a request is made on their behalf by someone of suitable academic standing. Access to non-government material, if granted, will normally be restricted to a few individuals at most. In broad terms, then, it is rarely worth trying to gain access to private material on which other researchers are already working.

Gathering Data by Questionnaires

Questionnaires are a common method of gathering information. Their design is a large subject that will not be attempted here, and the reader is advised to consult a specialist text (some are listed in the bibliography in Appendix 2). The concern here is with some of the practical problems that occur in using questionnaires. Since the administration of questionnaires during an interview shares many of the problems of interviewing, we shall concentrate first on the use of questionnaires for postal surveys.

Postal surveys are a favoured way of seeking to acquire data from a large number of respondents. Inevitably, the quality of the data gathered is more superficial than that which can be collected during an interview so the tendency is for the study to be a large one. This in turn means that there will be large quantities of data to process. In almost all cases this favours the use of a computer, the implications of which have already been discussed.

The biggest problem with the postal questionnaire is that it is only somewhat tenuously a primary data gathering method. The investigator may have no direct contact with the respondents who may interpret the questions very differently from the researcher's intention. A pilot survey, however modest, is therefore essential. It need not observe the strict procedures necessary later with regard to sample selection providing it indicates realistically how the questions will be interpreted. Another less used procedure principally employed in cross-cultural studies is that of back translation. The questionnaire is translated from, say, English to Arabic by one person and then from Arabic to English by another and the resulting version compared with the original.

In a postal survey it would usually be considered unwise to have a questionnaire requiring more than about twenty minutes to fill in or covering more than, say, six A4 pages. Too long a questionnaire is likely to reduce markedly the percentage of responses and a low response rate always raises questions of bias. As outlined in the last chapter, this problem can to some extent be overcome by including additional questions that enable the researcher to check whether the returns are typical of the sampled population but this, of course, has the disadvantage of increasing the length of the questionnaire. Accordingly, other steps will often need to be taken too.

The demand for banking services in Russian roubles amongst small businesses is taken as an example. A small number of responding companies account for the bulk of the behaviour of interest and since they are likely to be large and efficient there may well be definite advantages in eschewing the traditional random sample in favour of 100 per cent coverage of this fairly small group.

> THE SUPPORT OF A PRESTIGIOUS BODY SUCH AS A PROFESSIONAL
> ASSOCIATION CAN IMPROVE RESPONSE TO A QUESTIONNAIRE

Where random samples are deemed necessary it may be possible to administer the questionnaire by telephone. Computer software for random digit dialling is available for this purpose. Certainly, a telephone call to enlist the cooperation of potential respondents often handsomely increases the response rate. The sponsorship of a prestigious body, such as a professional association, can also improve response considerably. In most circumstances it is usually necessary to send a suitably worded follow-up letter to non-respondents. Since response rates can vary from under 5 per cent to 80 per cent or so, depending on the above factors, it clearly behoves the researcher to consider these points. If this is not done the result may be a small number of possibly biased returns that are insufficient for the purposes of the analysis, and the researcher will also be in no position to draw up a realistic budget for the resources required during this part of the study.

Interviews

Most social scientists would see the interview as providing higher quality information that is freer from bias than many other methods available to them. Indeed, in a new field, a programme of interviews may be the only way of obtaining a realistic picture of the way people view it. Such rich potential does of course imply a need for planning and training, if the student is to make the most of the interview programme arranged. Many factors are relevant here: from basic points, like the need to be punctual, through to considerably more complex topics such as how to probe a particular subject in a non-directive way. A number of texts deal with these points (see bibliography in Appendix 2) and the reader is referred to these for further details.

The major data gathering problem in interviewing is to find adequate ways of recording all the data obtained. These problems in turn relate to the degree to which the interviewer wishes to structure the interview and in fact is permitted to do so (since the research student's control over an interview with, for example, a chief executive is somewhat limited). An interview can, in fact, be just a means of completing a lengthy and complex questionnaire. Usually, however, the student will wish to supplement this by open-ended discussion and a more common model is for the interviewer to define a schedule of topics to be covered and to explore them in whatever order appears natural in the course of the discussion. This situation is obviously more difficult to handle. At a very minimum two things are needed: firstly, some way of discreetly keeping a check that all topics have been covered; and, secondly, an initial icebreaking question that is almost guaranteed to evoke a response from the interviewee and that will encourage them to communicate freely thereafter. This problem is obviously exacerbated by the fact that, under most circumstances, interviews should probably not take much over an hour and, indeed, researchers may be given much less time if the subject is one that is of little interest to the interviewee.

Generally, it is not desirable to schedule more than two or three interviews a day, which implies that the typical student researcher cannot afford a very extensive programme for reasons of both time and money. This is obviously particularly the case in a dissertation project. Against that, the more modest aims of such research projects generally mean that the results of a few interesting interviews will form the basis of an acceptable dissertation where the topic being studied is relatively novel. In the longer research project for a research degree, thought also needs to be devoted as to how material gleaned from interviews is to be analysed in the final research report, otherwise the researcher runs the risk of having a wealth of data from a set of individually valuable interviews that collectively are very difficult to generalise from. The preparation of a realistic interview schedule in advance of the first interview is clearly a wise step.

Further Uses for Primary Data

Frequently, primary data gathered for one purpose turn out to be of great value for totally different purposes at a later date. It is by no means unknown for a researcher to return to the data years after the immediate objective of writing a thesis has been achieved. And, like bibliographies, the data may represent a tradeable commodity that will facilitate access to other researchers' data. It follows, then, that where possible primary data should be carefully filed away along with sufficient details to enable them to be used by someone else. Similarly, where some part of them has been transcribed on to the computer those data should be put on to some long-term storage medium, for example, a diskette, so that they are available for future use. If this is done, however, it must be borne in mind that such storage media do not last forever: there may be physical deterioration or the computer system used to write the data may become obsolete.

SECONDARY DATA SOURCES

Secondary data is data collected by others and published in some form that is fairly readily accessible. (See Figure 6.2.) Thus, in these terms company accounts that are published by law are secondary data. Although they are likely to be of subsidiary importance to laboratory-based science students, secondary data are almost always needed in student research and for students in the arts and humanities and the social sciences may well be the main source of data.

Source	Type of data
Books and journals	'Workhorse data' More esoteric quantitative data of all kinds Non-quantitative data
Technical publications (Manuals/handbooks/data sheets/ standards)	Physical/chemical constants Technical performance specifications
Official publications (e.g. central and local government)	Economic/social data
Trade association data	Technical or economic data
Private data services	Economic/product data
Information services	Bibliographic information, newspaper/journal articles
Internet/Web data	Databases worldwide

Figure 6.2 Some sources and types of secondary data

In general, the student may not know too much about the hidden assumptions, corrections or distortions that go into the production of a particular set of secondary data unless trouble is taken to find out what these were. Such data tend to have the beguiling look of the printed page or the PC screen about them and may thus appear far removed from the messy imperfections and inconsistencies that researchers may know to exist in their primary data. Whatever the researcher's interest, it is always wise to ascertain the basis on which measurements are compiled since otherwise different sets taken under different conditions or using different methods may well not be comparable. In addition, many data involve substantial measurement error and it may well be important in the analysis to be aware of this.

On the other side of the coin, secondary data have considerable attractions for students especially if they are engaged in a short research project. They are usually more quickly available than primary data and much less organisation is required to obtain them. Furthermore, they exist in considerable quantities and may contain information that is fairly easy for a government agency with legal backing to collect; something that would be very difficult for the lone researcher.

A type of secondary data that is increasing considerably in importance with the expansion of research internationally and the trend to storing research data in internationally available databases, is that from previous researchers' studies. If the basis on which previous studies have been conducted has been properly documented, and there has been reasonable standardisation in the way data were collected, then it becomes possible for the researchers to base the analysis entirely on the data from previous studies. This approach, known as meta-analysis, is extensively used in fields such as epidemiology. If the data involved are quantitative, then there are statistical methods that can be applied to enable the data to be analysed efficiently (see bibliography in Appendix 2).

Figure 6.2 lists a number of important sources and types of secondary data, and these are reviewed briefly paying attention to some of the main advantages and problems of each source and referring the reader where desirable to more specialist sources for discussions of particular types. It will be noted that all the categories of data involve the storage of the data on computer databases. This, in turn, has greatly facilitated the use of secondary data via the Internet using a Web browser.

Books and Journals

For many researchers, books and journals are likely to be the major source of data. Furthermore, they are by far the most important source of what we have called textual data.

One major use of books and journals is in providing certain standard sets of 'workhorse data' that are used by all investigators in a field as test beds for new methods and techniques so that their performance can be compared with well-established ones. Very often they will be found in the literature of a subject, for example the various time series, such as IBM common stock price, used to compare different computer methods of forecasting.

The data presented in a book or paper have typically received more processing and may therefore be subject to more qualifications than other types of secondary data. Indeed, they are frequently based on refinements and reworking of existing secondary data though this may not be readily apparent.

On the whole, unless the research project is short or the data are only of peripheral interest the use of books as sources of other than 'workhorse data' is perhaps best restricted to those which focus on the assumptions and processes by which the data were generated or to those providing expensive or esoteric data not readily available elsewhere.

Technical Publications

A host of data, from physical and chemical constants to performance data for particular items of equipment, were traditionally to be found in handbooks and manuals. Nowadays, they are most likely to be found on a website. Publications of this type are familiar names to workers in a particular field: for example, *Spon's Landscape and External Works Price Book*. Similar information may be published by equipment manufacturers in the form of detailed performance specifications, or by trade associations or bodies such as the British Standards Institution. Most data of this sort are relatively easily found using a search engine. They are often compiled as a commercial service, however, and therefore may not be free.

Official Publications

The volume and diversity of government publications has already been remarked on in Chapter 4. In advanced economies these are a major source of social and economic data of all kinds as well as design and performance specifications for many fields of engineering, and so forth. The most frequently useful official data are probably the various statistics compiled by government departments.

Though discovering what official sources are available is usually relatively straightforward, and such publications are increasingly to be found on the Web, guidance as to how to make effective use of the information is, in our experience, more difficult to come by. Frequently, the researcher needs to carry out further manipulations of the data listed, perhaps by comparing data in one source with those in another. Such are the diversity of uses of government statistics that even the experienced researcher is only likely to know a few of the sources well. The student researcher can probably learn much about how to exploit such data from talks and seminars given by those who make regular use of them, such as market researchers, economists, educational sociologists and so forth.

There are many other public bodies that publish statistics of importance to the researcher. In the UK, for instance, organisations such as the Chartered Institute of Public Finance and Accountancy (CIPFA) publish much material of a statistical nature, and the reports of public sector industries go far beyond the provision of statutory accounting data in describing their operations.

The official statistics of other countries are another useful source for the researcher, as are those of international bodies such as OECD and UNESCO, all of which can provide important data for comparative purposes. Many of these find their way into the United Nations Statistical Yearbook and thence to its website. Lists of the official statistics of various countries can also be found, for example, in publications intended for market researchers.

Data of this type come in the category of those that researchers could not possibly collect for themselves. Rather, researchers must make the best use of what exists and from the point of view of the research report that means critically appraising the data available to them, assessing their defects and correcting or allowing for them as best they can.

There are many types of research that require historical data. Numerous official statistics have been collected in the past in connection with a decennial census or a particular survey. Certain data series, such as wheat prices, extend back over a substantial period. Also, such historical data series are often readily available from the Web.

Trade Association Data

> TRADE ASSOCIATIONS AND SIMILAR BODIES CAN BE AN EXCELLENT
> SOURCE OF BOTH TECHNICAL AND ECONOMIC DATA

Both technical and economic data about the operations of members can be obtained from trade associations and similar bodies. For obvious reasons the economic data they publish are more detailed than those available through official statistics. Information on UK trade associations can be found in the Directory of British Associations and the availability of data can be checked with the relevant association.

Private Data Services

Data that are of interest to the researcher can often be of considerable use to researchers in general, particularly those working in the private sector in market research, investment analysis, and so on. Data of this type are, accordingly, a commercial proposition and there are many different services available. Sometimes access to these services is free, as with trade catalogues and permanent exhibitions. More usually they cost money. Many are available on a subscription basis, for example, the Datastream service giving details of the accounts of companies listed on UK Stock Exchanges, and are to be found in larger public libraries as well as academic libraries. Some appear regularly –

often annually – for example, guides to UK markets. Other data are produced only on a one-off basis and tend to be far more expensive, for example, the multi-client studies produced by certain organisations giving data on various products and markets that typically are intended to be sold only to a few dozen organisations. Often, those services providing information not readily accessible to the academic researcher, for example, details of executive remuneration in different countries, are likely to be most useful and for that reason expensive, so their use has to be budgeted for at the planning stage.

Computer Databases

A source of secondary data that is of considerable importance is the computer database. In the UK, many Central Statistical Office Series are available on computer bureaux or on CD-ROM, as are accounting data for listed public companies. The fundamental importance of bibliographic databases and the possibility of using them as a data source has been noted in Chapter 4. Similar remarks apply to the databases for products and services now available in a variety of fields. International bodies also maintain important databases, for example, the United Nations database on trade flows. Many have been developed directly by universities and other institutions for research purposes and will often be available to researchers from elsewhere. Databases of textual information, for example newspapers, were extensively discussed in Chapter 4. It is worth noting the increasing availability of concordances or specialist literatures (such as the complete corpus of known works in Middle English) in database form.

Where they exist, databases are a very valuable form of secondary data. They usually contain far more observations than the individual student could collect and the basis on which the data have been gathered and the adjustments made is usually explicit. Most importantly, databases are ideally suited to computer analysis and make it quite feasible for the individual student to contemplate types of analysis and research topics that once would have been considered hopelessly ambitious.

Data From the Internet

During the past decade the advent of a single, international standard interface for accessing computer databases, the Web browser, has revolutionised the provision of secondary data. Although most forms of secondary data listed in Figure 6.2 were held as computer databases before the advent of the Web browser, the would-be user had to contend with a variety of different ways of accessing the data depending on which database management system was being used to store the data. Although databases are still stored in many different formats, the Web allows this fact to be disguised from the user. This means that many previously relatively inaccessible databases are now easily accessed via the Internet using a Web browser. This, in turn, has spawned the provision of many different types of information content via the Web. Moreover, for governments and other organisations that wish to communicate reports to the public, dissemination via the Web has become the favoured method. As we saw in Chapter 4, Web content is generally easy to locate using a search engine. However, the Web is not without its drawbacks. Data may be biased or of dubious quality, and the cost of some items may be beyond the student researcher.

Ideally, the student researcher needs free access to the data in order to experiment with different ways of processing them. This usually means transferring the details onto the researcher's own computer system. Nowadays, this transfer will be effected directly via the Internet, when the database owner is another university (particularly an American one) or some public body. Where the data are provided on a commercial basis there will be a cost, (if the owner is willing to make a copy available) because payment is expected for the data themselves. Additionally, there are almost always restrictions on the use researchers may make of the information; for example, it is unlikely that it will be licensed for resale. Whatever the source, it is probable that the researcher will need to budget for further copies of the database at regular intervals so that the version can be kept up to date.

Locating suitable secondary data sources and gaining access to them may have time and cost implications. Prospective use of secondary databases has, therefore, important implications for the planning of the research.

CHAPTER SUMMARY

DATA MAY BE DISTINGUISHED AS: primary data (data gathered by the researcher) and secondary data (data gathered by others).

THE DATA TO BE GATHERED ARE RELATED TO THE PURPOSES OF THE ANALYSIS: it follows that the type and quantity of data are affected by that purpose and therefore, indirectly, by the level of the research project.

DATA MUST BE: located
assessed
collected and checked
recorded in a form suitable for subsequent analysis.

MEASUREMENT ERROR: affects much data and must be reduced to an acceptable level, possibly by increasing the sample size.

DATA GATHERING: is a demanding activity when primary data are involved and time should be allocated for training in collection. Secondary data are usually easier to collect and use although the assumptions on which this type of data are based may be unclear. Their use may involve costs that must be budgeted for.

THE WEB has made a huge difference to the ease with which secondary data can be accessed and used.

DATA ORGANISATION: thought should be given to how best to organise the data and associated notes on them to avoid wasted effort through reduplication of analyses, etc.

Part C

Producing the
Research Results

7

Executing the Research

This chapter discusses issues associated with execution of the research, in particular some common problems which occur in research projects, and relationships with supervisors.

The chapter has four main objectives:

1. To identify problems which, with hindsight, could have been avoided and to suggest anticipatory action which should be adopted.
2. To suggest ways of coping with unavoidable or unexpected problems which may arise.
3. To make positive suggestions which will facilitate research progress.
4. To discuss in depth the role and responsibilities of the research supervisor and how he or she can be used effectively in executing the research.

We consider various problems which may be encountered in student research, discuss them, and suggest solutions. These are:

a) departure from the research plan;
b) overcommitment;
c) individual problems of illness and motivation;
d) problems threatening continuation of the study;

e)   problems which cause serious delays;

f)   general support problems;

g)   harassment and intimidation;

h)   supervision issues, including working with supervisors, and common problems with supervision.

THE RESEARCH PLAN

Creating an effective research plan is the most important positive step towards successfully completing a research project. But it is unusual for any research project to go completely according to plan. Plans change, and need constant and regular revision.

In large part, avoidable problems should be anticipated by the systematic planning process described in Chapter 3, which involves:

a)   clarifying aims and objectives;

b)   defining activities required to meet the aims and their duration and order;

c)   identifying 'milestones' and review points;

d)   producing time estimates when milestones will be reached;

e)   planning to use resources effectively;

f)   defining priorities once the research is underway.

In Chapter 3 the importance of fixing 'milestones' in the project was discussed, and in particular their use for ensuring that progress is maintained. Experience suggests that many students do not place sufficient weight on meeting the deadlines they identify, or on redefining and re-planning the research if for some reason a milestone is missed by any considerable length of time. This is particularly so at the doctoral level where there are few natural markers of the passage of time. The end result can be that each stage takes longer than planned and, eventually, what once seemed a leisurely schedule now seems hopelessly optimistic given the time remaining.

> FACE UP TO PROBLEMS. USE THE PLAN TO IDENTIFY WHEN SOMETHING IS TAKING TOO LONG OR ISN'T WORKING OUT WELL, AND ASK FOR HELP.

A further and often more serious variant of this problem is to refuse to admit that a significant snag has been encountered. Surprisingly often, research students find that a particular stage in the research is more difficult than was envisaged but are unwilling to admit to themselves that the problem is a major one. Instead they begin to look a day or two ahead to the time when the bug will certainly have been

170

removed from a computer program or their apparatus will finally begin to work, and eventually many months can be wasted in a welter of misplaced optimism.

Such situations can be avoided if students realise that they have a problem and seek advice about it. If they continually review their progress against a plan it is unlikely that they will seriously deceive themselves, whereas if they do not they will almost certainly find it far more difficult to seek help given the embarrassingly long time it took to see the need.

OVERCOMMITMENT

It is not suggested that once students embark upon a research project they should turn their backs on all other types of activity; there should be scope for both leisure and the pursuit of other interests. Opportunities will often present themselves to full-time research students which may be contributors to self-development in a career sense, or simply as a means of generating much-needed income.

Tutorial Work

DON'T OVERCOMMIT ON TEACHING WORK. A ONE-HOUR TUTORIAL MAY INVOLVE THREE HOURS OF PREPARATION AND TWO HOURS OF MARKING

A difficult decision for some research degree students to take is the extent to which they accept tutorial or demonstrating work offered to them. Many research students have ambitions to pursue a career in education, and apart from financial benefits, see the experience as being of much potential value. It is important that before accepting a teaching commitment students should investigate the total demand which it will make on their time. A one-hour tutorial may involve three hours' preparation and two hours' marking. Ten hours' commitment arising from, a regular teaching assignment of, say, two one-hour lectures would be a substantial proportion of a working week. Certainly, time in excess of this could have a major adverse effect on the rate of progress of the study itself (see Figure 1.4). If possible, tutorial work commitments should be built up gradually.

Students who anticipate that they will from time to time present the findings of their work in a more or less formal setting would do well to read one of the many short guidebooks on making effective presentations.

Writing Papers

The writing of papers on topics arising from the research has much to commend it. In addition to gaining valuable experience of the writing process itself the acceptance of articles for publication or conference presentation is probably the main way in which academic reputations are established. Additionally, a measure of substance is added to research theses if students can reference their own work which has been published in journals of repute. It would therefore be quite reasonable for a student to think in terms of submitting articles for publication at a rate of about one per year of full-time study. Again, though, be realistic about the time writing a paper for publication can take. A 5000-word paper will normally take a minimum of 25 hours of dedicated work to get it into a format acceptable for a scholarly publication, even when most of the background research has been done in the course of a student's project.

Organising Time

> DON'T LET A RESEARCH PROJECT GET OUT OF CONTROL. KEEP A SCHEDULE CHART AND UPDATE IT FREQUENTLY. LEARN HOW TO ORGANISE YOUR TIME TO KEEP CONTROL OF A PROJECT

In practice, the most important determinant of the amount of outside (non-leisure) activity in which research students can safely engage, is their ability to organise their own time effectively. There are students who manage a substantial part-time commitment to research while at the same time occupying very senior positions in organisations or working in professional practice. Conversely, many research students, particularly younger ones, find considerable difficulty in organising their own time effectively enough to carry on the single task of research.

The assumption that major diversions can be absorbed without prejudicing successful completion is a dangerous one. It is vital that the research should never get out of control. We strongly recommend, therefore, the maintenance of schedule charts that are updated frequently, at least every two weeks, during the course of doctoral research and a realistic approach to any binding commitment.

INDIVIDUAL PROBLEMS

Illness and loss of motivation are the two main ways in which research progress may be affected by what may be termed 'personal' factors.

Illness

> ALWAYS INFORM SUPERVISORS AND/OR HEADS OF DEPARTMENT IF RESEARCH TIME IS LIKELY TO BE SIGNIFICANTLY AFFECTED BY ILLNESS

Illness affecting the student or close relatives is always a possibility. It is likely to have an adversely non-linear effect as the duration of illness increases. Probably the maximum which the student can accommodate is 10 per cent, or about one month for each year of study. Supervisors or examiners should be made aware if a significant amount of research time is likely to be affected by illness.

Institutions and grant-awarding bodies are invariably sympathetic towards students who suffer certified illness and it is much to be preferred that such incidence is notified. If the illness is of long duration the decision to take is clear-cut. Students should seek to have their registration suspended and, if they are full-time students, to have part of any support they receive deferred. The decision becomes more difficult if shorter periods of illness are involved when there may be an inclination to absorb the time lost and at the same time retain any grant payment. The proportion of the planned period remaining will obviously be an important factor. If the student is in doubt, the inclination should be towards delaying the planned completion date.

Loss of Motivation

> A DROP IN MOTIVATION AND FEELING THAT 'THIS IS GOING NOWHERE' ARE NORMAL IN ANY RESEARCH PROJECT. TRY SWITCHING TEMPORARILY TO ANOTHER ASPECT OF THE PROJECT

Without self-motivation research can be extremely laborious, but no student can maintain the same pitch of enthusiasm throughout a study particularly if it is of several years duration. A range of factors may lead to a loss of motivation. These include tedium, frustration, lack of progress and a reduction in interest. There is little need to give examples. Of more importance is how problems of this type might be overcome.

The first recommendation is that these problems should be discussed informally with someone else; preferably the supervisor in the first instance, but also with students who have themselves experienced and overcome similar difficulties. If informal discussions do not help, then a second possibility is that the student should suggest to the supervisor that an ad hoc committee should be set up to review progress. Some institutions use this practice routinely and it is usually found to be very effective. Two or three faculty members (one of whom may have no experience in the field of research) are often able to generate suggestions which indicate how problems may be resolved or which rekindle the student's interest in the topic.

A third possibility which may help in overcoming low motivation, in particular during the early stages of research, is to leave aside the task in hand and switch to another element of the research study. In Chapter 3 we saw how several activities can run in parallel (see Figure 3.2).

Unless the activity creating the problem is 'critical' the student can probably find something completely different to pursue and, importantly, will be able to assess how long a task may be deferred before it becomes critical. As argued above, one activity which can be both motivating and rewarding is the writing of a paper on a distinct phase of the work which has been completed. Even though the paper may be a general one reviewing the current situation in the area, or a descriptive account of the response to a survey, acceptance for publication can be a spur to renewed effort besides having other advantages.

The ability to 'stand back', particularly during longer studies, and view tedium and frustration as being inevitable from time to time should go some way to overcoming motivational problems. To this end the use of some type of chart as described in Chapter 3 will emphasise progress which has been made.

The student should always look to the research supervisor for advice and support. On first being acquainted with motivational difficulties, an experienced supervisor should be able to make a number of suggestions for the student to follow up. This is only possible, of course, if the supervisor is kept fully informed.

THREATS TO THE CONTINUATION OF THE STUDY

Although the future can never be predicted with certainty, students who set out on research studies will normally expect (particularly if they have undertaken thorough topic analyses and/or research proposals) to achieve a successful outcome. To some degree the prospects of success are related to the level and duration, and also the nature, of the research (see Chapter 1). All types of research may, however, be brought to a halt by factors outside the control of the student. These factors include: loss of data; the realisation that substantial conclusions cannot be drawn; the withdrawal of facilities; or evidence that some other researcher has successfully covered the same ground.

Loss of Data

Computers can be stolen; files become corrupted; notes and index cards lost or destroyed. The solution to the threat of lost data is simple – back everything up onto disk and keep the copies somewhere away from the computer where work is being held on a hard drive. Never keep research work on a single floppy disk alone. Print hard copies on occasion – the words can always be re-keyed or scanned if needs be. Make photocopies of vital notes. Losing a week's worth of writing is recoverable (though intensely annoying). Losing a year's worth would, for most people, be irrecoverable.

Lack of Conclusions

> WHERE FINDINGS HAVE LITTLE VALUE OR ARE INCONCLUSIVE, THE RESEARCH CAN OFTEN BE RESCUED BY SOME LATERAL THINKING AND A CHANGE OF FOCUS

If researchers find that their efforts are likely to be fruitless there is little point in reminding them that their research design should have been more symmetrical, with a low probability of an inconclusive outcome. An example is a student in the marketing area who felt quite confident of achieving a valuable outcome from a study of the importance of attitudes of potential customers in relation to the promotion of different makes of car. Having collected a large volume of data and having subjected it to analysis it remained unclear as to whether any relationship exists; an outcome which was unacceptable.

In terms of the model of research presented in Chapter 2, the problem in this situation is one where the research has insufficient value. Major changes would therefore need to be explored and made to the line of the research and the way it has been viewed. These changes could be:

1. Reflections on the process and question: examining why success was not achieved when it was expected, possibly by going outside the original field of research and relating it to other theories.
2. Investigation of a 'common error': showing that similar assumptions to those underlying the original research are widely employed by practitioners and pointing out the consequences of their erroneous use. If the student can show that car design is strongly influenced by similar (incorrect) beliefs then the research has strong implications for the design policy of car manufacturers and this may well make a sufficiently weighty set of findings.

175

3. Identification and investigation of other variables: perhaps the lack of success is explicable in terms of the high percentage of cars purchased by companies rather than by individuals?

In cases where inconclusive findings deliver no obvious research benefit (when research design is *asymmetrical* – see Chapter 2) students need to think laterally in consultation with supervisors and others to create something valid from the data.

Withdrawal of Facilities

IF ACCESS TO DATA OR RESOURCES IS WITHDRAWN, CAN THE SAME INVESTIGATIONS BE FOLLOWED USING OTHER, SIMILAR ONES?

The withdrawal of facilities will primarily affect research studies which depend upon external co-operation. For example, an organisation which hitherto had been collaborating by permitting access to its research and development department may decide to withdraw from the arrangement. In such cases the important question to be resolved is how far the value of the research is dependent on the resource concerned.

For example, it is easy to forget, as commitment to a particular path of research develops, the extent to which expediency dictated earlier choices. Examples of such expediency would be the support of a company with which the institution has close links, or access to a private collection situated near to the researcher's home. Neither is necessarily unique and there may well be other possibilities of carrying out essentially the original research plan but using some other resource. Alternatively, it may be possible to adopt a comparative stance in the research, for example, by looking at several other organisations and seeing how they cope with similar problems to those studied in the original company, or by examining how one sequence of events uncovered in the examination of family papers impinged on others who were involved in them.

A more insidious problem than withdrawal of key resources is the inability of those resources to function as planned. Most engineering laboratories have test rigs that may never have worked at all or have at least required several generations of research students to get them to perform as intended. Computer software, surprisingly often, refuses to work in accordance with its specification. The difficulty here is that while the student can clearly see that in the future the hoped-for results will emerge, in the meantime there is little to show for their efforts. Sooner or later, therefore, it is necessary to call a halt and make a decision as to whether to change the direction of the research or focus on getting the resource to function as planned.

At the master's level and below, change of direction is frequently a sensible strategy since the work could well be of an acceptable standard. At the doctoral level this is more rarely the case and so the decision will probably be to treat the resource as if withdrawn, in which case the earlier remarks apply.

Parallel Studies

Despite the increasing efficiency of information transfer it is still possible that two researchers will cover, in ignorance, the same ground. If this proves to be so when basic research at the doctoral level, with its emphasis on generalisability, is involved, there may be little that the 'second past the post' can do about it. There are, fortunately, relatively few situations where the difficulties are so extreme. In the experimental sciences, confirmatory evidence would be considered very desirable and in most situations in the social sciences and humanities exact and irremediable overlap is most unlikely. Much more likely is that the research provides an alternative view with sufficient incremental value.

Dealing with a Crisis

> IF A PROBLEM ARISES WHICH SEEMS TO THREATEN THE COMPLETION OF THE STUDY – STAY CALM. TAKE ADVICE. SEEK AN ALTERNATIVE FOCUS (USING AS MUCH ORIGINAL DATA AS POSSIBLE)

In each of the above cases, student researchers may initially feel that the ground has fallen away from under them. This will be the case particularly if the major part of the period of the study has been completed. Given the catastrophe that appears to have befallen them it is unlikely that their judgement will be sound. Their primary need is for detached, expert advice from outsiders. The first source of help is the supervisor, although the supervisor may be too closely involved to offer impartial guidance. A useful strategy is for the student to discuss the problem informally with acquaintances who are also involved in research, who can offer a variety of perspectives on the problem.

Ideally, they should all be familiar with the field of research but have related rather than similar interests. Such a group needs to focus on whether: a) there is a serious problem; and b) if so, can it be overcome with as little waste of previous work as possible?

Where the answer to question b) is 'No', the positive options open to the student would seem to be as follows:

a) try to define rapidly a new research topic which will have as much overlap as possible with the redundant topic;
b) consider conversion (in the case of the doctoral student) to an acceptable master's thesis;
c) drop the idea of completing a research degree and write papers for both academic and (if appropriate) professional journals; or, possibly, a book.

Much will depend on how much research time is left and on the enthusiasm which the student can retain. The experience gained from undertaking earlier research stages should be of considerable benefit if the student has to retrace steps. Which of the options listed is to be preferred will depend on the individual, but if at least one year of the study period remains consideration should be given to working up a new topic, despite the knowledge that it may be necessary to write a large part of the thesis after the formal completion of the programme. These options are considered, briefly, below.

New topic

It is not easy to make more than general recommendations on the development of a new topic as so much depends on the line of research which has been abandoned. Nor is it suggested that the latter is a common experience. Students may, however, comfort themselves with the thought that the greater the experience they have gained the easier it should be to both define and follow a new direction of study.

Switch to a masters'

One situation in which some consolation may be derived from the frustration of a study arises when a student working for a doctorate has done sufficient work to satisfy the requirements of a masters' degree. Much depends on the student's objectives. If, for instance, a future in tertiary education or in research is envisaged the student may be more inclined to use the time remaining to work towards a redefined doctorate. If not, the prospect of a master's degree may be more appealing.

Publish the findings

There are few students who would accept that there should be no tangible outcome of, perhaps, three years of study. Most students would see as desirable the establishment of a reputation primarily through publication in academic journals, and perhaps a measure of lecturing or consultancy. If, therefore, the student has made substantial progress but has fallen short of the requirements of a PhD the acceptance of a few well-written papers by academic journals of standing may offer some compensation. In any event, research students are unlikely to communicate with the world at large through their thesis and if it is an academic reputation they seek they must be prepared to write either books or papers or both (see Chapter 8).

Increasingly, similar comments apply to non-doctoral students. If, as we have suggested, they have selected their dissertation topic with an eye to their career objectives it may well be of benefit to derive one or more publications from their research project.

SERIOUS DELAY

> THE TYPE OF ANALYSIS TO BE EMPLOYED SHOULD BE ANTICIPATED AS MUCH AS POSSIBLE. DATA ANALYSIS PLANNING SHOULD PRECEDE DATA COLLECTION

The above comments refer to circumstances in which a particular course of study is terminated for unpredicted reasons. More frequently encountered, and linked to poor rates of research degree completion, are those studies which are significantly delayed not so much by inefficient research management but by the occurrence of a specific problem. The most usual hurdle to be overcome faces students who have collected large volumes of data but who are unable to analyse them in sufficient depth. This reinforces the argument that the type of analysis to be employed should be anticipated as much as possible. Data analysis planning should precede data collection.

It is to be hoped that constructive advice will be available from the supervisor on analytical approaches but it should be recognised that in many instances the supervisor may not possess the requisite skills. If this is so the student should seek assistance from other sources. The academic world has within it many people who can provide guidance, and it is a measure of the student's initiative to be able to make effective contact. What can almost be guaranteed is that assistance will be forthcoming on request, provided the student demonstrates an intent to solve the problem. An approach of 'I've got a problem and now it's your job to sort it out for me' will not be well regarded.

Another major cause of delay arises from dependence on other people's reactions to a researcher's initiatives. The estimated duration of activities used to develop schedules in Chapter 3 assumes 'normal' speeds of response but from time to time these will not be achieved. There may be lengthy delays in gaining approval from a collaborating body, items of equipment may not be delivered on time, questionnaires sent out for pilot test may not be returned and so on.

The risk is largely the extent to which parts of the study lie outside the direct control of the student. If there is much of this the need to adopt a formalised approach to planning can only be stressed. It is not so much a matter of normal 'lead time' (the interval between requesting something to be done and its occurrence) but a matter of considering in advance of a specific request whether the ground can be prepared in any way. For example, it would be worthwhile determining the frequency of meetings of an external body which will give approval for a study to be undertaken, or when a key individual is likely to take holidays, or whether an alternative supplier for a piece of equipment can be identified.

The consequences of delays such as those caused by some aspect of the process of the research or the research design may be absorbed during the remainder of the study. But if delay is substantial a student working for a research degree may have to resort to the second and third options (conversion, if appropriate, to a master's degree, or writing papers instead) mentioned above.

GENERAL SUPPORT PROBLEMS

The vast majority of students who commence a research study do so in the expectation that sufficient support will be available for them to achieve their objectives. Thus, they anticipate that appropriate funds will be forthcoming and that at the least they will be provided with minimum facilities such as desk space. The sensible student will have established what will be available in terms of accommodation, telephone, filing space, laboratory, library, computer facilities, and so on. The question is whether there is a possibility that any of this support will be withdrawn or will prove to be insufficient. In grant-funded research, it is possible that some activities may not qualify for funding (for example, the transcription of interview tapes, or overseas travel).

If financial support is provided externally there may be some risk of discontinuation. This has been a not uncommon occurrence for government-funded students from developing countries, when political changes have led to a withdrawal of funding. In the UK, many students are funded by private sector organisations and economic recession and company closure or merger can lead to similar problems arising.

Many institutions of further and higher education have 'hardship committees' which are often able to give practical support to those students who, through no fault of their own, find that sponsorship is withdrawn, but this support may be limited to fees only (not living expenses).

Although support problems are dominated by issues relating to fees or grants, some students continue to experience difficulties through the data collection and analysis stages. Costs and facilities associated with the former should be capable of reasonable estimation and should be highlighted during the assessment of topic feasibility. Thus questions as to whether funds will be available to purchase equipment and materials, to cover travel, or to pay for the mailing of several hundred questionnaires will need to be resolved.

> GIVE PLENTY OF NOTICE OF REQUIREMENTS FROM CENTRALISED SUPPORT DEPARTMENTS SUCH AS INFORMATION TECHNOLOGY OR LABORATORY ANALYSIS

Less easy to assess will be whether appropriate support for analysis will be forth-coming. Many students rely heavily on IT facilities and it is wise to anticipate as far as is possible the likely extent of what will be needed. Lengthy delays may arise if the student does nothing until on the point of requiring analysis to be undertaken. In large part, therefore, this type of problem should be anticipated at the planning stage and should not fall within the 'unavoidable or unexpected' category. Usually, for example, ample notification will be given of the upgrading of an education institution's IT services so that students will be able to reschedule their analysis if facilities are to be temporarily withdrawn or make alternative arrangements if software becomes unavailable.

Employment Opportunities

Full-time research students are sometimes confronted with another type of problem: an offer of employment. Few prospective employers are prepared to make an open-ended job offer that will allow students to complete their research before taking up an appointment. Employers may well allow some time to be spent during the early months of employment on completing the study. Our experience has shown though that the completion of research within, say, six months of taking up an appointment is extremely rare. Despite every intention, the demands of a (presumably) responsible position preclude other types of activity. This is one reason for poor completion rates, as commented upon in Chapter 1. Erstwhile full-time students discover that research is not something which can be easily picked up at any time and one consequence is that the longer the period taken the lower the probability of completion.

It is difficult for the young student to make a choice between what might be an attractive job opportunity and the completion of a degree. The attraction of a high salary after months or years spent at subsistence level while working on the completion of a thesis is difficult to resist. But whatever the economic climate the possession of a research degree is likely to continue to enhance the prospects of employment throughout a student's later career.

Part-time students quite often experience a change in employment during their studies; such a change of circumstances is likely to affect their schedules detrimentally. For this reason they need to push ahead rapidly whenever work pressures allow. The only way to ensure that research work does not cause conflict when an attractive posting is offered is to have completed it.

Searching for Employment

> EXTRA TIME SHOULD BE INCORPORATED WITHIN THE RESEARCH PLAN TO ACCOMMODATE ACTIVITIES SUCH AS THE PREPARATION OF JOB APPLICATIONS AND ATTENDANCE AT INTERVIEWS

A related problem is that of trying to schedule the transition from study to employment. Thinking about, applying for and attending interviews for jobs can have a very damaging effect on schedules during the later part of a student's research when it is likely that most of a contingency allocation will have been used up. It is therefore sensible that extra time should be incorporated within the research plan to accommodate activities such as the preparation of job applications and attendance at interviews.

HARASSMENT AND INTIMIDATION

> STUDENTS WHO FEEL THEY ARE BEING HARASSED, INTIMIDATED OR PRESSURED MUST SEEK ADVICE IMMEDIATELY FROM A UNIVERSITY (STUDENT) COUNSELLING BODY

Problems of a very different nature are those involving harassment and intimidation. These are not new problems, but there is a much-raised awareness of them now, so most university policy on them is recent. It is difficult to offer generalised advice in this area except to say that every university has policy guidelines, and every university has advice centres to deal with concerns about gender, race, religious or disability issues on behalf of students. Such advisors can be used for confidential conversations about matters of concern to a student. A conversation with an advisor is a long way from a formal complaint. Students should not feel that expressing concerns will invariably lead to a confrontation with authorities.

Most universities specifically advise against (or forbid) intimate relationships between faculty members and students. Shared interests and sheer physical proximity can encourage such relationships, but university regulations tend to contractually forbid them for a number of reasons. The relative power of a senior faculty member or supervisor over a student means that the university itself can be (and has been, on occasions) challenged in a court of law by an unhappy student. Even without that ultimate recourse, the practical difficulty of continuing to study alongside or under the direction of a former intimate means that the research is likely to be adversely affected.

Students who feel harassed or intimidated by fellow research students should also talk in confidence to advisors. Again, university regulations will specifically protect students against harassment on the grounds of gender, religion, disability or race, and no student should feel that they have to suffer this kind of problem alone. A student who is concerned or frightened about such issues will not be the first or only person the university has encountered in these situations, and there will be sympathetic advisors in place to help.

PROBLEMS AND ISSUES IN WORKING WITH A SUPERVISOR

This section examines, in five sub-sections, some common problems and issues in working with a supervisor:

1.   Managing the supervisor relationship.
2.   The key roles of the supervisor.
3.   Six areas for a student to manage.
4.   Common problems regarding supervisors.
5.   Summary – avoiding supervision problems.

Managing the Supervisor Relationship

Students undertaking research projects have a right to expect to receive advice, supervision or direction, but the relationship should not be a passive one. A supervisor should be looked on as a useful and scarce resource, like a research budget, to be 'spent' wisely. Research students should plan for good use of their supervisor and take responsibility for getting the most from a relationship. A student normally only has one supervisor; a supervisor may have several students.

The word 'supervision' is a fairly accurate reflection of the context in which research is most appropriately conducted, containing elements of both 'advice' when requested and 'direction' when deemed apposite by the supervisor. In the initial stages of the research, at least, the student should look to the supervisor for guidance and direction on appropriate standards. A word of warning is necessary as many supervisors see their role in standard setting as advisory, and do not feel it appropriate to direct the student as to what needs to be done to achieve the right level. Rather they see themselves as indicating directions through comments or queries. If these are disregarded they may, eventually, cease to give such advice.

> STUDENTS SHOULD ENSURE THEY ARE GIVEN A COPY OF THE UNIVERSITY'S GUIDELINES FOR SUPERVISION, SO THEY KNOW WHAT TO EXPECT FROM THEIR SUPERVISOR

It is important for students to understand the expectation of the relationship as perceived by the supervisor and the institution, and to bear in mind that in the end the student, not the supervisor, has the responsibility to demonstrate learning and quality of research to the appropriate level. A research student should quickly end up with much more specialist knowledge on their research topic than their supervisor. Whether a student–supervisor relationship starts as 'advisory or 'directive', it should always move towards the advisory as the student gets into the rhythm of the research. A supervisor should never create dependency, and a student should never seek it.

In long-term research especially, a working relationship between student and supervisor is important. That does not mean students and supervisors need to be friends, or to socialise, but it does mean that a student needs to feel personally comfortable with the supervisor (and vice versa) and his or her knowledge, reputation and views. For shorter-term research (an MBA dissertation, for example) this is less important as the level of guidance and contact expected will be much lower.

Supervisors may be appointed at different stages of the research according to the approach used by the particular institution. Different institutions have different approaches to supervision of research projects. The link between student and supervisor may be established prior to topic selection, between topic selection and the research proposal, or after the proposal has been agreed. In some cases, part-time students may not be accepted until they have presented a carefully argued research proposal.

The assumption is that the student will be working with a single supervisor. However, it may be desirable to appoint a second, or indeed the institution may require it. At its best such a supervisory relationship can be of considerable benefit to the student. The calibre of advice received and the additional scrutiny given to the work increase the chance of turning out high quality research. On the other hand such a relationship can create problems that do not exist with a single supervisor. It is more difficult to organise meetings at which both supervisors can be present. The responses to work submitted may differ. To gain the full benefit of such an arrangement will usually involve the student in more managerial effort.

184

The Key Roles Of The Supervisor

It is assumed that (at least for research degree students) the supervisor satisfies all of the requirements listed in Chapter 2 and that the student sees a reasonable prospect of a satisfactory relationship. These requirements are, in outline:

1. Good record of completions of students.
2. Clarity on the supervisor's view of the supervisor–student relationship.
3. Supervisor's subject competence and eminence.
4. Supervisor's research methodology competence.
5. Supervisor's accessibility.

If there are doubts about any of these, the student should not hesitate to attempt to find an alternative. In some cases the provision of two supervisors ensures that all the criteria above are met between them (for example, teaming up an eminent but hard-to-access subject expert with an accessible research methods expert).

The supervisor fulfils a number of key roles in any research project, though naturally the balance varies depending on the level of research. In general a supervisor should:

1. Get the student to define objectives at each stage of the work.
2. Check to see that those objectives are met.
3. Verify with the student that the work is of the right standard.

More fundamental is the degree of obligation which the supervisor carries for the successful completion of a research study. Below research degree level, two conditions need to be met: firstly, the report or dissertation must be handed in by a particular date; and, secondly, minimum standards should be satisfied. Postgraduate degrees based wholly or in part on dissertations or theses often specify a submission date within what might be quite an extended period.

STUDENTS MUST TAKE THE INITIATIVE TO MANAGE THEIR SUPERVISION TOWARDS AN EFFECTIVE END RESULT

Although degree-awarding institutions define the latest date of normal submission, extensions are usually granted if students can provide evidence that they are continuing to make some progress. In these circumstances (even though the student may be paying substantial fees) supervision can become lax and solely reactive. This is, to an extent, understandable as staff members move to new interests, and new students arrive. Therefore, students taking an inordinate time to complete their projects must expect the initiative for supervision to be largely their responsibility.

Part-time students

The position of students registered for a part-time research degree is rather different from that of the full-time student. Very often their research will be related to their work in which case they may expect reasonable support from their organisation. In fact some statement to this effect from their employer will often be required by the institution with which they are registered. In many cases an industry supervisor may be appointed or, if the candidate is located in a different country, an additional academic supervisor may need to be found locally. Meetings and discussions with the supervisor should, desirably, take place at least quarterly; in many cases, these will be supplemented by submission of written material particularly in the writing-up stage.

In the case of dissertation projects the 'budget' for supervision may be very limited. Contractually, this may mean, for example, a supervisor is directed to spend say six hours per dissertation student, composed of two one-hour meetings and four hours of reading and commenting on written work. It is always a good idea for a student to read the institution's guidelines on what support to expect, and to agree a working pattern with a supervisor, even for a short dissertation project.

Six Areas a Student Should Manage

It is recommended that the student should:

1. Attempt at the outset to ascertain the supervisor's own views of the staff–student relationship.
2. Agree with the supervisor the routine aspects of the relationship (and take responsibility for their implementation).
3. Produce written lists of queries prior to meetings with the supervisor.
4. Keep written notes of meetings with the supervisor and submit copies.
5. Agree with the supervisor the nature and timing of progress reports to be submitted.
6. Agree with the supervisor the nature and timing of draft chapters to be submitted.

Each of these points needs to be couched within an institution's stated requirements as specified in the institutional, departmental or faculty handbook/regulations.

The supervisor's views

Even though both student and supervisor find a mutual interest in the research the relationship can be soured if, in particular, there are a number of counts on which the supervisor has strong feelings, which may not necessarily be about the research topic (though the same cautions apply). If, for example, the supervisor has high standards of punctuality, the relationship would rapidly deteriorate if a student were to be persistently late in keeping appointments or broke them altogether. Some supervisors welcome their students 'dropping in' on occasion for an informal update on progress; others prefer arrangements to be made by prior appointment or through a secretary. Preferences should be established and appropriate behaviour followed.

Establishing routines

Regular contact between student and supervisor is very desirable. It is accepted that a small proportion of students may have sufficient competence and motivation to complete even a doctorate unaided, but the large majority will rely heavily on expert guidance, mainly from the supervisor. In the latter respect a prime requirement is that the supervisor should not lose touch with progress. Therefore, it should be agreed that the interval between meetings should not exceed a certain period. At some stages of the research frequent discussions will be required but, ideally, routine contact should be maintained with the interval between meetings not exceeding four weeks. The supervisor has a definite responsibility to comply with such an arrangement but as the person to suffer if regular contact breaks down, it is the student who should take the initiative in rearranging dates if a meeting has to be postponed. If a supervisor proves impossible to pin down to appointments, a student should seek advice from their research department and explore a change of supervisor.

Listing queries

It is helpful to the supervisor if the student submits a brief list of any queries or problems before routine meetings. This serves a number of purposes: it provides a basic agenda for the meeting; it forces the student to properly define what might otherwise remain a vague, unvoiced unease; it prevents the accretion of small difficulties into a single insuperable obstacle, and it fulfils a primary need for successful project management, namely the recognition of problems that need to be resolved. Obviously, in many types of research the student will also need to bring along to meetings supplementary material such as questionnaires or laboratory reports that bear on the issues raised.

> WHETHER OR NOT SUPERVISORS KEEP THEIR OWN WRITTEN RECORD OF MEETINGS STUDENTS SHOULD CERTAINLY DO SO, AND SHOULD PROVIDE THEIR SUPERVISOR WITH A COPY OF THE NOTES OF THEIR MEETINGS

Something positive should emerge from most meetings between student and supervisor. This may take the form of questions answered or suggestions to follow. It is all too easy to assume that these will be remembered but the nature of research makes it quite probable that they will not be. Whether or not supervisors keep their own written record of meetings students should certainly do so, and should provide their supervisor with a copy of the notes of their meetings.

Scheduling and submitting progress reports

Students should be prepared to submit progress reports at a frequency as high as once per month until the writing-up phase proper of the research is entered. They should be as succinct as possible unless the supervisor requests that a particular issue should be enlarged upon. Progress reports should record what work has been done since the previous report and show the relationship of this work to the following:

a) the latest version of the research plan;
b) whether a milestone event in the project has been reached;
c) action points agreed at the last progress meeting;
d) queries raised by the student or suggestions from the supervisor at routine meetings in the intervening period.

Where necessary the assumptions on which the work is based and the ways they were checked should be clearly laid out. This makes it possible to verify at each stage that the work is of the requisite quality and should avoid the disastrous discovery in the final stages that it is based on untenable assumptions. The submission of progress reports is the primary mechanism by which the student ensures that the research plan remains feasible or discovers when it needs amendment. Most successfully managed research projects use some device as discussed in Chapter 3.

Scheduling and submitting draft chapters

Students should seek to draft out chapters of the report at an early stage in the research. Our example research project (Chapter 3) is based on a research plan in which the writing of draft chapters is seen to be realistic after only four weeks of the execution phase. What might be attempted here is the 'Introduction' or 'Background to the Research'. In large part, the writing may ultimately be redundant due to a shift in the direction of the research or simply by becoming out of date. The major advantages are that the supervisor will be able to assess and react to the content of the material submitted, and that the student will be able to gauge the magnitude of the writing-up task, at the same time coming to grips with the demands of format and style.

An obvious point which applies to the submission of any written material is that the supervisor should have had the opportunity of reading it before meeting the student.

Common Problems Regarding Supervisors

Change of supervisor

Ideally, a student should relate to one supervisor throughout the project. For students undertaking two- or three-year projects there exists, however, the possibility that staff mobility, or study leave, will prevent this from being achieved. In these circumstances the supervisor has a responsibility to ensure that new arrangements are made which will have as little effect as possible upon the progress of the research. If the supervisor is staying in academic life it may be possible for the student to change from one institution to another (research councils will permit this). For a variety of reasons the student may be unwilling or unable to accept a transfer and in these circumstances the supervisor and colleagues should endeavour to effect a move to another member of staff who is able to satisfy the range of requirements. Obviously, the host institution will carry responsibility whatever the reason (for example, retirement or death in service) for the breaking of a supervisory arrangement.

Shortfalls in a supervisor's knowledge

> A RESEARCH SUPERVISOR MAY NOT BE AN EXPERT ON DATA ANALYSIS OR RESEARCH METHODOLOGY

It is sometimes the case that a supervisor does not have all the necessary skills to advise the student. This situation is most commonly encountered during the analysis phase when knowledge of mathematical, statistical or computing techniques is required. It is far from certain that a supervisor will be an expert on data analysis or research methodology and it is important that students appreciate that, and learn where a supervisor's skills and interests lie in order to be able to get the most out of the supervisory relationship. Supervisors should not attempt to conceal their ignorance in such matters as these and will ideally direct the student to the appropriate quarters. The student should, however, never be diffident about approaching other members of staff, at the same time keeping their own supervisor informed.

In the longer research project, thesis committees are an effective way of revealing areas that have not received sufficient attention during supervisory meetings and many institutions use them on a regular basis for this reason. No matter how excellent the working relationship, it is rare at the doctoral level at least that every need of the student is recognised by the supervisor or that the supervisor is in a position to respond effectively to every request for assistance. Often, the help needed from outsiders is small – a key reference, a suggestion as to methods of analysis – nonetheless, it can well be of major benefit. The thesis committee therefore provides an excellent way of supplementing supervision and in addition may lead to the uncovering of serious difficulties of the type discussed below. If an institution offers participation in a thesis committee, a research student should take up the offer.

Failure of supervision

The most regrettable situation arises when a supervisor falls below what is acceptable in terms of both the quality and quantity of supervision. If students feel that their research progress is being marred for this reason they should not hesitate to take informal and then, if necessary, formal steps in an attempt to resolve the situation. All of this assumes that the supervisor has not responded to concerns expressed, and may involve the matter being taken successively higher in the institutional hierarchy. Action of this type though unpalatable, may, if not taken by students, adversely affect their prospects.

Summary – Avoiding Supervision Problems

A SUPERVISOR SHOULD BE LOOKED ON AS A USEFUL AND SCARCE RESOURCE, LIKE A RESEARCH BUDGET, TO BE 'SPENT' WISELY

Students should remember that although their research may constitute the whole world as far as they are concerned, this will not be so in the case of their supervisor. Nevertheless, most supervisors are more likely to respond positively and effectively if they are to some extent 'managed' and the student should not be diffident about adopting the courses of action described above. Most supervisory relationships work very effectively.

It is easier to avoid problems with supervision, rather than to try to fix them once they have occurred. To seek to avoid problems, students should:

1. Understand the contractual guidelines a supervisor is given by the institution.
2. Plan to make effective use of the time given.
3. Understand their supervisor's skills, limitations and preferences.
4. Manage the relationship and take the initiative for it working effectively.
5. Especially in long-term study, make a particular effort to keep regular contact with a supervisor.

CONCLUSION

Virtually the whole of this chapter has been concerned with problems which the research student may encounter, suggesting perhaps that the successful completion of a research project is comparable with the crossing of a minefield. The student should be aware of various types of pitfall – and to be forewarned is to be forearmed – but there is much that can be done to promote progress, and that has been the primary aim of this chapter.

Research rarely proceeds without some kind of difficulty, whether it is a feeling of becoming bogged down and going nowhere, to a disk crash, to a supervisor who is out of the country at the wrong time. But a good research plan will build in contingency time for minor emergencies, and even major ones can be overcome with planning, determination and early mobilisation of supervisors and university departments in support.

By recognising and facing up to the problems which will inevitably occur and then taking action of the type we have proposed, the prospect of successful completion will be greatly enhanced.

CHAPTER SUMMARY

THE CONSIDERATIONS IN THE EXECUTION PHASE ARE SIMILAR FOR RESEARCH STUDENTS AND DISSERTATION STUDENTS: the biggest difference is that the supervisor plays a much less important role in the dissertation project. Because of the short time-scales, problems encountered in dissertation projects can be more difficult to overcome.

RESEARCH RARELY PROCEEDS SMOOTHLY: students will at some stage encounter – and if they are to be successful must overcome – a range of problems.

MANY PROBLEMS ARE AVOIDABLE: careful planning should high-light this type of problem. Two aspects, over-commitment and supervisory arrangements, should be given much consideration.

UNEXPECTED PROBLEMS MAY ARISE: these may relate to the student, the supervisor, the research, or support for it.

RESEARCH PROGRESS CAN BE FACILITATED: by continually adopting a positive attitude towards it and identifying and pursuing activities which are consistent with effective and timely completion.

8

Presentation of the Research Findings

INTRODUCTION

The evaluation of student research is nearly always made through an assessment of the written account of the work undertaken and the conclusions reached. In addition, students are often required to explain or defend verbally their findings. This chapter will be concerned with the two aspects and will consider the steps which need to be taken to ensure that both written and verbal presentation satisfy requirements.

After emphasising the need to take proper account of institutional guidelines the chapter will cover advice on writing the thesis, dissertation or project in four main areas:

1. The style and structure of a report.
2. Guidelines on citations and references, including the citing of on-line material.
3. Writing chapters and sections.
4. Editing and proofreading.

In addition it covers:

5. Copying, printing and binding the report.
6. The oral defence of the work (the *'viva voce'* or *'viva'*).
7. Publishing parts of the work.

The chapter begins with a short review of institutions' research guidelines.

Student research ranges from undergraduate students who have one or two months in which to conduct and report on a project to doctoral students who have three years or more at their disposal. Although some of the topics covered would not normally apply to shorter projects – the *viva voce* for example – most of them, including subsequent publishing opportunities, do.

INSTITUTIONAL GUIDELINES

> READ INSTITUTIONAL GUIDELINES CAREFULLY AND ANNOTATE THEM. MAKE THE GUIDELINES A TOPIC OF AN EARLY MEETING WITH A SUPERVISOR OR HEAD OF RESEARCH, AND KEEP NOTES ON THE MEETING FOR FUTURE REFERENCE

All institutions that offer degrees publish regulations for the guidance of candidates. Before beginning a research project, it is clearly important for a student to read carefully and annotate the guidelines, and we would strongly recommend that the guidelines are again read carefully before beginning to write the project. Not all guidelines express clearly and precisely what is expected, and in any case, students should always make the institution's expectations of standards an early (and documented) topic of discussion with a supervisor or department head. For example, one criterion for the degree of Master of Philosophy by research at York University was that an MPhil thesis should display:

> a good general knowledge of the field of study; a comprehensively particular knowledge of some part or aspect of the field of study; some original contribution to knowledge or understanding.

and a PhD Thesis should display:

> an original contribution to knowledge or understanding
> (www.york.ac.uk/admin/gso/guidance.htm – accessed September
> 2001)

Figure 8.1 lists the criteria relevant to each type of report. Questions and clarifications which might arise from these stated requirements might be, for example:

Level	Description	Criteria
First degrees and some Masters' degrees which require the completion of a project	Project report	1. A well structured convincing account of a study, the resolution of a problem, or the outcome of an experiment
Master's degree by study and dissertation	Dissertation	1. An ordered, critical and reasoned exposition of knowledge gained through the student's efforts
		2. Evidence of awareness of the literature
Master's degree by research	Thesis	1. Evidence of an original investigation or the testing of ideas
		2. Competence in independent work or experimentation
		3. An understanding of appropriate techniques
		4. Ability to make critical use of published work and source materials
		5. Appreciation of the relationship of the special theme to the wider field of knowledge
		6. Worthy, in part, of publication
Doctoral degree	Thesis	1. to 6. As for Master's degrees by research
		7. Originality as shown by the topic researched or the methodology employed
		8. Distinct contribution to knowledge

Figure 8.1 Criteria to be satisfied by reports on student research

1. How comprehensive is a 'comprehensively particular knowledge' expected to be?
2. Is the PhD also expected to demonstrate a 'good general knowledge in the field of study'?
3. How should the difference between 'some original contribution' and 'an original contribution' be judged? Is this the only significant difference of depth between the two?

Guidelines will always embody both 'compulsory' elements which require students to conform to some standard, and 'free' elements where students can display their own approach. Thus, under compulsory elements the need to observe certain typographical standards – for example, that text be typed double-spaced with at least a 40mm margin on the left and a 25mm margin on the right – should be noted. Similarly, the work of others must be properly referenced, with some institutions prescribing the form that citation of particular types of work such as journal articles should take. Non-negotiable guidelines on matters such as binding, appendices, margins, figures, and pictures are almost always given. Students should simply note and conform to them. Not to do so will usually automatically lose marks.

A useful way of coming to grips with requirements is for a student to scrutinise theses or dissertations in their library. However, the research reports produced by students who were successful in the past can for a variety of reasons be an imperfect guide to present standards. Modestly written reports may have been redeemed by a brilliant defence at an oral examination. The standards of the field may have changed as more research has been completed.

IF WORD LIMITS HAVE BEEN EXCEEDED, CONSIDER PLACING SOME LESS IMPORTANT BACKGROUND MATERIAL IN AN APPENDIX

A question frequently asked by students is: 'How long should a report be?' If their institution prescribes the length of a report, students should, unless otherwise instructed, work to a 10 per cent margin of error. In other words, if the length is specified at 20,000 words, 18,000 to 22,000 will normally be taken as hitting the specified target. Shorter or longer may be seen as evidence of not achieving the requisite depth, or not being able to focus, and be penalised as such. If no length is specified, the only real answer to this question is that the thesis should be of sufficient length to accommodate everything which is needed for students to discuss and prove within a context any proposition which they put forward. An examination of university library shelves will show the wide variations in length which have arisen in order to satisfy this general requirement. Experience has, however, indicated that the vast majority of successful doctoral theses do not exceed 100,000 words (500 pages of A4 size double-spaced). Because of a tendency of some research students towards 'overkill' most universities now place an upper limit on wordage.

Appendices may not be considered as part of the word count in which case material in excess of limits can usually be accommodated by relegating less important material to an appendix. This needs to be done with care, so as not to disrupt the argument and flow of the work.

STYLE

> WHAT IS IN THEORY A GOOD ARGUMENT MAY NOT BE PERCEIVED AS SUCH IF IT IS NOT ORGANISED AND COMMUNICATED WELL

The prime aim of writing research is to convince examiners that the student has satisfied the appropriate criteria to gain a qualification. Therefore, it can be said that students are not writing for the world at large but, in the first instance, for one or two individuals who will be acting for the institution or the degree-awarding body in the examining process.

Having said that, a report which communicates good information effectively will be perceived as far superior to one which suggests it might contain information of value, but is unable to communicate it with any clarity. What is in theory a good argument may not be perceived as such if it is not organised and communicated well.

The development of style is an important educational objective. There is a danger that the ultimate written account, if weak in other aspects, may fail because it is not easily readable. A short time spent in developing an attractive and communicative style will be of much benefit both in writing about the research and thereafter.

Gunning (1952) developed a useful measure known as the 'fog index'. This description was used because it was felt that long words and sentences made for 'foggy' reading. Briefly:

> Fog index = 0.4 (Average sentence length plus per cent of words more than two syllables in length.)

Words that are capitalised, are combinations of short simple words, or, for example, arise because of the use of the past tense, are excluded from the calculation. Gunning regarded a 'fog index' of 12 as the danger point, beyond which text becomes difficult to read. The grammar check feature in Microsoft Word also provides summary statistics using similar calculations.

As would be expected, writers on style also express views on paragraph length.

The general recommendation is that paragraphs should be short, both for clarity and textual appearance. They should, however, be long enough to accommodate a particular idea. Very short paragraphs of one or two sentences should be avoided both for reasons of appearance and to avoid the reader having to switch too rapidly from one point to another.

Attention to the suggestions made in this section will only help towards achieving good style. Students should not be under the impression that there is a common style which they should seek to attain. Cooper (1990) states:

> Good style is one which makes some impact on the reader. The author's personality comes through. Poor style usually refers to writing which is involved, where there is little attempt to structure the writing, and usually where the vocabulary range is limited.

Monroe, Meredith and Fisher (1977) refer to 'stimulus-response' patterns in their book *The Science of Scientific Writing* which, although addressed to scientists, makes many points of general relevance. Some common patterns which they select are:

Question–Answer: When you generate a question in writing, the reader will expect you to answer the question soon.
Problem–Solution: If you present a problem the reader will expect a solution or an explanation of why no solution is forthcoming.
Cause–Effect, Effect–Cause: Whether you have mentioned a cause first or an effect first, once you have mentioned one, the reader will surely expect you to mention the other.
General–Specific: When you make a general statement, the reader will expect to be supplied with specifics, which clarify, qualify or explain the general statement.

Although the presentation of ideas is the very nub of the process of writing there is little that can be added here except, again, to encourage students to devote some of their time to reading literature which has been written specifically on the topic of report writing.

It should always be remembered that the greatest interest to students will be whether or not their report has reached the required standard. At research degree level it will not be possible to assess beforehand the reaction of the examiner and it is therefore essential that a comparable level of criticism is obtained from other sources. Obviously, there will be much dependence on the supervisor but this should not preclude students from seeking expert opinion elsewhere. Colleagues, family and friends will often be able to spot illogicalities or omissions in the argument and to give useful criticism of readability and style.

Students should not be too disappointed if their first attempts to convey their ideas and arguments are heavily criticised. People often need time to develop the requisite skills. This reinforces the need to start writing as early as possible.

One aspect of style on which students often seek guidance is the use of personal pronouns. Because student projects are usually of a personal nature there is obviously much scope for 'I' to be used throughout the report. This may be avoided by the use of the passive voice. Thus, 'It was found that...' is used instead of 'I found that...'. Traditionally, in most fields of research, the use of the passive voice has been favoured with the major exception being the use of 'we' in mathematics. In recent times, however, limited use of the first person has been accepted, if only to break up the monotonous effect of continued use of the passive voice. In terms of readability, passive sentences tend to correlate with less reading ease; again, Microsoft Word's grammar check feature suggests changes to the passive voice and indicates the percentage of passive voice sentences.

Writers on style such as Cooper make a number of suggestions as to how impact may be increased. Thus Cooper (1990, pp. 127–36) stresses the importance of analogy, metaphorical language, repetition for emphasis, rhythm, and the avoidance of cacophony and 'phoney' style. Broehl and Shurter (1965, pp. 81–7) argue that writers should make effective use of verbs, be direct, use an appropriate tone, and be specific. Students should give consideration to suggestions of this type.

It may be useful to adopt as a model the writings of a specific author or of workers in a particular field such as economics that maintains a tradition of clear communication of technically difficult subjects. It should be remembered, however, that the research report is typically aimed at a narrower audience and that certain knowledge and predispositions on the part of the reader can be assumed. Thus, though jargon would usually be frowned on in a text that was to have wide non-specialist readership, it may be used in a research report in order that it be clear what the report is about, avoiding the ambiguities that are often associated with everyday language.

ABBREVIATIONS AND ACRONYMS SHOULD BE USED WITH CARE. MANY OF THESE MAKE FOR VERY DIFFICULT READING

Abbreviations and acronyms should be used with care. Abbreviations and acronyms in common currency ('the EU' for the European Union) may be used freely, but a high quantity of abbreviations make for very difficult reading. Students should be aware that although they know their work inside out, an examiner will not, and it is distracting in the extreme to keep having to refer to a glossary to figure out what is meant by multitudes of abbreviations. If in doubt, even with the addition of a few more words into a restricted word limit, students should spell abbreviations out in full.

Apostrophes are commonly misused, and can provide an annoyance if not an actual change in meaning. Apostrophes are only used to denote possession (the girl's bike) or missing letters (wasn't) but not plurals ('the girl's cakes' is correct, not 'the girl's cake's'). They are not used for the possessive for his, hers or its (the bike is hers/its wheels are broken). When 'it's' is used for 'it is' (a letter is excluded) then an apostrophe is used (it's raining/it is raining). A good tip is to spell out in full 'it is', 'do not' and so on, rather than use 'it's', 'don't', etc. Apostrophes are often, incorrectly, used in dates ('the 1960s' is correct; 'the 1960's' is not).

Tables and Figures

Students are often confused by the difference between a table and a figure. The simplest rule is that, apart from the descriptive margins, tables are composed wholly of numerical data whereas, with certain exceptions, all other items of this form are figures. It should be remembered that figures or tables which have not been originated by the writer should be acknowledged and full details of sources given within the figure or table itself. These should be cited in the same way as a reference – for example, a figure of the three main types of competitive strategy should give the source in something resembling the following way: 'Source: Porter, M., *Competitive Strategy*, 1980, page number' with the full reference, in the appropriate style, given in the reference list.

Increasingly, students wish to include computer output in their writings. It is usually necessary to prune such output drastically and a decision is often needed as to whether selected pages should be incorporated as figures or whether larger quantities should be bound in as appendices or presented as a separate portfolio.

CITATION

A research report differs from many other forms of writing (a newspaper article, for example) in that it should make clear what material and ideas have been originated by the student and what is owed to the work of others. At most levels of research, it is important that students show that they have understood the ideas of others and this they can only do by demonstrating their ability to summarise and present them within their own framework. This means that under most circumstances the amount of direct quotation should be fairly small.

Quotations are extracts (usually short) from someone else's work. References give source information for quotations or ideas. These are discussed in some detail below. A bibliography is a list of all books consulted (but not necessarily referenced). The level of degree sought will govern how full and comprehensive a listing of all relevant literature in the field should be. At doctoral level, students are normally expected to demonstrate that they have understood the body of relevant literature in full.

Direct Quotations

Obviously, there are situations where direct quotation is necessary. For example, a study of the impact of Kierkegaard on 20th-century writers on existentialism would be strange indeed without substantial quotations of Kierkegaard himself and sections of text from later authors that appear to have been influenced by him. Equally, much theory in applied mathematics, say, is of such elegance that it would be foolish to rewrite it in a different notation. It would not be acceptable to produce a research report dominated by quotations from various authors glued together by an occasional sentence supplied by the researcher.

Quotations

Quotations should be properly differentiated from the main body of the research report. Indented, single-spaced text is perhaps the easiest way of clearly differentiating the longer passage. Quotation marks are generally used for a short passage or a single sentence. Variations such as a different typeface (for example, italic), may also be used. In either case, the work from which the quotation is drawn should be clearly referenced as discussed below. Institutions often give guidelines for quotations similar to the above, which should, of course, be followed.

Citation Guidelines

PROVIDE A REFERENCE IN CASES WHERE AN INEXPERT READER MIGHT THINK IDEAS WERE THE WRITER'S OWN WHEN THEY ARE NOT

Where other authors are drawn on for ideas rather than direct quotation, things can be a little more difficult. Many ideas are in the public domain. The rules about referencing other work to some extent depend on the customs of the field in which the student is writing. On the whole, a defensible approach would be to reference only those ideas which an inexpert reader might think were the researcher's own even though they are not. In such cases the researcher should try to give the original source of the idea and also the place where it was found. Thus, if the researcher has become familiar with, for instance, information theory and the work of Shannon through reading someone else's introduction, the following practice should normally be used:

> As Brillouin's (1962, pp. 13–20) account of Shannon's (1948) work shows, the theory of information has much in common with ideas from fields of physics such as thermodynamics.

Although it may seem pedantic, students are well advised to treat the matter of citation with considerable care. An examiner is likely, for instance, to consider that a student who consistently attributes ideas to later workers, rather than the person who actually originated them, has conducted an inadequate literature search. Thus, in the example above, attributing Shannon's theory to Brillouin may give a poor impression.

A poorer impression still is created by students who use the ideas of others without attribution. Indeed, if this is done by directly using someone else's writings without due attribution this constitutes plagiarism, which all academic institutions consider a serious offence against academic regulations. See Chapter 4 for further discussion on this.

Concern has recently grown about increasing incidences of plagiarism in theses and dissertations and it seems likely that there will be growing pressures to test them for plagiarism using the software that is available for this purpose.

Reference Style

Citation style must comply with whatever standards are prescribed by the institution. As far as citation in the body of the text is concerned there are two broad schemes in use: the Harvard method as followed in this book (last name of author plus date) or the numerical approach (also called the Vancouver method) in which each reference is given a specific number. The former approach is simpler and permits the insertion or deletion of references at will, whereas in the latter case any references which are introduced or deleted at a later stage will necessitate all of the subsequent numbers being changed. The Harvard method is predominantly the one required by institutions and publishers. In some cases a research institution will also ask for the page number of the work cited to appear in the text reference (name/date/page(s)) if it can be specifically attributed to a page or pages.

In a reference, emphasis may be given to the idea or to the author, as:

> ... a strong claim is made that a system of equity must exist within every society (Smith, 1999, p. 63) [idea emphasis]
> ... Smith (1999, p. 63) has argued that every society should have within it a system of equity [author emphasis]

Initials or first names should *not* be included in citations. Where there is a possibility of confusion – if there were two or more Smiths working in the field then the following form should be adopted:

> ... Alan Smith (1999) has argued ...

If an author has written two works in the same year, these are usually distinguished by an a or b suffix:

Smith (1999a) has argued that every society ...
Societies institutionalise ethical systems through legal frameworks
(Smith, 1999b)

These should be similarly cited in the reference list at the end of the report (see below).

Some institutions specify that references in the text should always be complete in themselves, with name, date, page information even if that leads to repetition of a name already mentioned:

Alan Smith (Smith, 1999, pp. 26–36) has argued ...

Otherwise it would be normal to complete the reference information from the text flow:

As Alan Smith (1999, pp, 26–36) argued ...

Numbered references (the Vancouver method) appear in the order of appearance, that is, the first reference in a work is numbered '1', the second '2' and so on. If reference 1 is cited later in the work, it still carries a number 1:

Smith[17] continues and develops the argument proposed by Martyn[1]

With a numerical approach it is better to make reference to a name as well, where possible. For example:

Smith[17] argued that every society should have within it a system of equity

is preferable to

It has been argued[17] that every society ...

WHATEVER REFERENCE STYE IS ADOPTED – STAY CONSISTENT. FOLLOW THE INSTITUTION'S GUIDELINES

Students should read and follow an institution's guidance notes on reference style, and if in doubt, ask their supervisor for clarification.

Reference List

References within the body of the text confirm that students are able to relate their thoughts to the body of knowledge. These must relate exactly to the list which will be positioned at the end of their report. External examiners usually scrutinise the list of references very carefully and will be critical of lists which are not comprehensive, accurate and well presented.

If the numerical approach is adopted the text and reference can be linked easily in either direction. One limitation is that a reader may not be able to establish quickly whether a particular author has been referenced. As numerical lists run in number this means that listings of authors will not be alphabetical, and an author with several different (non-sequential) citations will appear in different places in the list.

With the Harvard name/date approach someone reading through the list of references will not be able to turn immediately to that part of the text to establish what ideas have been taken from the author in question unless an electronic version is being read. The alphabetic listing does, however, allow the reader to see very quickly and easily which authors (and which works of these authors) have been cited.

A standard procedure should be adopted for references. A commonly employed approach is:

a) *for books:* author followed by initials (in capitals), year of publication (in brackets), title of book (underlined or in italics, with edition if any), page numbers, place of publication (if known), publisher:

> Smith, A. (1999), *Exploring Social Theories* (2nd Edition), pp. 61–63,
> New York: Rothwell Press.

b) *for articles:* author followed by initials (in capitals), year of publication (in brackets), title of article in single quotation marks, name of journal (underlined or in italics), volume number, issue, page number:

> Smith, A. (1999), 'Systems of Equity; a New Paradigm', *Journal of Social Theory*, Vol. 22 issue 3, p. 42.

THE IMPORTANT ISSUE IS TO PROVIDE A REFERENCE TO A WEBSITE WHICH CAN BE LOCATED EASILY IN THE REFERENCE LIST AND EXPLORED BY OTHER RESEARCHERS

At the time of writing, no standard protocol for website referencing has been widely accepted. It is sensible to treat web references as nearly as possible like textual references. Again, one consistent style should be followed, which will be the one prescribed for textual references by the institution. Page numbers would not be cited. The important issue is to provide a reference which can be located as easily as possible in the reference list and which can be followed by other researchers if desired.

A website reference would make reference to the author if known, or the title of the site if not. It should always include the date accessed. The reference in the reference list should cite the URL (unique resource locator) in full. It is usual form never to cite the http:// part, but always to cite the www. part:

> *In text:* 'The approach made by just-desserts.com (2001) is of particular interest here.'
> *Reference list:* Just-desserts.com (accessed 24 April 2001) *The Perfect Tiramisu*, www.just-desserts.com/recipes/tiramisu

Students should note that website URLs change frequently, and a website reference will not usually provide as permanent a reference source for future researchers as will a text reference.

Reference Shortcuts

Certain Latin words and phrases encountered in scholarly works can be useful in referencing. These are normally italicised, as are other foreign language phrases not in common currency.

Sometimes a student may wish to quote something which contains an obvious grammatical, typographical or numerical error. In this case '(*sic*)' typed as here within brackets and placed immediately after the error will demonstrate that the error was from the original source and not the writer's error ('Senator Quayle's often-quoted 'Potatoe' (*sic*) reference was widely seen to be . . .').

Other Latin abbreviations are:

a) *Et alia* (abbreviated to *et al.*): and others. This allows multiple authors (Smith, Kelly, Martyn and Robinson, 1998) to be referenced as (Smith *et al.*, 1998). *Et al.* is normally used beyond two authors – Smith and Kelly would appear as (Smith and Kelly, 1998).

b) *Ibidem* (abbreviated to *ibid.*): in the same work. This allows *successive* reference to the same work without repeating the name each time. This replaces all details in the immediately preceding reference, but should be followed by page number:

> Owen's later work was strongly challenged by Fowler (1998, p. 34). Fowler further makes the point that ritual involves a change in the individual's position within a society, not just to the individual in isolation (*ibid.*, p. 38).

c) *Opere citato* (abbreviated to *op. cit.*): in the work cited. This requires the author's name and page number, and refers to a *work already cited* (but not a sequential reference):

> Fowler (1998, p. 34) disagrees strongly with Owen's later works, particularly his 'Magic and Ritual' (Owen, 1966), a position also endorsed by MacAlister and Murphy (1999) and Hamman (1999). Fowler further makes the point that ritual involves a change in the individual's position within a society, not just to the individual in isolation (Fowler, *op. cit.*, p. 38)

d) *Loco citato* (abbreviated to *loc. cit.*): in the place cited. This is used with the author's name and is similar to op. cit. but is more precise as it refers to the same passage in a book already cited:

> Fowler (1998, p. 34) disagrees strongly with Owen's later work. Fowler further makes the point that ritual involves a change in the individual's position within a society, not just to the individual in isolation (Fowler, *loc. cit.*).

e) *Confer* (abbreviated to *cf.*): compare.

> Fowler (1998, p. 34) disagrees strongly with Owen's later works particularly his 'Magic and Ritual' (Owen, 1966), *cf.* MacAlister and Murphy (1999).

Doctoral theses often contain several hundred references and the work involved in ensuring that these are systematically presented and are error free can be formidable. There are advantages at this level in using bibliographic software of the type referred to in Chapter 4 or of utilising some of the facilities of word processing packages which will be discussed later in this chapter.

References to Reports with Unknown Authors

Reports should be referenced as with authors except that the title of the report, in full or in clearly understandable and identifiable abbreviated form, should feature in the text and the reference list instead of the name of the author. Thus:

> The population of Germany grew by 6.2% between 1988 and 1998 but is forecast to grow at only 1.1% between 1998 and 2008 (OECD Population Report, 2000).

Bibliography

As discussed in Chapter 4, students should make the compilation of a final bibliographic listing as easy as possible by keeping notes in proper format as they go.

As new references are added, the bibliography will need to be extended.

Bibliographies should always be alphabetically listed, using the surname of the first author. Students who use Microsoft Word can use the Table – Sort AZ command to order a list alphabetically so long as it is prepared in the right format in the first place (last name, initial, etc).

CHAPTERS AND SECTIONS

Order of Chapters

There is a logical order with which (subject to variations imposed by local regulations) most written reports on research should conform:

Title page
Acknowledgements
Preface
Contents page
List of tables
List of figures
List of other types of materials
Chapters
Appendices
List of references
Bibliography
Index

All of these sections need not necessarily appear. Undergraduate reports, for example, may include only the title page, contents and chapters. Because of the need to relate the research to a body of knowledge, a list of references will be a vital element of masters' and doctoral theses. Such a list will include all relevant works which have been consulted by the author and which have been cited in the text. The emphasised distinction is between a 'List of References' and a 'Bibliography': the latter is normally a comprehensive coverage of books and journals in an area, even though these may not have been cited in the text.

Chapter headings should have been suggested by students as part of their research proposal and will probably be consistent with the following logical order:

1. Introduction – the aims and the context of the research.
2. Survey of prior research – normally as a review of relevant literature.
3. Methodology/research design – how the study was planned and why it was planned that way.
4. Results of the research – what was found.
5. Analysis – discussion about the meaning of what was found.
6. Summary, conclusions and recommendations for further research.

As an example, we can look at a student research project that has been concerned with an in-depth study of the use of Web-based marketing in four organisations, the end purpose of which is to suggest criteria that distinguish successful from unsuccessful applications. At a minimum it would probably contain the following material which will eventually need to be assembled into chapters:

1. Prior research on Web-based marketing.
2. Prior research on factors affecting the success of Web-based marketing approaches.
3. Prior research on factors affecting the success of other marketing approaches.
4. Account of study in organisation A.
5. Account of study in organisation B.
6. Account of study in organisation C.
7. Account of study in organisation D.
8. Analysis of the individual case studies and construction of an overall scheme for the prediction of success.
9. Conclusions.

In this example, many implicit decisions have been made about topics that will *not* be explored. For example, no reference is apparently made to the literature on the management of innovations, though this might well be relevant.

ABOVE ALL, CHAPTERS SHOULD BE ORDERED LOGICALLY

There are a number of problems on how this material should be combined into chapters. Should items 1 and 2 be combined into one chapter – probably the best way if the factors affecting success appear to be highly specific to Internet marketing – or should they be separated? If, however, the factors affecting success seem to be relatively consistent across various marketing approaches, there may well be a case for combining items 2 and 3. Similarly items 4, 5, 6 and 7 could be run in parallel through several chapters looking at applications of different types of model in each of the four organisations in turn or, alternatively, each item could form a single chapter. The most important determinant of the choice should be the way in which the material will be analysed (but above all, chapter order should be logical and draw on common sense).

A further important concern is the degree to which the ground will be prepared in earlier chapters for what is to come later. Some of the previous work on factors determining success will be highly relevant; and some of the field observations will be more appropriate than others. In either case it is sensible to highlight these particular aspects as they are dealt with so that the readers know that they should pay especial attention to them.

Order of Chapter Sections

The ordering of the sections within each individual chapter is a continuation of the process of logically structuring the report. Let us return to our example of the project on factors affecting the success of Web-based marketing. The chapter on prior research could be presented, for example, chronologically, categorically, sequentially, or in order of perceived importance.

A decision on the nature of the major chapter sections will not be sufficient for students to commence writing the body of the text. It will be necessary to continue the process of subdivision once or even twice further. Again, a number of options are available with, probably, categorical and chronological ordering being most appropriate in the marketing example being used.

In our example on Web-based marketing, the major sections might be:

1. The extent and range of Web-based applications in marketing.
2. Major successes and failures of Web-based marketing applications.
3. Suggestions in the literature for new Web-based developments in marketing.

Major section 1 may then be subdivided into market research, advertising, and sales transactions (*by categories*), each of which in turn may be discussed under the headings of 'early applications', 'recent developments', and 'likely future developments' (*chronological*).

Probably the most common (and least ambiguous) method of referring to each separate section is to use hierarchical numbering. This enables students' approach to the logical breakdown of their writings to be clearly seen, particularly in the contents page. Thus, if in our example 'Survey of prior research' is Chapter 2 of the thesis the early sections of that chapter would appear in the contents page numbered as:

2. Survey of prior research.
   2.1   The extent and range of Web-based applications in marketing
      2.1.1 Market research.
         2.1.1.1   Early applications
         2.1.1.2   Recent applications
         2.1.1.3   Likely future developments
      2.1.2 Advertising
         2.1.2.1   Early applications
         2.1.2.2   Recent applications

and so on.

Different hierarchies of headings should be differentiated by different type-styles (size, emboldening, italicising, underlining, etc.) as well as by numbers. These should of course be kept absolutely consistent throughout the report.

It is not customary to subdivide chapters further than is indicated above; to do this would result in too fragmented an approach causing the reader to be in some difficulty in remaining with the main theme being propounded.

Detailed guidance on format is often provided by a student's institution. For example, chapter titles may be required to be 14 point upper case and centred, and main sections 12 point bold, ranged left.

Report Organisation

An approach that many students find useful for identifying the chapters and breaking them down into subsections is to depict the structure of the report in the form of an outline.

Figure 8.2 shows the structure already discussed for our Web-based marketing example. Note that the section, subsection and sub-subsection numbering suggested for Chapter 2 would also be continued into other chapters.

Where to Start

The first chapters written will almost always undergo several redrafts. It may well be that much of what is written will be excluded altogether, as an argument matures. Also, material which seemed to be best placed in one section may evidently be better in another.

All this is to be expected. Research and its writing does not often progress in a linear and orderly way.

Although the introductory chapter probably suffers more revision than any other, research students should endeavour to write this as soon as is feasible together with chapters which review the current state of knowledge, and describe what the approach to their research will be.

To receive supervisor feedback at an early stage on style and coherence, it may be better to start writing a chapter at the heart of the work. This also has the advantage of giving some feel for what needs to be introduced prior to this chapter.

STUDENTS SHOULD EXPECT TO HAVE TO REORGANISE THEIR MATERIAL AND SHOULD THEREFORE ALLOW TIME FOR THIS IN THEIR PLANNING

Effective strategy in report writing requires that the student has a clear picture of the report as a whole. As indicated earlier, however, this will continue to evolve until a great deal has already been written. In reality, then, it is unlikely that the

```
┌─────────────────────────────────────────────────────────────────────┐
│                                                                       │
│  1  Introduction                                                      │
│                                                                       │
│  2  Survey of prior research                                          │
│     2.1   The extent and range of Web-based applications in marketing │
│           2.1.1   Market research                                     │
│                   2.1.1.1 Early applications                          │
│                   2.1.1.2 Recent applications                         │
│                   2.1.1.3 Likely future developments                  │
│           2.1.2   Advertising                                         │
│                   2.1.2.1 Early applications                          │
│                   2.1.2.2 Recent applications                         │
│                   2.1.2.3 Likely future developments                  │
│           2.1.3   Logistics                                           │
│                                                                       │
│  3  Success factors for Web-based marketing                           │
│                                                                       │
│  4  Success factors for Web-based applications outside marketing      │
│                                                                       │
│  5  Case study A                                                      │
│                                                                       │
│  6  Case study B                                                      │
│                                                                       │
│  7  Case study C                                                      │
│                                                                       │
│  8  Case study D                                                      │
│                                                                       │
│  9  Analysis of case studies to determine success factors in the      │
│     implementation of Web-based marketing                             │
│                                                                       │
└─────────────────────────────────────────────────────────────────────┘
```

Figure 8.2 An example of hierarchical headings using numbered sections

final result will closely resemble the initial structure proposed. Students should expect to have to reorganise some of their material and should therefore allow time for this in their planning.

The Preface

There may be a number of observations which students would like to make which are not part of the research proper. These observations will include introductory or explanatory remarks which students would communicate verbally if the opportunity were available.

In a scholarly research work, it would be normal to confine these personal observations to scene-setting comments related to the research process or the work itself. Examples of preface material might include comments about finding an initial topic unprofitable before turning to the research which is to be reported on; or that a foundation for the research had been achieved by the completion of a dissertation in a similar field for the purpose of satisfying the requirements of a lower-level degree course.

If joint work has been involved the extent of the collaboration can be clearly stated in the preface. It will usually contain brief thanks and acknowledgements which as a matter of courtesy should range from academic to material helpers. In the former category would come experts in the subject area who may have carried no responsibility for the student but gave of their time to provide advice, or perhaps computer specialists who put considerable effort into sorting out some of the difficulties which are often encountered in using or developing software. Material help may include people who have helped with transcription, editing or proof-checking. Supervisors should, of course, justify acknowledgement if they have carried out their responsibilities effectively.

Depth of Coverage

The point in writing a student report is to demonstrate knowledge, ability, and – depending on the level of research degree being followed – comprehensiveness. In a higher degree, argument must be supported appropriately, leaving students who must comply with a constraint on length in some difficulty as to what can be included. If, therefore, it is felt that the thesis will probably be too lengthy it may be decided to omit whole sections (and justify the omission if called upon at an oral examination) rather than reduce the level of detail throughout.

> A PAGE BUDGET SPECIFYING THE NUMBER OF PAGES TO BE DEVOTED TO EACH SECTION IS A USEFUL DEVICE

Students who are unhappy at the thought of taking a prior decision to delete sections may choose to edit the paper at the end to achieve reductions in length to comply with word limits. Nevertheless, they should not pose themselves an impossible task. Coverage in depth clearly reduces the scope for breadth of discussion, and some students do encounter problems by attempting too broad a coverage. As well as leading to excessive length such an approach also carries the risk of superficiality. A page budget specifying the number of pages to be devoted to each section is a useful device for identifying this problem in advance.

Among the possible cures are:

a)   the researcher becomes less ambitious;

b) the researcher relies more heavily on summaries and reviews by previous authors rather than attempting to evaluate peripherally related areas of previous work;

c) reference is made to the researcher's own work published elsewhere;

d) whole sections may be omitted.

Interpretation of Data

STUDENTS SHOULD ALWAYS BE CONSCIOUS OF THE PERSON OR TYPE OF PERSON WHO WILL BE RESPONSIBLE FOR EVALUATING THEIR WORK

Student report writing is a very specific form of communication, with the final product initially forming a one-to-one link between the student and the examiner. Particular note must therefore be taken of interpretation of data. Students should always be conscious of the person or type of person who will be responsible for evaluating their work.

Obviously, if the examiner is on the staff of the student's institution and there is no external assessment, the student should seek guidance before commencing writing. If external assessment is involved, students could sensibly make 'behind the scenes' enquiries to establish whether the examiner has any pronounced views on writing or content.

It may perhaps appear to be a little cynical to suggest the need to seek to satisfy the examiner of the report. Research theses in particular should after all be seen as an addition to the general body of knowledge, available to all. Research students are nevertheless undertaking an examination and their primary objective to achieve success is quite clear. The publication of books and articles based on the material contained within the research report can come later.

Selection from the Data

By the time students have completed their reading, data collection and analysis this will have resulted in the accumulation of a mass of data held in one form or another. The problem is to transform the data into a well-ordered, appropriately interpreted account written at the requisite level.

Although students should have been selective at the data gathering phase some material will probably be superfluous to the requirements of the report. Thus, as stated earlier, if the fieldwork has involved a large sample survey it would be inappropriate to include all completed questionnaires in the report (although these should be retained as primary source material which may be called for at an oral examination). One example of the questionnaire should be included. If, say, several in-depth interviews have been tape recorded it may be desirable to include the transcripts of some or all of these in an appendix (or, again, retain the transcripts for possible use in an oral defence). Computer-based statistical analyses will probably lead to many different outputs. If a representative example of a set of outputs conveys the point the researcher wishes to make then there is no need to include every page of output in the report.

In purely scientific terms an important question with research theses is the degree to which the findings would be repeatable if the work were to be undertaken by another researcher. This implies that as well as an adequate description of the methods of analysis, primary data should ideally also be made available to the reader. Chapter 6 contains observations on how researchers might make their data more widely available.

IF THERE IS A DOUBT AS TO WHETHER A PARTICULAR SET OF DATA
SHOULD BE INCLUDED, THEN INCLUDE IT (SPACE PERMITTING)

Taking into account comments made earlier on the level of presentation a reasonable rule for research degree students to follow is that if there is any doubt as to whether a particular piece of data should be included, then include it; deletion is always possible at the editing stage. In reality, the final versions of most theses will omit material that was included at the draft stage, or relegate supporting material to appendices.

EDITING AND PROOFREADING

In writing a research report for examination, students should tend to include rather than exclude material which may support their arguments. If this policy has been adopted it is reasonable to assume that when all the chapters have been written there will be much scope for pruning.

Editing is, however, not simply a matter of eliminating text but is designed to ensure that the research findings are rewritten and presented in as effective a manner as is possible.

Editing the Individual Chapter

Monroe *et al.* (1977) have suggested that good style emerges from naming, predicating and modifying. The first two of these suggestions are the basis of the 'core' elements of a sentence, which comprise the subject, verb and object. The core is then expanded by adding modifiers:

a) '... inflation is created' (the core idea);
b) '... inflation is created by excessive wage demands' (the core idea has been modified);
c) '... inflation is created by excessive wage demands rather than by an increase in money supply' (the modifier has been modified).

With each sentence being made up of a core idea and modifiers, Monroe *et al.* then proceed to recommend a procedure for editing:

1. Underline the core elements of every sentence. Find the subject, the verb and the object of the sentence. If there is more than one subject, verb or object, underline all of them.
2. Look for the core idea. Make sure that the main idea is expressed in the core of the sentence and that this basic idea makes sense by itself.
3. Check for modifiers between the core elements. As a general rule, ten or more words between the subject and the verb is too many.
4. Look for misplaced modifiers. When you come across a potential problem, draw an arrow from the modifier to what it modifies. A long arrow means that you should rework the sentence.
5. Check items for precision. Have you previously defined the specialised terms? Examine all words representing qualitative judgements. Check to make sure that you have used these correctly, that the reader will understand what specific qualities are being summed up in each word.
6. Avoid ambiguity. Rather than referring to the 'Health Service' stipulate the 'UK National Health Service'.

This technique is primarily concerned with the writing of articles, so the sentence-by-sentence procedure might be too laborious to apply to a lengthy report.

A HIGH-QUALITY ARGUMENT SHOULD ALSO BE PRESENTED IN HIGHLY READABLE FORM, BUT READABILITY DOES NOT IN ITSELF GUARANTEE QUALITY OF ARGUMENT

Readability does not in itself guarantee quality of argument. Students should be prepared to undertake a substantial rewrite of sections of a chapter if the whole reads unsatisfactorily. In doctoral or part-time research an interval of perhaps two years may have elapsed between the writing of early chapters on the literature survey and research methodology and the final chapters on analysis and the conclusions. Editing will include the task of incorporating additional and newer material into the body of the text and revising the structure as appropriate.

Editing the Full Report

If researching and writing simultaneously has been followed, students will eventually have assembled all sections of their report. Students with supervisors should have obtained regular guidance from them and this guidance will be reflected in the writing. Neither student nor supervisor will, however, be able to assess the whole report until the last section has been written and it is important that plans for final editing are clear.

Students should not expect more than one careful full reading from their supervisor. This should occur at the well-edited draft stage, in what the student considers final form, with no obvious errors or gaps. If editing alone is insufficient at that stage, and additional analysis is called for, project completion may be delayed significantly. In the absence of a supervisor the whole responsibility rests with the student although it may be possible to prevail upon an acquaintance (including a staff member) to assist.

The research degree student will appreciate that although a thesis will be examined as an exclusively individual effort (unless collaborative work is acknowledged) a bad fail will reflect adversely on the student's supervisor. This would be the case particularly if it is evident that little guidance has been given. If, however, a poor piece of work, supposedly in near-final form, is submitted to the supervisor, he or she will probably communicate this fact to an external examiner (particularly if the supervisor believes the relationship to have been a troublesome one).

Proofreading

The task of proofreading is the final stage of writing before the report is bound into its covers. In publishing, a 'proof' is original text which has been typeset and output for checking. Proofreading is the process in which the typeset material is checked for deviation from the original copy.

Two types of errors are recognised. *Systematic errors* are consistent misuse of, for example, apostrophes or the consistent misspelling of an author's name. *Random errors* would be, for example, the attribution of an article to the wrong author or a one-off misspelling.

A WORD-PROCESSING SPELLCHECKER IS NO SUBSTITUTE FOR CAREFUL PROOFREADING

Provided that students are aware of systematic errors and how to correct them, they are readily removed from a word processed text by a simple global edit. Most random errors that involve spelling mistakes will be detected by a spellchecker (though care still needs to be taken with word pairs such as 'practice' and 'practise' and grammatically logical sentences containing incorrect, but not misspelt words, will not be picked up). It is, therefore, useful as a preliminary to proofreading to spellcheck the text. A spellchecker alone is not sufficient.

Some further points to be noted on spellcheckers are:

1. Packages may be geared to USA or UK spellings. Most institutions are willing to accept USA spellings providing that they are used consistently. Students may need to obtain a USA dictionary, if they have learnt USA rather than UK English.
2. Students should be able to add technical terms, and so on, to the thesaurus used by the spellchecker.

Every student who writes a report for presentation should endeavour to ensure that, at least in the typographical sense, the report is perfect. It is reasonable to expect that 98 per cent of pages should be error free and that if this figure drops to 95 per cent students can expect adverse comment from the examiner.

A word of caution: proofreading one's own work is notoriously difficult. It is a much better idea to have someone – it can be a friend or colleague, rather than a professional proofreader – do it for you. Some useful rules for people who will be proofing their own material are:

a) read each line in turn;
b) recognise that intense concentration is needed and break off every few minutes;
c) read aloud;
d) take a sample (say 5 per cent) of those pages on which no errors have been noted and re-read them.

Particular attention should be paid to: spelling errors; faults in grammar, inconsistencies, for example, where the same reference is cited with a variety of different dates; and to omissions.

This stage of the writing is tedious but important. In contrast to the irritation created by numerous typographical mistakes, readers are much impressed by text which is error free.

COPYING, PRINTING AND BINDING

Proofreading is, of course, just one aspect of an important last stage of the report. Reproduction from the original text is now put in hand, determined by the several copies required by the institution's regulations and by the students them-selves. Usually a report will be word processed and printed on a desktop printer, then photocopied as necessary. Since it is one of these copies that will go to the examiner the impression created by it is important. In particular, it makes little sense to devote enormous care to structuring, editing and proofreading the report and then to obscure this by presenting a finished article which has been poorly reproduced.

As well as textual material, most research reports will contain a variety of tables, drawings and graphs. These are most conveniently produced using a spreadsheet package and should, where possible, be output directly into the word processor file containing the report. All non-textual material should be of good quality; clear, well-labelled and carefully produced.

The easiest way to import non-computer generated material such as drawings or photographs into a report is through a good quality scanner.

Copying

Once the finished text is assembled it usually needs to be photocopied. Where diagrams are to be separately incorporated into a printed text (that is, not scanned), blank pages should be left in the word-processed original to preserve the report pagination and to allow for gluing diagrams in afterwards.

It is sensible to use a reasonably sophisticated copier. Such a copier will also offer reduction facilities which are useful where diagrams and drawings need to be reduced to fit into the standard A4 format likely to be specified in most UK regulations.

Sometimes a student will wish to include photographs in the report. These should, if possible, be scanned into the report and printed, then copied. If the photographs are in colour, a colour printer and copier should be used if possible. Alternatively the photographs may be contained within a folder. Maps and photographs may be subject to copyright restrictions, and any such restrictions should be checked and complied with before they are used.

ALWAYS BACK FILES UP. ALSO, KEEP A PAPER COPY

Many students are subject to nightmare visions of draft chapters or even the whole draft report being destroyed by damage to the hard disk on which their word processed file is stored. Such accidents do happen and are perhaps more likely than might be expected. It is sensible therefore to backup copies of files onto disk. Provided there are at least two copies of the work in different physical locations, one should survive.

Further protection can be obtained by producing a paper copy for the supervisor. If all computer files are lost, it should still be possible to reconstitute the file by document scanning.

It is perhaps worth noting that in cases where computer files are erased by mistake they may be able to be restored by an expert. Files that have been lost by physical damage to the hard disk can sometimes also be recovered. If the student is uncertain how to proceed, which will almost certainly be the position in the latter case, it is better to approach an expert in data recovery.

PREPARING FOR A *VIVA VOCE* OR ORAL EXAMINATION

The doctoral student (and possibly master's student) will have to undergo a *viva voce* or oral examination (the two terms are normally used interchangeably). This, along North American lines, is often viewed as a 'thesis defence'. Doctoral students must always have this in mind during their writing and their draft chapters should include all supportive evidence needed. The defence of their argument should be concerned with the methodologies which were employed, the value claimed for their findings, and their recommendations for future work, and not with explaining and justifying the omission of corroborative material which should have been included in their thesis.

However long it may last, the oral examination will only require a fraction of the time that the research project as a whole will take. Nevertheless, it is far from a formality and should be prepared for thoroughly with a view to reinforcing the good opinion that the examiners should have formed from the study of the written report.

The wise student will also, at the earliest possible stage, have done some homework on the examiners and will attempt in the writing of the report to accommodate the implications of any preferences and attitudes which they are thought to hold. It is not too cynical to suggest either, particularly at doctoral level when the examiner will be an expert in the field, that references to the examiner's own work should be made. The academic world is, of course, well known for its conflicts of opinion on topics; students should accordingly do their best to ensure that there will be no antipathy towards them simply because of the line of argument they have pursued or the way they have presented it.

Students should, therefore, attempt to place themselves in the position of the examiners and consider the type of question which may be put in order to evaluate the report. To provide a systematic basis for anticipating how their research may be evaluated, a number of questions under each of those eight criteria of Figure 8.1 are posed here which the doctoral student should seek to satisfy. To do this a checklist proposed by Hansen and Waterman (1966) is drawn upon in part. In relating it to their own situation, students may find it useful to remember that for higher degrees individual examiners may well seek the advice of colleagues on particular aspects of the research outside their own sphere of interest or understanding.

Defining Criteria

Evidence of an original investigation or the testing of ideas

1. Was the aim of the research clearly described?
2. Were the hypotheses to be tested, questions to be answered, or the methods to be developed clearly stated?
3. Was the relationship between the current and previous research in related topic areas defined, with similarities and differences stressed?
4. Are the nature and extent of the original contribution clear?

Competence in independent work or experimentation

1. Was the methodology employed appropriate? Was its use justified and was the way it was applied adequately described?
2. Were variables that might influence the study recognised and either controlled in the research design or properly measured?
3. Were valid and reliable instruments used to collect the data?
4. Was there evidence of care and accuracy in recording and summarising the data?
5. Is evidence displayed of knowledge of and the ability to use all relevant data sources?
6. Were limitations inherent in the study recognised and stated?
7. Were the conclusions reached justifiable in the light of the data and the way they were analysed?

An understanding of appropriate techniques

1. Given the facilities available, did it seem that the best possible techniques were employed to gather and analyse data?
2. Was full justification given for the use of the techniques selected and were they adequately described? In particular were they properly related to the stated aims of the research?

Ability to make critical use of published work and source materials

1. Was the literature referenced pertinent to the research?

2. To what extent could general reference to the literature be criticised on the grounds of insufficiency or excessiveness?
3. Was evidence presented of skills in searching the literature?
4. Was due credit given to previous workers for ideas and techniques used by the author?
5. Is evidence displayed of the ability to identify key items in the literature and to compare, contrast and critically review them?

Appreciation of the relationship of the special theme to the wider field of knowledge

1. Was the relationship between the current and previous research in related topic areas defined, with similarities and differences stressed?
2. Was literature in related disciplines reviewed?
3. Was an attempt made to present previous work within an overall conceptual framework and in a systematic way?

Worthy, in part, of publication

1. Was the organisation of the report logical and was the style attractive?
2. With appropriate extraction and editing could the basis of articles or a book be identified?

Originality as shown by the topic researched or the methodology employed

1. To what extent was the topic selected novel?
2. Was there evidence of innovation in research methodology compared with previous practice in the field?

Distinct contribution to knowledge

1. What new material was reported?
2. To what extent would the new material be perceived as a valuable addition to a field of knowledge?
3. To what extent do the conclusions overturn or challenge previous beliefs?
4. Were the findings compared with the findings of any similar studies?
5. Was the new contribution clearly delimited and prospects for further work identified?
6. To what extent does the work open up whole new areas for future research?

Students should rehearse their answers to an appropriate selection from the above list of questions. This procedure should indicate what additional evidence will need to be taken into the examination. In the main, any supplementary material will relate to the data gathering and analytical phases, but may also include papers which students have written during their research.

BE PREPARED TO DEFEND, EXPLAIN, ELABORATE OR EVEN APOLOGISE FOR ANY PART OF YOUR WORK AT AN ORAL EXAMINATION

Whatever the level of the examination it should go without saying that students if called upon should be able to defend, explain, elaborate or even apologise for any part of it. In the last-mentioned respect, tolerance which may be extended towards the undergraduate is unlikely to apply in the case of the doctoral student. If an unacceptable weakness is found by such a student after a thesis has been submitted criticism is best anticipated and coped with by preparing a typed statement for distribution in advance of the examination.

The Oral Examination

Though practice varies depending on the level of the research project the oral examination will almost always involve at least two examiners. Usually, there will be at least one external examiner present for a postgraduate project and this may also be the case at undergraduate level.

In most UK universities the supervisor will not be appointed as the internal examiner for doctoral theses. Undergraduate or masters' students may, however, find that their supervisor happens to be functioning as an internal examiner and this will lead to a definite difference in attitude to that to which the student has been accustomed. At doctoral level in most UK universities the role of internal examiner is taken by another member of staff, perhaps with the supervisor's formal role being that of 'in attendance'. In addition, for a research project that has involved collaboration with outside bodies, various people not on the staff of the institution may also function as examiners.

The prime purpose of an oral examination is to satisfy the examiners that the report presented represents individual or acceptably collaborative effort. If collaboration has been involved evidence of the degree of cooperation will be considered.

The main concern of the examiners is to ensure that any claims made in writing can be justified and that the analytical methods used are understood. In part, the examiners are adding credibility to the report by approving it, particularly in the case of the research thesis which will then be included in bibliographies.

During the examination, however, students should expect to have to express opinions on topics which they may feel are peripheral to their studies in order to convince the examiners of their expertise in the wider field which includes their area of study. Although well able to defend their written arguments, uncertainty as to where the discussion might lead may give cause for prior concern. In particular, the student's craftsmanship and honesty are to some extent on trial as well as the merit of the research report itself.

As far as preparation is concerned individual students must decide what best suits them. It is obviously sensible to set aside a period of time beforehand so as to put oneself into the right frame of mind for the oral examination and reacquaint oneself with the details of a research report that may have been completed a significant number of weeks before. To provide such a period may cause difficulty for part-time students or those students who are now working in a full-time job. Perhaps the best mental preparation of all is for students to be in a position to exploit the strengths of their writing and to pre-empt criticism of its weaknesses. Obviously, the advice of a friend or colleague or even better a rehearsal for the oral examination can be of great help here. Doctoral students must remind themselves that insofar as their conclusions are concerned they should be original. They should have developed considerable expertise in their chosen topic area and be able to defend their thesis from a position of some strength. They must, however, expect questions which probe the scope of the topic, the nature of the target population, the type of cross-sectional comparison selected, and so on, at whatever level is appropriate for the type of research that has been conducted.

DO NOT TRY TO BLUFF AN EXTERNAL EXAMINER – IT IS USUALLY NOT POSSIBLE TO GET AWAY WITH IT

With regard to the examination itself possibly the most important advice that can be offered is that students should not attempt to 'pull the wool' over the examiners' eyes. Very rarely will it be possible to get away with this in front of experts.

Initially at least, the meeting will be conducted by the examiners with the student playing a very reactive role. At this stage it is important that students answer concisely but completely the questions put to them by the examiners, since the nature of their replies will be taken as a guide to the way in which the research itself was conducted. Therefore, where they are uncertain as to exactly what is meant by a question students should request further clarification before attempting to answer. Nor, where the question is difficult or subtle, should they hesitate to reflect so that they can give a considered reply. Though examiners are likely to concentrate on what they perceive to be the key strengths and weaknesses of the work in question, various examiners may differ as to what these are. Accordingly, students must anticipate that discussion will range widely and that questions will be posed on many different aspects of the research.

PUBLISHING THE RESEARCH

Once research is successfully completed it may be used as a basis for publication. Having the results of research published can be very satisfying. Most of the hard work has already been done and with a little time and effort it should be possible to transform a report, dissertation or thesis into a publishable form as a journal article, a book, or a chapter of a book.

Why Publish?

> PUBLISHING RESEARCH MEANS THAT OTHERS CAN SEE TANGIBLE EVIDENCE OF THE EFFORT AND INTELLIGENCE PUT INTO THE WORK

Getting into print is something that most researchers who care about their work and their ideas look to do at some point. It means that others can see tangible evidence of the effort and intelligence put into research, leading, possibly, to recognition both nationally and internationally. It can help in gaining promotion and job-seeking and, for those interested in becoming a consultant, teacher or speaker, it is invaluable in getting both name and ideas known. Above all, it can be very satisfying to see one's name in print on something that represents much time and effort, and in which pride can be taken. Published research creates professional pride in the achievement, and the institutions or organisations within which an author studies or works will share in the esteem.

In every case when publishing (other than those cases where the author acts as publisher also), consideration and approval will be needed from another party. For journal articles (assuming that they comply with the style requirements of the particular journal), the subject matter will be the dominant concern. This will also be pertinent in the case of a bibliography which is included within a journal. For 'stand-alone' books (and bibliographies, monographs, etc.) commercial considerations will arise.

Journals

Typically, scholarly journals carry papers of around 5000 words in length, accompanied by an abstract of around 100 words, which summarises the topics explored and key findings. Despite the many differences of emphasis across different journals and in different subject areas, four considerations should be universally sought:

1. *Weight:* Coverage should be substantive and significant. In most instances an article submitted to a scholarly journal will be subjected to external review. It should state clearly how the paper contributes to the wider body of knowledge – in other words, why it has been written and why the reader should read it.
2. *Accessibility:* All but the more esoteric journals appeal to practitioners, teachers and students as well as to researchers. An article must be comprehensible to the main audiences of the journal.
3. *Ease of decision making:* Publishers and editors tend to have many papers submitted to them. Make sure that when they receive an article and covering letter they want to read on.
4. *Relevance and implications for readers:* Papers should always state what it is about a study or findings that is relevant to readers. It is good practice to point to areas for further research, and to point to questions or implications for practitioners.

In the case of scholarly journals, a literature review should have identified some obvious recipients for a paper derived from a thesis. Failing that, advice is normally available from supervisors. Most publishers will have an extensive catalogue of information on their journals on the Internet, with sample copies normally available. Two or three target journals should be selected and scanned to gain a feel for the style. It is most important to read the 'Notes for Authors' which appear in almost all journals (again, these are normally found on journal websites). Contact the editor, who will usually be delighted that you are interested, and will be genuinely pleased to talk through the journal's editorial policy and give help and ideas.

Certain 'rules' should be adopted, which are largely common sense and apply equally to reports, speeches, presentations, and the like.

1. Plan. Construct the skeleton of your article before starting the article proper.
2. Introduce. Incorporate the purpose, the objectives and the message of your article into your opening paragraphs.
3. Discuss. Run through your findings or argument as outlined in your introduction.
4. Break. Use headings and subheadings to break up the text.

5. Illustrate. Use charts, tables or graphs (and/or illustrations) to explain difficult points, present data or simply to make the text more readable.
6. Illuminate. If at all possible bring your points to life by using case histories, quotes and anecdotes to enliven an article.
7. Summarise. Present, clearly and concisely, the key conclusions and recommendations arising from your research.
8. Conclude. Finish with recommendations as to how the conclusions might stimulate eventual application and further research.

If an article is rejected without reasons being given, ask why. Editors will usually offer honest and constructive criticism which can help in the future. If it is simply because the editor has an overabundance of copy, or does not feel that the article fits the journal, try one of the other publications identified initially.

It is often possible to prepare more than one article for prospective publication. This may be achieved by dividing up the research report content in order that distinctly different topics can be addressed. Alternatively, a topic may be written up at two levels: one directed towards academics and the other towards practitioners.

Books

Taking length into account, the longer form of research report may be seen to equate with a book. A scholarly book normally comprises about 60–80,000 words. Before publication of the findings in this form is achieved, however, two major hurdles must be surmounted: a publisher has to be found, and the work will need to be rewritten to become 'reader friendly'.

Very few instances of a thesis being published as it stands are known to the authors. The requirements of the target market for a book will usually differ considerably from those of the examiners. Further, though the publication lead time for an article appearing in a journal may be long, the corresponding period for the publication of a book is usually longer still. But the publisher will be much concerned with the commercial prospects of a book and substantial time may be taken in evaluating what those might be. It behoves the aspirant to plan well in advance if publication in book form is sought and, if a publisher can be found, to recognise the demands of rewriting not long after completing the thesis.

Most of the advice on style and submission for journals relates also to books.

Monographs

The term 'monograph' may be open to a number of interpretations. A monograph may be viewed as a short book to which the comments made in the previous sections may apply. Alternatively, organisations which support research may be prepared, for altruistic reasons, to facilitate the production and distribution of a monograph based on the research report.

Some journal editors and publishers are willing to include 'monographs' alongside standard issues within a particular volume of a journal. Such 'extended articles' of, say, 40,000 words satisfy the publisher's requirements for original copy and the researcher's desire to promote the findings, often in an attractive format, more quickly than would be possible through a book.

Review Articles and Bibliographies

Researchers should, as a routine part of their studies, establish and appraise current thinking in the area that they are exploring. At doctoral level their search of existing literature should be thorough and may well support the production of a review article on the field. Equally, publication may be possible as a bibliography in book form or as a bibliographic article to be included within a journal. As far as bibliographies are concerned, they are more valuable if the compiler presents the material thematically and supplements the list of sources with a synthesis and a critique.

CONCLUSION

This chapter has dealt with the communication of the research work to an audience. Primarily, in the first instance at least, this audience consists of university examiners. But in a wider sense, a research student's output joins the scholarly body of knowledge and should be able to communicate to others in the research community. To this end, we specifically addressed the issue of scholarly publication.

Communicating ideas clearly is far more important than literary brilliance. The student should make sure to situate the written work within the institution's regulations, and conform to guidelines on word limits, page layout, reference style and so on.

Most research students will be asked to discuss their work at an oral examination or *viva voce*. Preparation is vital for such an event, and to this end we have set out a number of 'generic' questions and topic areas which may well be explored by an examiner at a *viva*.

Finally, and by no means least, we have discussed a number of issues relating to publication. Bringing one's work to a wider audience, and thus adding to the body of accessible research knowledge is, in a sense, where the research student started. Without knowledge being captured in a way that others can build on, disagree with or have insights and ideas sparked from it, scholarship itself would hardly exist.

CHAPTER SUMMARY

EVALUATION OF A RESEARCH REPORT: will involve certain criteria that depend, in part, on the level of the research. Students should be familiar with these.

STUDENTS AT LOWER LEVELS: may have only a very limited opportunity for feedback from their supervisors on their research. It is especially important for such students, therefore, to assume as much responsibility as they can for their research report.

STUDENTS SHOULD START WRITING THE REPORT AS EARLY AS POSSIBLE: accepting that initial drafts are readily modified later in the light of comments received.

THE WRITTEN ACCOUNT OF RESEARCH: should be of sufficient quality in respect of structure, style and content.

THE QUALITY OF PRESENTATION: of a report can be an important factor in influencing an examiner and should be given full consideration.

AN ORAL EXAMINATION: will certainly be required at doctoral level and may be required at lower levels. As far as possible, it should be carefully planned for and students should rehearse answers to questions that might be put to them.

> PUBLICATION: of your research findings, whenever appropriate, should be sought as the final outcome of your research studies.

Appendices

Appendix 1

AN EXAMPLE OF TOPIC ANALYSIS

In this appendix we provide an example of topic analysis as a student would present it in the initial stage of a research degree.

Student's Name:

Date:

Area of proposed study:

THE IMPACT OF E-BUSINESS ON DEMAND FOR ACCOMMODATION IN CENTRAL LONDON FROM THE UK FINANCIAL SERVICES INDUSTRY

1. Introduction

The adoption of the Internet Protocol as a basis for communication among organisations has meant a massive reduction in the cost of computer communication between those inside the organisation and those outside. This has led to Internet-based communication via the Web now being a relatively low cost option for such communication. As a result, organisations operating within the Financial Services Industry (FSI) all operate intranets. This makes it even easier than in the early 1990s to relocate back office functions, such as call centres, to low cost regions. Intranets might also be expected to encourage home working (teleworking), defined for the purposes of this study as working part or all of one's time from home, within the industry. Much of the work of financial analysts and consultants is knowledge intensive and might be pursued more effectively at home. Indeed, in the early 1990s in the pre-Internet era this led to many management consultancy firms adopting hot-desking. Nonetheless, there remain issues, such as security, which might lessen the impact of e-business on the encouragement of home working.

The Internet and intranets could, potentially, have a large impact on the extent to which employees in the City of London financial services sector work in Central London (recognising that substantial activities are carried out outside the City itself in areas such as Docklands).

2. Research Questions

The proposed study would be concerned with the following research questions:[1]

a) Will the development of e-business and, in particular, the development of Internet-based information services and company intranets really encourage home working (teleworking) in the financial services industry?
b) What is the likely growth in home working in the City of London FSI over the next few years?
c) How will the development of e-business and, in particular, the development of Internet-based information services and company intranets affect the relocation of back offices outside Central London?
d) Where will back offices be relocated?
e) What are the factors encouraging greater growth of home working in the financial services industry?
f) What are the implications of changes to the amount of home working in London and to the extent of relocation of back office functions by the London FSI brought about by e-business?[2]

3. Prior Research in the Area[3]

There seems to be little published academic research on the social impacts of e-commerce or e-business. The literature, which appears to be mainly geographical, on the impact of information (and communication) technologies relates to the pre e-commerce era. A typical, and useful, example is the paper by Longcore and Rees (1996) that considers IT-induced restructuring in New York's financial district from the perspective of the impact on building construction and back-office location decisions. A more quantitative study by Sivitanidou (1997) of the impact of the information revolution in Los Angeles finds clear evidence of a decreasing attractiveness of Central Los Angeles relative to the outer regions. Such findings might be expected to translate in the case of the City of London to a tendency to decentralisation into South East England. Michie (1997) considered the impact of IT on the London Stock Exchange in the context of a historical study. Aside from the fact that this study deals with an important City institution it raises the issue of the conflict between the globalisation of financial markets and the need for them to be locally regulated. This may have implications for the location of intranet Web servers, etc. Two studies were founded on call centres: Richardson and Marshall (1996) and Bristow *et al.* (2000). These, however, are focused mainly on the implications of call centres for regional development outside London, the former with Tyne and Wear, the other more general. They deal then with the obverse of the problem of interest in this topic analysis.[4]

Much more academic research has been published on home working/teleworking. A fairly recent review was provided by Shin *et al.* (2000), while Lococo *et al.* (2001) discuss some of the drivers of teleworking. Authors such as Vilhelmson and Thulin (2001) and Makridakis (1995) raise the issue of telework as the forthcoming form of work that will supplant existing organisational forms. The latter paper is particularly interesting given Makridakis's long association with forecasting research. A number of other authors explore the organisational implications of teleworking, which are likely to be a major issue addressed by the proposed mail questionnaire. Thus Duxbury and Neufeld (1999) consider how teleworking affects communication within the organisation, while Ruppel and Harrington (2001) consider the interesting, from a City perspective, question of the role of intranets in information sharing. Lindstrom *et al.* (1997) provide a classification of telework that is likely to be useful in the proposed exploratory interviews. Another aspect of teleworking explored by Stanworth (1998) is its relative lack of success compared with the claims of its proponents; this is a possible issue with regard to the London FSI. In addition, the teleworking literature contains important strands dealing with teleworking from employees' and from a feminist perspective. Since these are not so relevant to this topic analysis they are not presented here.[5]

A further literature that may well be relevant in assessing the implications of the findings of the study proposed is that concerned with the modelling of the London office market, e.g. Daniels and Bobe (1993); Wheaton *et al.* (1997); Hendershott *et al.* (1999).[6]

4. Value of the Research

Academic value

There appears to be little published research on the impact of e-business/ e-commerce on industry. The FSI is a particularly interesting one in that it is: a) knowledge intensive; b) a major UK industry; c) comprises a number of very diverse sectors; and d) has particular concerns of security and regulation. As an industry, it also appears under-researched. The study would contribute to the body of academic knowledge.

Although there has been more research on teleworking most of it is general rather than industry specific. Teleworking's impacts on the FSI might be considered to be of particular academic interest. On the one hand, it is a wealthy industry with a large proportion of knowledge workers who might be expected to embrace teleworking. On the other hand, the special considerations of security and confidentiality and regulatory constraints might be seen to reduce teleworking's attractiveness, as might the benefits of working in close physical proximity to other financial services professionals.

The impact of information and communication technologies (ICT) and e-business on the London office market seems to have attracted relatively little attention. The findings of the study would have a bearing on that.

Social value

Financial services is an industry in which London is a world leader. For that reason the London office market is a valuable one. The potential impacts of e-business through changes to the rate of back office relocation and home working are of interest not only to firms in the FSI, that have to plan for their Central London accommodation needs but also property market professionals such as large, international firms of estate agents. Given the long time-scales for office construction or refurbishment, forecasts of those changes are important. Moreover, if the predicted effects are negligible it is important to know this too.

Again, the findings of the study are of potential interest to those concerned with the planning and development of transport in the London region.

Relocation of back offices from London has important implications for UK regional development. Increases in home working would influence development in the South East and, possibly, elsewhere in the UK. It follows that the findings of the study have interest from a wider perspective of UK regional planning.

Personal value

The study would be of personal value to the researcher, since it is linked to anticipated career development and would take advantage of the researcher's existing contacts.

5. Proposed Research Design

Data collection would involve three main stages:

1. A programme of exploratory interviews with firms operating in each of

the main sectors of the FSI as defined by the Financial Services Authority.[7] These interviews would be aimed at identifying what questions should go into the questionnaire. It is considered important to interview respondents in each of the main FSI sectors since, in principle, the scope for home working and/or back office relocation in, say, retail banking may differ from that of, for example, pensions fund consultancy. It should be possible to arrange these initial interviews through personal contacts.

2. The distribution of a mailed questionnaire to human resource directors in major firms in all the sectors of the FSI. It is the intention that this would contain mostly closed questions to be analysed using SPSS.[8]

3. The carrying out of a number of in-depth interviews with firms in each of the main sectors of the FSI. These firms would be recruited through the Stage 2 survey.[9]

Analysis of the survey data would be by means of SPSS. The interviews would be analysed to identify the main influences on FSI firms' location decisions.[10]

NOTES

1. This particular set of research questions is oriented towards the demand for office space. Obviously, other focuses could have been adopted, e.g. looking at employee attitudes to home working, the organisational implications of back office relocation, etc.

   If this topic analysis is accepted then these research questions will need to be refined after an in-depth literature review and, possibly, the Stage 1 interviews.

2. In refining this topic analysis into a research proposal it would be necessary to look at how the recipients of the mail questionnaire would be selected.

3. All the literature searches reported in this section were reported using *Web of Science*. Attempts to use various search engines proved completely unsuccessful. All searches generated thousands of apparently irrelevant references and the poor facilities for sophisticated Boolean searching offered by most search engines meant that it was impossible to refine these searches to make them useful. This is the opposite to the situation in Chapter 4 but, as pointed out there, it is a common experience. *Web of Science* is a much more reliable starting point in most cases.

4. The references discussed in this paragraph were generated using a title, abstract and keyword search on *Web of Science* search using the search term: **(E?business OR E?Commerce OR Internet OR Intranet* OR IT OR Information Technolog* OR ICT OR Information and Communication Technolog*) AND (Business* OR Office* OR Compan* OR organi?* Work*).**

5. The literature described in this paragraph was found using a title, abstract and keyword search on *Web of Science* using the search term: **(telework* OR Home?work*) AND (Work OR Business* OR Organi?ation*).**

6. The references discussed in this paragraph were generated using a title search on *Web of Science* search using the search term: **London AND Office.**

7. These interviews might under some circumstances be replaced by a set of focus group discussions.

8. To maximise the response from busy, senior people it is best to avoid very many open ended questions. However, a question on *important issues not covered by the questionnaire* at the end of it may provide useful guidance for Stage 3.

9. Recruiting firms to be studied in more depth on the back of a mailed survey is often the easiest approach to adopt. Whether that will be the case here is another matter. It may be necessary to make use of personal contacts and if they are not sufficiently good the viability of the topic may be in doubt.

10. If the topic analysis is accepted further thought will need to be given to how the interview data will be analysed when the research proposal is worked up. NUD.IST and Decision Explorer would, for instance, be computer tools that might be used for this purpose.

NB: Notes are provided here for explanation of the inclusion of the various aspects featured in this example. They would not normally be used in a topic analysis document.

References

Bristow, G., Munday, M. and Gripaios, P. (2000), 'Call centre growth and location: corporate strategy and the spatial division of labour', *Environment and Planning A*, **32,** 3, 519–38.

Daniels, P.W. and Bobe, J.M. (1993), 'Extending the boundary of the City of London – the development of Canary Wharf', *Environment and Planning A*, **25,** 4, 539–52.

Duxbury, L. and Neufeld, D. (1999), 'An empirical evaluation of the impacts of telecommuting on intra-organizational communication', *Journal of Engineering and Technology Management*, **16**, 1, 1–28.

Hendershott, P.H., Lizieri, C.M. and Matysiak, G.A. (1999), 'The workings of the London office market', *Real Estate Economics*, **27**, 2, 365–87.

Lindstrom, J., Moberg, A. and Rapp, B. (1997), 'On the classification of telework', *European Journal of Information Systems*, **6**, 4, 243–55.

Lococo, A., Yen, D.C. and Chou, D.V. (2001), 'Telecommuting: its structure, options and business implications', *International Journal of Technology Management*, **21**, 5–6, 475–86.

Longcore, T.R. and Rees, P.W. (1996), 'Information technology and downtown restructuring: The case of New York City's financial district', *Urban Geography*, **17**, 4, 354–72.

Makridakis, S. (1995), 'The forthcoming information revolution – its impact on society and firms', *Futures*, **27**, 8, 799–821.

Michie, R.C. (1997), 'Information technology and the London Stock Exchange since 1700', *Journal of Historical Geography*, **23**, 3, 304–26.

Richardson, R. and Marshall, J.N. (1996), 'The growth of telephone call centres in peripheral areas of Britain: Evidence from Tyne and Wear', *Area*, **28**, 3, 308–17.

Ruppel, C.P. and Harrington, S.J. (2001), 'Sharing knowledge through intranets: A study of organizational culture and intranet implementation', *IEEE Transactions on Professional Communication*, **44**, 1, 37–52.

Shin, B., Sheng, O.R.L. and Higa, K. (2000), 'Telework: Existing research and future directions', *Journal of Organizational Computing and Electronic Commerce*, **10**, 2, 85–101.

Sivitanidou, R. (1997), 'Are center access advantages weakening? The case of office-commercial markets', *Journal of Urban Economics*, **42**, 1, 79–97.

Stanworth, C. (1998), 'Telework and the Information Age', *New Technology Work and Employment*, **13**, 1, 51–62.

Vilhelmson, B. and Thulin, E. (2001), 'Is regular work at fixed places fading away? The development of ICT-based and travel-based modes of work in Sweden', *Environment and Planning A*, **33**, 6, 1015–29.

Wheaton, W.C., Torto, R.G. and Evans, P. (1997), 'The cyclic behavior of the Greater London office market', *Journal of Real Estate Finance and Economics*, **15**, 1, 77–92.

Appendix 2

A SELECT BIBLIOGRAPHY ON STUDENT RESEARCH

As elsewhere, this bibliography is aimed at doctoral students. However, many of the texts are suitable for students on undergraduate or taught postgraduate programmes.

Topic selection and development

Ackoff, R.L. (1978), *The Art of Problem Solving Accompanied by Ackoffs Fables*, New York: Wiley.
Buzan, T. (1995), *The Mind Map Book* (Revised Edition), London: BBC Books.
Checkland, P. (1981), *Systems Thinking, Systems Practice*, Chichester: Wiley. A book that provides a different way of thinking about social systems. It deals with one of the well-known methodologies used in social sciences.
de Bono, E. (1994), *De Bono's Thinking Course* (Revised Edition), London: BBC Books.
Van Grundy, Jr, A.B. (1988), *Techniques of Structured Problem Solving*, New York: Van Nostrand Reinhold.

Theory of knowledge

Cohen, M.R. and Nagel, E. (1934), *An Introduction to Logic and Scientific Method*, London: Routledge & Kegan Paul. A standard text on scientific method. Considers both experimental and observational studies and history. Useful discussion on principles of measurement.

Gardiner, P.L. (1959), *Theories of History*, New York: Free Press. Comprehensive set of readings on what is meant by historical knowledge with applications to other fields also.

Kuhn, T.S. (1962), *The Structure of Scientific Revolutions*, Chicago IL: University of Chicago Press. The classic text on the role of paradigm shifts in scientific discovery.

Popper, K. (1968), *The Logic of Scientific Discovery* (2nd Edition), London: Hutchinson. The classic logical positivist account of scientific method including the notion of falsifiability.

General texts on research methodology

Behavioural research

Cherulnik, P.D. (2001), *Methods for Behavioral Research: A Systematic Approach*, London: Sage Publications. A text for researchers in psychology.

Cohen, M.Z., Kahn, D.I. and Steeves, R.H. (2000), *Hermeneutic Phenomenological Research: A Practical Guide for Nurse Researchers*, London: Sage Publications.

Kerlinger, E.N. (1992), *Foundations of Behavioural Research* (3rd Edition), London: Harcourt Brace. General discussion of the underlying philosophy of behavioural and related research plus useful introduction to discriminant analysis, factor analysis, experimental design, etc.

Thines, G. (1977), *Phenomenology and the Science of Behaviour*, London: Allen & Unwin. An account of psychological research from the phenomenological perspective of the philosopher Husserl.

Educational research

Cohen, L., Manion, L. and Morrison, K. (2000), *Research Methods in Education* (Fifth Edition), London: Routledge.

Maruyama, G. and Deno, S. (1992), *Research in Educational Settings*, London: Sage Publications.

Health care research

Peat, J. (2001), *Health Science Research: A Handbook of Practical Methods*, London: Allen & Unwin.

Management research

Easterby-Smith, M., Thorpe, R. and Lowe, A. (2001), *Management Research: An Introduction*, London: Sage Publications. An overview of a variety of different approaches to management and organisational research and issues in their application in practice.

Policy research

Judd, C.M. and Kenny, D.A. (1981), *Estimating the Effects of Social Interventions*, Cambridge: Cambridge University Press. The title reflects a central concern of policy researchers.

Rossi, P., Freeman, H.E. and Lipsey, M.W. (1999), *Evaluation: A Systematic Approach* (6th Edition), Thousand Oaks, CA: Sage Publications. A comprehensive account of policy evaluation methods.

Social research

Robson, C. (1993), *Real World Research: A Resource for Social Scientists and Practitioner Researchers*, Oxford: Blackwell. A useful guide to social science student researchers especially practitioners such as teachers.

Rubin, A. and Babbie, E.R. (2001), *Research Methods for Social Work (with Infotrac)*, London: Wadsworth Publishing.

Texts on specific aspects of research methodology

Burrell, G. and Morgan, G. (1979), *Sociological Paradigms and Organisational Analysis: Elements of the Sociology of Corporate Life*, London: Heinemann. A classic account of types of knowledge about social systems.

Dubin, R. (1978), *Theory Building* (Revised Edition), London: Collier Macmillan. An examination of the construction of various types of theory in the social sciences but relevant to many other fields.

Glaser, B.G. and Strauss, A.L. (1968), *The Discovery of Grounded Theory: Strategies for Qualitative Research*, London: Weidenfeld & Nicholson. A key reference for the student engaged in exploratory research. Distinguished by its insistence on the interaction between data gathering and theory development. Also contains novel ideas on data sources. Intended for social scientists but of interest to all researchers making use of field observations.

Hantrais, L. and Mangen, S. (eds) (1996), *Cross National Research Methods in the Social Sciences*, London: Pinter. A text on a particular form of comparative research of especial interest to sociologists and policy researchers.

Kvale, S. (ed.) (1992), *Psychology and Postmodernism*, London: Sage Publications. Despite its title, the various contributions in this volume provide a good overview of the relevance of postmodernist ideas in both the humanities and the social sciences.

Schön, D.A. (1991), *The Reflective Practitioner*, Aldershot: Ashgate Publishing. The book for professionals engaged in research based on their own practice, e.g. architects.

Strauss, A.L. and Corbin, J. (1990), *Basics of Qualitative Research: Grounded Theory Procedures and Techniques*, London: Sage Publications. Grounded theory approaches have become very popular in the social sciences of recent years. A more up-to-date account of the ideas.

Warwick, D.P. and Osherson, S. (eds) (1973), *Comparative Research Methods*, Englewood Cliffs, NJ: Prentice Hall. Excellent set of readings on methodological problems in an important area of social science research.

Data sources and data gathering

Research in progress

Current Research in Britain: the Humanities, Boston Spa: British Library.
Current Research in Britain: Biological Sciences, Boston Spa: British Library.
Current Research in Britain: Physical Sciences, Boston Spa: British Library.
Current Research in Britain: Social Sciences, Boston Spa: British Library.

Theses

www.theses.com, *index to theses with abstracts accepted for higher degrees in the universities of Great Britain and Ireland.*

BRITS (1989), *The BRITS Index: an index to the British thesis collections held at the British Library Document Supply Centre and London University/British Theses Service (1971–1987)*. Godstone: BRITS/IPI.

wwwlib.umi.com/dissertations/, *Dissertation Abstracts.*

Official publications/statistics

British Library, *British National Bibliography for Report Literature.*
www.fedworld.gov/onow/, ordering service for US Government reports.
www.open.gov.uk, reports, etc. from UK Government departments.
www.un.org/depts/unsd/, United Nations statistics.

Europa.eu.int/comm/eurostat/, European Union statistics.
www.fedstats.gov, US Government statistics.
www.statistics.gov.uk, UK Government statistics.

Data archives/publicly available datasets

Elder, G.H., Pavalko, E.K. and Clipp, E.C. (1993), *Working with Archival Data – Studying Lives*, London: Sage Publications.

Foster, J. (1995), *British Archives – a Guide to Archival Sources in the UK*, London: Macmillan.

Levitas, R. and Guy, W. (eds) (1996), *Interpreting Official Statistics*, London: Routledge.

Surveys and questionnaire design

De Vaus, D. (1998), *Surveys in Social Research* (4th Edition), London: Allen & Unwin. Oriented to the use of surveys.

Oppenheim, A.N. (1992), *Questionnaire Design, Interviewing and Attitude Measurement* (New Edition), London: Pinter Publishers. A standard text on questionnaire design and administration.

Thompson, M.E. (1997), *Theory of Sample Surveys*, London: Chapman & Hall. The statistical theory.

Interviewing

Gubrium, J.F. and Holstein, J.A. (eds) (2001), *The Handbook of Interviewing: Context and Method*, London: Sage Publications.

Less conventional data gathering

Lee, R.M. (2000), *Unobtrusive Methods in Social Research*, Buckingham: Open University Press. A focus on methods rather than measures.

Simpson, D.K. (1990), *Psychology, Science and History: an Introduction to Historiometry*, New Haven, CT: Yale University Press. The methods are mainly conventional statistics as used by psychologists but applied to a field (history) where data are usually seen as primarily qualitative.

Webb, E.J., Campbell, D.T., Schwartz, R.D. and Sechrest, L. (1966), *Unobtrusive Measures: Non Reactive Research in the Social Sciences*, Chicago IL: Rand McNally. A classic compendium of imaginative approaches to gathering social data without causing bias in the observations.

Webb, E.J., Campbell, D.T., Schwartz, R.D., Sechrest, L. and Grove, J.B. (1981), *Non-Reactive Measures in the Social Sciences*, Dallas: Houghton Mifflin. Elaboration of the earlier ideas.

Analysis and analytical techniques

We have attempted, somewhat arbitrarily, to distinguish analysis techniques that are not necessarily statistical in nature from those that undoubtedly are. However, many of our 'non-statistical' techniques make extensive use of statistical methods.

Case studies

Hammersley, M., Foster, P. and Gomm, R. (eds) (2000), *Case Study Method: Key Issues, Key Texts*, London: Sage Publications.

Yin, R.K. (1994), *Case Study Research: Design and Methods*, (2nd Edition) London: Sage Publications. The standard text in fields such as business and management and information systems.

Content analysis

Gahan, C. and Hannibal, M. (1998), *Doing Qualitative Research Using QSR NUD·IST*, London: Sage Publications. N-VIVO is a PC-based tool that is much used nowadays for the content analysis of written and interview data.

Titscher, S., Meyer, M., Wodak, R. and Vetter, E. (2000), *Methods of Text and Discourse Analysis: In Search of Meaning*, London: Sage Publications.

Meta-analysis

An approach to the consolidation of data from a number of studies conducted by previous researchers.

Noblit, N. and Hare, R.D. (1988), *Meta-Ethnography Synthesising Qualitative Studies*, London: Sage Publications.

Rosenthal, R. (1991), *Meta-analytic Procedures for Social Research* (Revised Edition), London: Sage Publications.

Pattern recognition

Everitt, B. (1978), *Graphical Techniques for Multivariate Data*, London: Heinemann. A classic statistical approach supplemented by pictorial techniques.

McLachlan, G.J. (1992), *Discriminant Analysis and Statistical Pattern Recognition*, New York: Wiley. A statistical approach.

Qualitative analysis techniques

Denzin, N.K. and Lincoln, Y.S. (1998), *Collecting and Interpreting Qualitative Materials*, Thousand Oaks, CA: Sage Publications. A comprehensive overview that considers the use of computer methods also.

Silverman, D. (1999), *Doing Qualitative Research: A Practical Handbook*, London: Sage Publications. As the title implies a good account of a variety of approaches to the analysis of qualitative data.

Quasi-experiments

The idea of quasi-experimental designs is important to researchers in areas where control of all the experimental factors is not possible – for example, education, organisation studies.

Campbell, D.T. and Stanley, J.C. (1966), *Experimental and Quasi Experimental Designs for Research*, Boston, MA: Houghton Mifflin. Clear non-statistical discussion of ideas underlying experimental design model and of ways of extending it to field studies where not all factor levels can be controlled.

Cook, T.D. and Campbell, D.T. (1979). *Quasi Experimentation, Design and Analysis Issues Field Settings*, Chicago, IL: Rand McNally. Later, more comprehensive, examination of methodological problems of causal explanation based on field observations and ways of overcoming them.

General statistical texts

Reference is made to a number of statistical texts of a comprehensive nature. The level of mathematical/statistical knowledge required to use a text varies widely from one text to another in an era when statistical analyses are almost always carried out by students using a computer package.

Bagozzi, R.P. (ed.) (1994), *Advanced Methods of Marketing Research*, Oxford: Blackwell. A discussion of a wide variety of multivariate statistical methods and their application. Of interest to social scientists, information systems researchers, etc.

Box, G.E.P., Hunter, W.G. and Hunter, J.S. (1976), *Statistics for Experimenters: An Introduction to Design, Data Analysis, and Model Building*, New York: Wiley. A standard text on statistical methods for experimental scientists.

Green, P.E., Tull, D.S. and Albaum, G. (1988), *Research for Marketing Decisions* (5th Edition), Englewood Cliffs, NJ: Prentice Hall. Requires knowledge of elementary statistics but otherwise little mathematical expertise. Remarkably comprehensive, albeit a little dated, coverage of the underlying concepts and marketing applications of many different multivariate techniques including regression, experimental design, discriminant analysis, cluster analysis, etc. Particularly good on multidimensional and other scaling techniques. Still very useful to researchers in any field who are willing to make the effort to translate the examples into a context relevant to their research.

Tabachnik, B.G. and Fidell, L.S. (2001), *Using Multivariate Statistics* (4th Edition), Needham Heights, MA: Allyn & Bacon. A comprehensive text showing how the various statistical procedures can be implemented using a variety of standard statistical packages.

Statistical techniques

Cluster analysis

Everitt, Brian *et al.* (2001), *Cluster Analysis* (4th Revised Edition), London: Arnold.

Discriminant analysis

Klecka, W.R. (1980), *Discriminant Analysis*, London: Sage Publications. Covers practical application of classical techniques of discriminant analysis in the social sciences.

McLachlan, G.J. (1992), *Discriminant Analysis and Statistical Pattern Recognition*, New York: Wiley. Applications in computing and electronics and in pattern recognition.

Experimental design model

Cox, D.K. (1958), *Planning of Experiments*, New York: Wiley. A classic text that gives a clear description of the statistics of experimental design methods with a range of applications in the physical, biomedical and agricultural sciences.

Hinkelmann, K. and Kempthorne, O. (1994), *Design and Analysis of Experiments*, Chichester: Wiley. A more up-to-date text.

Keppel, G. and Saufley, W.H. Jr (1980), *Design and Analysis: A Student's Handbook*, San Francisco, CA: W.H. Freeman. A guide to the use of experimental design methods in practice with particular reference to applications in psychology.

Factor analysis

Bartholomew, D.J. (1987), *Latent Variable Models and Factor Analysis*, London: Griffin.

Lewis-Beck, M.S. (ed.) (1993), *Factor Analysis and Related Techniques*, London: Sage Publications.

Kaplan, D. (2000), *Structural Equation Modeling: Foundations and Extensions*, London: Sage Publications. Of recent years, structural equation modelling has emerged as the preferred approach to latent variable models such as factor analysis.

Loglinear analysis

A technique for the analysis of tabulated data that has grown greatly in popularity in recent years.

Agresti, A. (1996), *An Introduction to Categorical Data Analysis*, New York: Wiley.

Hagenaars, J.A. (1990), *Categorical Longitudinal Data: Log-Linear Panel Trend and Cohort Analysis*, London: Sage Publications. Applications in the analysis of social surveys.

Regression analysis

Allen, D.M. and Cady, E.B. (1982), *Analyzing Experimental Data by Regression*, Belmont, CA: Lifetime Learning. A book aimed at experimental scientists.

Doran, H.E. (1989), *Applied Regression Analysis in Econometrics*, New York: Dekker. Econometricians are amongst the largest users of regression methods. Furthermore, their applications of the technique are often sophisticated.

Edwards, A.L. (1985), *Multiple Regression and the Analysis of Variance and Covariance* (2nd Edition), New York: Freeman. Broader coverage of the regression model taking in its relationship with Analysis of Variance.

Jaccard, J., Turrisi, I.L. and Won, C.K. (1990), *Interaction Effects In Multiple Regression*, London: Sage Publications. An important topic in the practical application of the regression model

Kaplan, D. (2000), *Structural Equation Modeling: Foundations and Extensions*, London: Sage Publications. Nowadays, a common approach to the examination of sets of regressions.

Pedhazur, E.J. (1982), *Multiple Regression in Behavioural Research: Explanation and Prediction* (2nd Edition), New York: Holt Rinehart & Winston. Good discussion of applications of regression in the social sciences including path analysis.

Scaling

Cox, T.F. and Michael, A.A. (1994), *Multidimensional Scaling*, London: Chapman and Hall. Includes a disk with scaling software.

Green, P.E., Carmone, F. J. jr and Smith, S.M. (1989), *Multidimensional Scaling: Concepts and Applications*, Boston, MA: Allyn & Bacon. Covers the uses of multidimensional scaling in marketing and allied fields.

van der Ven, A.G.G.S. (1980), *Introduction to Scaling*, Chichester: Wiley. Clear account of both unidimensional and multidimensional scaling techniques.

Writing research reports

Becker, H.S. (1986), *Writing for Social Scientists: How to Start and Finish Your Thesis, Book or Article*, Chicago, IL: University of Chicago Press. An excellent guide on writing longer research reports in the social sciences. Particularly strong on the process of writing.

Day, A.F. (1996), *How to Get Research Published in Journals*, Aldershot: Gower.

Ebel, H.E, Bliefert, C. and Russey, W.E. (1990), *The Art of Scientific Writing: From Student Reports to Professional Publications in Chemistry and Related Fields*, Weinheim: VCH. Guide to writing research reports in the physical and biological sciences.

Turabian, K. (1996), *A Manual for Writers of Research Papers Theses and Dissertations* (6th Edition), Chicago, IL: University of Chicago Press.

Turk, C. and Kirkman, J. (1989), *Effective Writing*, London: E&FN Spon.

Williams, J.M. (1990), *Style: Toward Clarity and Grace*, Chicago, IL: University of Chicago Press. A very practical guide to effective scholarly writing based on theoretical considerations.

Appendix 3

BOOKS AND ARTICLES CITED IN THE MAIN TEXT (EXCLUDING THE TOPIC ANALYSIS)

Because many serial publications, such as dissertation abstracts, are now available in CD-ROM form we have not given frequencies of publication, since these are generally higher for the CD-ROM form than the paper form but may vary depending on the precise nature of the library subscription.

Ackoff, R.L. (1978), *The Art of Problem Solving Accompanied by Ackoffs Fables*, New York: Wiley.

Bolton, N. (1977), *Concept Formation*, Oxford: Pergamon.

Brillouin, L. (1962), *Science and Information Theory*, New York: Academic Press. British reports, translation and theses received at the British Library Lending Division, British Library, Boston Spa.

British Theses Service (1971–1987), *The BRITS Index*: an index to the British thesis collections held at the British Library Document Supply Centre and London University.

Broehl, W.G. and Shurter, R.L. (1965), *Business, Research and Report Writing*, New York: McGraw-Hill.

Calvert, P.J. (2001), *Scholarly Misconduct and Misinformation on the World Wide Web*, The Electronic Library, Vol. 19 number 4, pp. 232–40.

Checkland, P. (1999), *Systems Thinking Systems Practice*, John Wiley.

Clark, P.A. (1972), *Action Research and Organisational Change*, New York: Harper and Row.

Cook, T.D. and Campbell, D.T. (1979), *Quasi Experimentation: Design and Analysis Issues for Field Settings*, Chicago, IL: Rand McNally.

Cooper, B.M. (1990), *Writing Technical Reports* (2nd Edition), Harmondsworth: Penguin.

Critical Tools Inc. (2001), 'PERT Chart EXPERT', Austin,TX. h-w.critical-tools.com/ pertmain.htm.

de Bono, E. (1988), *Teaching Thinking* (2nd Edition), London: Temple Smith.

Fairbairn, G.J. and Winch, C. (1991), *Reading Writing and Reasoning. A Guide for Students*, Buckingham: Open University Press.

Glaser, B.G. and Strauss, A.L. (1967), *The Discovery of Grounded Theory: Strategies for Qualitative Research*, London: Weidenfeld & Nicholson.

Gowers, Sir E. (1954), *The Complete Plain Words*, London: HMSO.

Graduate Attrition Advisory Committee (1996), 'The path to the Ph.D', *National Research Council Report*, Washington, DC: National Academy Press. hw.nap.edv/readingroom/books/PhD/index.html.

Grinyer, P.H. (6/7 April 1981), Classification suggested at the 5th National Conference on Doctoral Research in Management and Industrial Relations. University of Aston Management Centre.

Gunning, R. (1952), *The Technique of Clear Writing*, New York: McGraw-Hill.

Hansen, K.J. and Waterman, R.C. (1966), 'Evaluation of research in business education', *National Business Education Quarterly*, Vol. 24, pp. 81–4.

Higher Education Funding Council for England (1999), 'Assessment panels' criteria and working methods, section I', *RAE Circular 5/99*, Bristol. h-w.rae.ac.uk/pubs/5.99/sectionI.html.

Higher Education Funding Council for England (1999), 'Assessment panels' criteria and working methods, section II', *RAE Circular 5/99*, Bristol. h-w.rae.ac.uk/pubs/5.99/sectionII.html.

Higher Education Funding Council for England (2001), 'Interdisciplinary research and the RAE', *Briefing Note 14*, Bristol. h-w.rae.ac.uk/pubs/ briefing/note14.htm.

Howard, K. (ed.) (1978), *Managing a Thesis*, Bradford: University of Bradford Management Centre.

Kraemer, H.C. (1987), *How Many Subjects? Statistical Power Analysis in Research*, London: Sage Publications.

Landwehr, C.E. (1983), 'The best available technologies for computer security', *Computer*, Vol. 16, No. 7, p. 86.

Lock, D. (2000), *Project Management* (7th Edition), Aldershot: Gower.

Monroe, J., Meredith, C. and Fisher, K. (1977), *The Science of Scientific Writing*, Dubuque, IA: Kendall Hurst.

Recommendations for the Presentation of Theses (1982), BS 4821, London: British Standards Institution.

Rummel, J.F. and Ballaine, W.C. (1963), *Research Methodology in Business*, New York: Harper and Row.

Saaty, T.L. (1980), *The Analytic Hierarchy Process*, New York, NY: McGraw-Hill.

Schön, D.A., (1984), *The Reflective Practitioner*, New York: Basic Books.

Science Citation Index, Philadelphia: Institute for Scientific Information.

Shannon, C.E. (1948), 'A mathematical theory of communication', *Bell System Technical Journal*, pp. 370–432 and pp. 623–59.

Spon's Landscape and External Works Price Book, London: Spon.

STAR (Scientific Technical and Aerospace Reports), Washington, DC: NASA.

Styles, I. and Radloff, A. (2000), 'Jabba the Hut; research students' feelings about doing a thesis', in Herrmann, A. and Kulski, M.H. (eds), *Flexible Futures in Tertiary Teaching, Proceedings of the 9th Annual Teaching and Learning Forum February 2000*, Perth, Australia: Curtin University of Technology.

United Nations Statistical Year Book, New York, NY: United Nations.

Universities Funding Council (1992), 'Research Assessment Exercise 1992', *Circular 5/92*, Bristol.

Universities Funding Council (1992), 'Research Assessment Exercise 1992: The Outcome', *Circular 26/92*, Bristol. h-w.niss.ac.uk/education/hefc/rae92/c26_92html.

University of Manchester (2000), *Regulations for Degree of Doctor of Philosophy*, Manchester. h-w.man.ac.uk/rgsv/academic/dr_philosophy/org_Reg.html.

US Naval Postgraduate School (2001), 'CPA/PERT'. h-w.ups.navy.mil.

Van Grundy jr. A. B. (1988) *Techniques of Structured Problem Solving*, New York: Van Nostrand Reinhold.

Webb, E.J., Campbell, D.T., Schwartz, R.D. and Sechrest, L. (1966), *Unobstrusive Measures: Non Reactive Research in the Social Sciences*, Chicago, IL: Rand McNally.

Index

descriptive research 14, 120
design
    of research projects 111, 113, 118, 153
    as subject of research 124–5
Dewey, J. 16
Dewey decimal system 74
dictionaries 81
digitisation 151
DIN standards 78
diploma projects 10
discriminant analysis 122, 126, 134
Dissertation Abstracts International 76–7
dissertation projects 5, 11, 26–7, 45,
    48–50, 69, 76, 112, 158, 184–6, 192
doctoral research 12, 76, 105–6, 117–18,
    125, 170, 177–8, 184, 200, 207, 219,
    222–3
'double blind' tests 155
durations of activities 60–3, 68, 71

earliest start times 63
Economic and Social Research Council
    136
    Data Archive 155
The Economist 79
editing of research reports 214–16
electronic conferencing 34
Emerald Independent Reviews 81
empirical relationships 125–9
employment opportunities for research
    students 181–2
encyclopaedias 81
EndNote 102, 152
ephemera 80
errors
    in data 145
    in text of research reports 216–17
    see also measurement errors
et al, use of 205
Ethnographer 123
European Union 78
evaluation research 131
evidence in support of arguments 117, 137
examiners 213, 219–23
experimental design model 129–30, 135,
    144
explanation and prediction
    in qualitative analysis 131–2
    in quantitative analysis 128–31
explanation as a purpose of research 14

exploratory research 116–17
extension of research duration 71, 185

facilities for research, withdrawal of 176
factor analysis 121, 134
factor levels 129–30, 144
failure to complete 4, 12, 71, 181
Fairbairn, G.J. 106
false drop problem 96
falsifiability 118
feasibility of research proposals 39–42
field experiments 15, 40
field observation 154–5
fields of research 13–14
    reviews of 33, 227
figures in reports 200
financial support for research students
    41, 156, 173, 180–1
The Financial Times 79
first degrees, research as part of *see* under-
    graduate-level research
Fisher, K. 198
float 63–5
'fog index' 197
Forrester Research 77

Germany 78
Glaser, B.G. 154
Google 98–100
government publications 77–8, 161
grey literature 80
Grinyer, P.H. 15–16
grounded theory 154
grouping techniques 126
guidelines
    for students 194–6, 203, 210
    for supervisors 184, 186, 191
Gunning, R. 197

Hansen, K.J. 219
harassment of students 182–3
hardship committees 180
Harvard method of referencing 202, 204
Her Majesty's Stationery Office 77
hierarchical numbering of sections in
    reports 209
Higher Education Funding Council for
    England (HEFCE) 8–9, 15
historical data 81, 162
hold-out methods 134–5

hours of work 66
hypertext markup language (html) 150

ibid, use of 205
illness of students 173
inconclusive research 44, 175–6
indexing services 79
information technology (IT) facilities 181
Institute of Chartered Accountants 78
interdisciplinary research 9, 13
International Bibliography of Social Science 81
International Standards Organisation (ISO) 78
Internet, the 5, 34, 73, 101, 145, 163–5
interpretation of data 118, 213
interval data 116
interview notes 149
interviews 157–8, 214
intimidation of students 182–3

job applications 182
journals
    academic 33, 73–5, 90, 160, 172, 178–9, 224–5
    for data recording 148

Kelly, J.L. 16
key transferable skills 73
keywords 83–5, 103–4, 107

laboratory experiments 14–15, 153
lagged relationships 126
lateral thinking 175–6
latest start times 63
Lexis-Nexis 80
libraries 33, 74, 105–6
light pens 151
listing of activities 54–7
literature
    access to 33
    use of 22
literature searches 32, 62, 73–107, 140, 225, 227
    reasons for 82
    serendipity in 105
    for subject matter or for methodology 83
loc cit, use of 206
logbooks 148–9

logic 117–18, 137
loglinear analysis 129
longitudinal studies 41, 135

management of research, meaning of 4–5
Manchester University 12
mark sense readers 150
master's level research 11, 112, 177, 207
mathematics, writing on 199, 201
measurement errors 142–3, 146, 165
measurement scales 123–4, 134
media, the (as a source of research topics) 34
meetings with supervisors, records of 188
Meredith, C. 198
meta-analysis 160
methodology for research
    application of 124
    choice of 22–3
microfilm or microfiche copies 79
Microsoft Word
    grammar checking 197, 199
    sort command 206
milestones 69–70, 170
mind maps 121
missing explanatory variables 135
monographs 75–6, 226–7
Monroe, J. 198, 214–15
morphological analysis 36–9
motivation 70
    loss of 173–4
multiple authors 205

nature of research, classification by 15–16
network analysis and planning 53–67
    by part-time students 70–1
    revision of 68–9
news groups 82
newspapers 79–80, 90
NEWSPLAN 79
nominal data 115–16
notes on research 148
NUD·IST 121, 123, 151–2
N-VIVO 121, 246

objectives *see* aims of research
occasional papers 77
official reports and statistics 33, 161–2
op cit, use of 205
opportunity cost of research 31

OR in search descriptors 90
oral examination 194, 213–14, 219–24,
    227–8
  criteria applied in 220–1
ordering of activities 57, 68
ordinal data 115–16
originality in research 15, 33, 76, 220–1
outcomes of research 43–4
overcommitment 171, 192

page budgets 212
paragraph length 197–8
parallel studies 177
part-time students 5, 12–13, 31, 41,
    70–1, 182, 186, 223
passive voice 199
patents 78
path analysis 126, 131
pattern recognition 125–6
perceptual maps 123
personal factors affecting research 172–4
personal pronouns 199
PERT (Programme Evaluation and Review
    Technique) 62, 67
phases of research 6–7, 17–18
PhD research 12, 30, 194
photographs in reports 218
pictorial data 121, 145, 151
pilot surveys 156
plagiarism 105, 107, 148, 202
planning of research 17–18, 182
  need for 69–70, 111, 170–1
  purposes served by 52
Polaris programme 62
policy analysis 131
'political' research 131–2
postal surveys 156
precedence relationships 126
prediction and explanation
  in qualitative analysis 131–2
  in quantitative analysis 128–31
prefaces to reports 211–12
presentations
  on research findings 171
  on research proposals 49
primary data 139, 144
  collection of 153–8
  further use of 158
  sources of 74–5
prior beliefs 44

prior research 47–8
process model of research 16–18, 20
professional associations 157
Profile 80
progress reports to supervisors 188
proofreading of research reports 216–17
proving of relationships 119
publication of research material 172,
    178–9, 224–7
publications, catalogues of 74, 77
purposes of research 14

qualitative analysis 114, 131–2
quality, assessment of 20–2
Quality Assurance Agency 136
quantitative analysis 128–31
quasi-experiments 130
queries raised with supervisors 187
questionnaires 149, 156–7, 213–14
quota sampling 133
quotations from other people's work 105,
    200–1

Radloff, A. 19–20
ranked data 115–16
ratio data 116
readability of research reports 215
reading skills 106
recording of data 144–6, 157
references, lists of 202–7
'reflective practitioner' concept 125
regression models 130, 134–5
relevance of research 9
relevance trees 36–7, 83–4, 88
report organisation charts 210
reports of research
  coverage of 212–14
  criteria to be satisfied by 194–6
  draft chapters of 188–9
  final preparation of 214–218
  length of 196–7
  structuring of 209–12
representativeness, checking of 133
research
  definitions of 7–8
  different levels of 112–13
Research Assessment Exercise 8–9, 15
research councils 42, 136
research groups 34
research proposals 45–9, 82

259

units of measurement 146
Universities Funding Council 15
University of Bradford Management
  Centre 19
URLs (unique resource locators) 204–5
usefulness of research 14

validation of data 145–6
Vancouver method of referencing 202–3
variability of variables 119
verification of data 145–6, 151
video material 150
viva voce see oral examination

Waterman, R.C. 219
Web of Science 81, 90–8
Webb, E.J. 143
websites, referencing of 204–5
White Paper on science policy (1993) 42
Winch, C. 106
word counts 196–7, 212
'workhorse data' 160
World Bank 77
writing of papers 172, 174, 180

Yahoo 98
York University 194